The Science of
Science-Fiction Writing

The Science of Science-Fiction Writing

James Gunn

The Scarecrow Press, Inc.
Lanham, Maryland, and London
2000

SCARECROW PRESS, INC.

Published in the United States of America
by Scarecrow Press, Inc.
4720 Boston Way, Lanham, Maryland 20706
www.scarecrowpress.com

4 Pleydell Gardens, Folkestone
Kent CT20 2DN, England

British Library Cataloguing in Publication Information Available

Library of Congress Cataloging-in-Publication Data

Gunn, James, 1923–
    The science of science-fiction writing / James Gunn.
        p.   cm.
    ISBN 1-57886-011-3 (paper : alk. paper)
    1. Science fiction—Authorship.   I. Title.
    PN3377.5.S3   G86   2000
    808.3'8762—dc21
                                                                00-026016

⊖™ The paper used in this publication meets the minimum requirements of
American National Standard for Information Sciences—Permanence of
Paper for Printed Library Materials, ANSI/NISO Z39.48–1992.
Manufactured in the United States of America.

Contents

Acknowledgments

"The Anatomy of a Short Story" was published in *Writer's Digest*, April 1986.

"The Issue Is Character" was published in *Writer's Digest*, December 1992.

"The World View of Science Fiction" was published as "The Worldview of Science Fiction" in *Extrapolation*, Summer 1995.

"Where Do You Get Those Crazy Ideas?" was published in *Writing and Selling Science Fiction*, Writer's Digest Books, 1976.

"Heroes, Heroines, Villains: The Characters in Science fiction" was published in *The Craft of Science Fiction*, edited by Reginald Bretnor, Harper & Row, 1976.

"Robert A. Heinlein: The Grand Master" was published as an introduction titled "The Grand Master" for *The Puppet Masters*, Gregg Press, 1979.

"Isaac Asimov: The Foundations of Science Fiction" was published as the first chapter of *Isaac Asimov: The Foundations of Science Fiction*, Oxford University Press, 1982, and in revised form by Scarecrow Press, 1996.

"Henry Kuttner, C. L. More, et al." was published as "Henry Kuttner, C. L. Moore, Lewis Padgett, et al." in *Voices for the Future*, edited by Thomas Clareson, Bowling Green University Press, 1976.

Introduction

The September 1999 issue of *Analog* included a story by James Gunn called "The Giftie." Although I did not think about it until after the event, that publication marked, to the month, the publication of my first science-fiction story, "Communications," in the September 1949 *Startling Stories*. To be strictly accurate, it was my second story; it got published first, but the first one I wrote was "Paradox," which was published in the October *Thrilling Wonder Stories*. I didn't have a story published in *Astounding Science Fiction* until "Private Enterprise" in July 1950.

All those stories, like the rest of my first ten, were published under the pseudonym of "Edwin James," for reasons that now are difficult to recall. I think it had something to do with keeping my real name for writing about science fiction, which has something to do with the present book. The last story published under my pseudonym was "Survival Policy" in the October 1952 *Astounding*. The first story published under my real name was my eleventh, "The Misogynist," in the November 1952 *Galaxy*.

My experience as a full-time writer of science fiction lasted only four years, the first period between 1948 and 1949 and the second between late 1952 and mid-1955, although, since my retirement in 1993, I may be in my third. The 1950s were a difficult period to be a full-time writer; SF was supporting maybe half a dozen full-time writers at the time. In 1995, when my writing income was beginning to pick up, I moved my family to Lawrence, Kansas, where I had earned two degrees from the University of Kansas. Almost by accident I got involved with the University, first as a part-time teacher of freshman courses in composition, then as managing editor of its alumni publications. In 1958 I was invited to fill a new position writing feature articles about the University and the following year was hired as Administrative Assistant to the Chancellor for University Relations, eventually assuming responsibility for the University's public relations.

In that position I taught one course a year in fiction writing and kept up my contacts with the English Department. Meanwhile, throughout this period, I continued to write part-time, completing the stories for

Station in Space, *The Joy Makers*, *The Immortals*, and my first collection of short stories, *Future Imperfect*. For a few years during the tumultuous 1960s I found no time to write—I didn't even take the month's vacation to which I was entitled—but about 1967 I got back to it. I devoted my vacation to writing tasks that I had carefully laid out in the months before, and completed the last two novellas in *The Burning* and wrote the chapters and stories that eventually developed into *Kampus* and *The Listeners*.

In 1970 I decided to return to teaching and writing, and the English Department welcomed me. When he told me about the unanimous departmental vote, the Chairman also commented that "some of the younger faculty members hope you will teach a course in science fiction." I taught that course my first semester back, and the lectures became the chapters of *Alternate Worlds: The Illustrated History of Science Fiction*, the coffee-table book that Prentice-Hall published in 1975. It was the beginning of my writings about science fiction.

But teaching, and the time the University expected to be devoted to research, also liberated my fiction-writing energies, and I published two books a year for the first few years of my full-time teaching career. As a part-time writer, I was following a long tradition. Over the years most science-fiction writers have written in the time they could spare from full-time jobs or household duties. Part-time writing has its virtues; when money is not the primary concern, writers can devote themselves exclusively to what they want to write. Only in the last couple of decades, with the broad expansion of the book market from under 300 science-fiction and fantasy books a year in 1972 to about 2,000 books a year today, has the full-time writing of science-fiction become relatively common.

The 50th anniversary of the publication of my first story (it was my 96th published story) combined with a couple of earlier events to catalyze *The Science of Science-Fiction Writing*. A dozen years earlier I had begun gathering my various chapters and essays about science fiction into a thick folder under the title of *Inside Science Fiction*. When Robert Reginald asked me if I would be interested in publishing a book with Borgo Press, I thought of this folder. As I put the book together, however, I discovered that I had enough material for at least two books. Since Borgo Press was an academic publisher, I selected for *Inside Science Fiction* the essays and chapters about the literature and the teaching of science fiction. That book was published in 1992.

What I had left in the folder were the thoughts about the writing of science fiction that I had collected over a period of more than forty years of experience in teaching fiction writing and twenty years of teaching the writing of science fiction. The incentive to pull it together came in the late summer of 1998, when a writer and editor named Ted Rodriguez proposed an on-line writers workshop that he called the Soshin Distance Learning Center. He asked me if I would be willing to take charge of the science-fiction section. I had been exploring the Internet for four or five years and had subscribed to several serve lists as well as helping organize one for alumni of the workshops I held annually on campus during the summer. I was interested enough in how it would work to agree to a trial run, looked through my folder on writing and on writing science-fiction, and prepared readings and lesson plans.

The Soshin Distance Learning Center was a good idea that didn't work, but it led to a subsequent on-line workshop organized for me by a young writer who had seen the Soshin materials and, almost single-handed, got together a small group of writers for an experimental venture. Out of all these, and the writings put together for it, came *The Science of Science-Fiction Writing*.

Here you have it: forty years of reflections about the fiction-writing process and how to teach it, and the ideas I have shared with my students about how to do it effectively and how to get it published afterward.

Part 1

Writing Fiction

1

Why People Read Fiction
A New Look at the State of the Art

We live in an era in which fiction has been divided as rigorously as it has ever been into high and low art. High art has mostly dispensed with narrative and with the storyteller's tradition of entertaining, abandoning that activity to popular fiction, film, and television, much as painting abandoned portraiture and landscape to the photographer's camera. Literary fiction has even abandoned the illusion of reality, preferring to concern itself with the fictional process, with what has been called "metafiction"—not the relationship between the reader and reality as interpreted by the written word, but the relationship between the author and the story and the reader and the story.

What literary fiction offers in return may be witty, wise, intellectually stimulating, and otherwise wonderful, but it does not provide the reader the traditional rewards of narrative, or if it does—if somehow narrative creeps in—the work does not seem typical.

What is it that literary fiction has largely forsaken? What is narrative, and what does it do?

I have spent fifty years writing stories, constructing narratives that I hoped to sell, and have been reasonably successful: I have written nearly 100 stories, and published all of them. Being a professional writer has advantages and disadvantages: theory must meet the hard test of practice and be constantly corrected, but rewards and reinforcement come from art that is fully under control rather than from experiment. Nevertheless, I have been fortunate in that the category in which I have chosen to work—science fiction—always has been tolerant of experiment.

I must admit to a feeling of surprise, however, when, after a couple of decades of writing and selling stories and novels, I began to discover what narrative actually was and how it worked for the reader. I discovered it, over a period of years, from the process that many of my colleagues have found is the only way actually to learn anything: that is, by teaching others how to do it. When I was faced with the responsibility of teaching fiction-writing classes, I had to inspect my own writing experience—and even further back than that, my own reading experience.

Why do we read fiction? That is the question with which I began my fiction-writing classes. I get a lot of different answers: some students reply that they read for wisdom, for truth, for beauty; to meet different kinds of people and experience different emotions; to enjoy the pleasure of reading language well used; to learn about life. . . . My response to all of these is that if those things are what we are looking for we can find them in other places. Surely if we want wisdom we ought to go to philosophy, for truth to scientists or religious leaders, for beauty to poetry, for people to biography or character sketches or even the daily newspaper, for places to travel articles, for emotions to psychology; and for all of them to experience, to real life. If we can get these things as well or better from other sources, then it is not for this that we read fiction.

Why then do we read fiction? For entertainment. But it is not just any kind of entertainment: We can be entertained by many kinds of activities, even by many kinds of reading, and in many ways, but fiction offers a special kind of entertainment that depends upon special conditions. We read fiction because it affects us emotionally, and it affects us emotionally in specific ways that set it off from every other kind of emotional experience. Narrative generates a particular kind of emotional response that we can obtain from no other kind of experience except for comparable narratives in drama, film, television, or oral storytelling.

The emotional response of readers to narrative emerges, it seems to me, from a concern the reader feels for what happens to fictional people. Fiction has been defined as "interesting people in difficulties," or, as John Ciardi put it once, "character under stress." Stanley Elkin used similar words when he called fiction "character in crisis." The situation of the story, which introduces the reader to those "interesting people in difficulties," involves the reader initially with the characters. Why must they be interesting? Because we do not care, or we do not care enough, about uninteresting people. One of the commonest mistakes of beginning writers is to write about typical people, ordinary people, dull people. "He was a typical college freshman," my beginning students want to write, or "she was an ordinary housewife."

It isn't typical people we want to read about, or ordinary people—not because the world isn't made up of typical people or ordinary people, because it is; but only from the viewpoint of a writer who doesn't look deeply enough to detect the unusual qualities that lie beneath the surface of all of us. No, we want interesting people, because interesting people engage our attention and begin to involve us in the process of narrative.

We must care about them to want to know what is going to happen to them.

Moreover, interesting people have been made real for us, and we care about people, as readers, proportionately as we conceive of them as being real. At their best some characters begin to seem more real than the people around us; because we share their perceptions and even their thoughts, we actually *may* know them better than we can know anyone in the real world. Reality is the reason, as well, why we want the characters of stories to exist in places that we can sense. As the late Caroline Gordon once pointed out, Flaubert discovered that characters do not exist for the reader unless they have been put into a setting, and to make those settings seem real they must exist in three sensory dimensions—that is, with descriptions that appeal to at least three senses. Logically all places we know in real life have a visual attribute, but we don't know any that also does not have a characteristic sound or smell, and many also have touch or taste. Writers who describe their scenes in this way make the reader feel that they are describing the real world—and we care.

In the traditional analysis of fiction, situation is followed by complication. Complication is the natural consequence of situation: the character or characters, being placed under stress or in crisis by the situation, must try to relieve the stress by action; that action only makes the situation worse and increases the pressures upon the characters. The emotional basis for this is that the reader, once involved, must have his concern deepened by the efforts of the characters to resolve their situations, to solve their problems. If they do not attempt to solve their problems, the problems were not serious enough in the first place or the characters were too unperceptive to recognize their predicament or too defeated already to be moved to action, and the characters did not deserve our sympathy. If they solve their problems on the first attempt, their problems were not serious enough to test their characters or the characters were too strong to be tested by the problems. In either case our emotions do not become involved, and our involvement does not become properly developed.

Our narrative can have a series of complications—efforts by the characters to resolve their situation that fail, or succeed in part but fail in more serious and sometimes unforeseen ways, or succeed but reveal a more serious problem. Eventually—and how long eventually is depends upon the scope and hence the length of the story—the situation must be resolved; the characters must solve their problems or make a supreme effort that fails in some definitive way. The most effective narratives (and those readers prefer) are those in which the character or characters grow into a condition in which they can solve their problems, usually by developing the moral strength or the courage or the wisdom to tackle their predicaments in new ways or in old ways renewed. If character is under stress, we wish to see it respond, and only the most limited narratives offer us resolutions in which the situation is changed but the character remains the same.

In this moment of resolution, which has been preceded by the moment of crisis (or greatest tension), our concern—our caring about the characters—reaches its greatest peak, and from it we obtain our reward, our emotional response. Our tension, our caring, is released, and we experience this release as pleasure. It is for this feeling, finally, that we read—this almost physiological release of tension that Robert Scholes compares to sex. "Our sexual experiences," he says, "exhibit a narrative structure: a beginning, middle, and end—a tension, climax, and resolution."

This is not to deny the other gratifications. There is, of course, the foreplay of character building and plot development and the tactile pleasures of scene and setting. We can enjoy the textures of words and sentences, the mental stimulation of images and metaphors, even the intellectual pleasures of comparison and discovery. But without emotional release we do not enjoy the particular pleasure that only fiction can provide.

Everyone has experienced narratives that do not seem to display these characteristics. In some cases—like the slice-of-life story in which the characters do not change and in which there not only is no resolution but no complication and sometimes no situation—I think the words "short story" or even "fiction" are misapplied. If we are going to call these "stories," the term is too broad to be useful, and we will need another term for the narrative that provides the kind of emotional response that I have described. [All terminologies, to be sure, carry connotations of approval or disapproval; to withdraw the term "short story" from the plotless story seems to diminish it; on the other hand, the kind of story that I have been describing has been called the "formula story" by others.] In other cases the narrative seems to have eliminated the customary structure of situation, complication, and resolution (to rise, uncontaminated by fictional precedent, from the anything-can-happen magic of life itself) and yet provides for us, as readers, the emotional response we look for from fiction. I suggest that here we have a more artful art—perhaps unconscious, perhaps more sophisticated, and that if we inspect it closely we will find the basic structure existing still, perhaps with the elements rearranged, perhaps only better disguised, to give us art that avoids the appearance of art.

For, if I am right, narrative—story—has a basis in our existence as emotional creatures that cannot be denied or falsified.

Once we accept fiction as an emotional experience for the reader produced by inducing the reader to care about "interesting people in difficulty" and then releasing that caring through the resolution of those difficulties by the characters, then we can move on to the role of art and craft in fiction. Art and craft are terms whose meanings shift as we use them and often overlap; I will use them here to mean inspiration when I speak of art and the shaping of that inspiration when I speak of craft. In fiction, I consider art the conception of situation and the invention of character and incident and the initial choice of word and structure; craft is the shaping of situation, the selection and presentation of character, the description of place, the assemblage of incident into plot, and the refinement of word and sentence—all to the better service of the process that results in the enhanced pleasure of the reader. That is, the process itself, as a psychological equation, can be improved, though its essential nature cannot be altered.

In this process, with the writer considered as producer and the reader as consumer, one important aspect of the craft of the writer is the control of the reader's expectations. If pleasure is the goal of the process, the reader must be prepared for the release of caring that is interpreted as pleasure. The reader must care about the characters and hope they resolve their difficulties (or in a reversal of normal storytelling, hope a detested character does not succeed), so the craft of the writer lies in showing the reader whom to care about and what to hope for—and the sooner the better.

Caroline Gordon once said that the ending of a story should be implicit in its first sentence. One of my favorite examples of this principle in action is the opening sentence of Ernest Hemingway's *The Old Man and the Sea* (which I have long believed is itself a complete lesson in the craft of fiction): "He was an old man who fished alone in a skiff in the Gulf Stream, and he had gone eighty-four days now without catching a fish." That sentence tells the whole story that is to follow; it establishes and controls the reader's expectations. The reader has been told who and where and what to care about; now he will discover the how. The reader knows what to expect: a drama featuring a classic battle between a single old man and a great fish. And even if the reader cannot pick up from the tone of that first sentence that the drama is going to end in failure, by the end of the first page Hemingway has prepared the reader with such phrases as the "sail . . . looked like the flag of permanent defeat" and, on the next page, "his hands had the deep-creased scars from handling heavy fish on the cords."

I am discussing here basic responses to narrative that go deeper than conscious recognition—a psychological process (perhaps with physiological components) that does not have to be conscious to be effective. The reader's first response to narrative is untutored.

Every event in a story creates expectations in the reader, whether the reader is consciously aware of them or not. Every character is expected to do something, to be present for a purpose. This is one reason for the existence of flat characters and round characters: flat characters raise the expectation that they exist for the purpose of performing a single function, for carrying that spear and nothing else, and round characters for performing a series of actions—for imitating life. The consequence of this fact is that writers must be more careful about creating round characters than flat ones. Flat characters may not be adequate to sufficiently engage the reader's sympathies (they are not sufficiently "real"), but a round character who does not perform important actions disappoints the reader's expectations. [Thus, in *The Old Man and the Sea*, the tourists and the waiter who at the end comment on the skeleton of the fish exist in the story only for this purpose, and we know—and should know—no more about them than this.] This phenomenon lies at the heart of the detective story, where all suspects are (or ought to be) properly rounded—not simply to provide all the clues, as the detective story reader expects, but to give the characters the dimensions necessary for the reader to consider them legitimate suspects. And, of course, this response explains our groans of disappointment (like those at a shaggy dog story) when we learn that "the butler did it." We do not expect such actions of a spear carrier.

Characters alone, or even characters and events together, are not the only source of expectations. Settings demand appropriate actions ("some places cry out for a murder") or emphasize actions by contrast. If an author shows us a place in detail, just as if he presents a character in detail, we expect it to matter, to be of importance to the story the author chooses to tell.

Setting is part of the process of creating atmosphere, but so is the selection of words, which we call diction, and their arrangement in sentences, which we call style. Setting, diction, and style, too, create expectations that contribute to reader pleasure (or disappointment in ways that may be a failure of the author to master, or even understand, his craft, or may be a conscious effort to create a contrast often used for humor). I point out to my students that no word can be used without arousing expectations, that even the lowliest word in the language, the article, cannot be inserted into a story (or left in revision) without raising the reader's expectation that very soon a noun will follow.

What keeps readers reading a story is questions for which they want answers. Customarily these concern plot (what is going to happen to these characters? or how are these people going to get out of their difficulties?) but may also concern character (why are these characters behaving in these strange ways? or what do they need to learn or what do they need to be able to do that will get them out of their difficulties?) or setting (why is this place important?) or atmosphere (how is this feeling going to be translated into action?), or even diction and style (why is the author using these words? why are he or she adopting this style?). The rewarding experience provides satisfying answers to all questions raised. The disappointing experience leaves questions unanswered. The dull story raises no questions. The skillful writer raises no questions (and allows none to be raised) that he does not intend to answer. In this way he controls the reader's expectations.

The writer who understands his craft, then, permits no word, no character, no event to enter his story that does not arouse (or satisfy) the intended expectation. But if this is true, what is the role of surprise in fiction? How can we justify the De Maupassant surprise ending and the O. Henry twist? The ending that is totally a surprise is unacceptable; somewhere in the conditions and events of the story must be preparation for the ending, justification for what happens. Otherwise we feel cheated, as if we have been told in the poorly crafted detective story that "the butler did it." What we want as readers, science-fiction writer Poul Anderson has pointed out, are the twin pleasures of surprise and rightness. This requires even greater craft: to prepare readers for what will happen but to prepare them in such a manner that they do not know they have been prepared until the moment arrives. The ideal reaction to the resolution is, as Anderson says, "How surprising but how natural! Why didn't I see it coming?" The challenge of the author is to tell the reader what is going to happen but in such a way that the reader doesn't understand until after the reading has been finished.

This raises another question for the craft of writing: the sophistication of the reader and the question of readership. Although literary critics often look down on writing for a specific level of reader, not to write with an estimation of a level of reader sophistication is to surrender all thoughts of craft (if we define craft as not shaping fiction to the satisfaction of the author but to the understanding of the reader). Events that may be skillfully "undercut" for one reader may seem totally surprising to a less skillful or sophisticated reader, and events that are foreshadowed but not obviously revealed for one reader may be given away for one more sophisticated in the ways of fiction writers. [Writers, therefore—and perhaps critics as well—tend to surrender the innocent pleasures of reading unless they are able to turn off the mental tools of their trades.] The detective-story reader enjoys the game of guessing the culprit before that person is unveiled by the author, but the reader doesn't want it to be too easy and he admires the author who can present a logical perpetrator who has been concealed so cleverly that the person's identity is difficult to guess but the clues to whose identify have all been fairly presented.

Here, too, we might venture a speculation about the relationship between a reader and an author. Reading something by an author whose writing previously has given pleasure through craft as well as character and subject, a reader may relax in the confidence that the author will not lead a reader astray but will guide him carefully and without false trails to the promised reward. With an unfamiliar author, on the other hand, a reader may be constantly on guard, questioning his authority as well as his skill, unable to enjoy the experience fully because he doesn't know if the author knows what he is doing. A new author (or one new to any particular reader) must establish his authority quickly and make clear his grasp of the fictional craft.

Sophisticated readers also are capable of enjoying variations of the fiction-reading process for the sake of variety alone. They may perceive that the author is inverting story order, for instance, saving the statement of the situation until last, perhaps, or presenting uninteresting characters, or characters without problems or whose problems are so insoluble that attempts to resolve them are futile, as a commentary on life or on the process of fiction. The sophisticated readers' enjoyment of these variations, however, is in spite of, rather than because of, the fiction-reading process. The author is playing an intellectual game with the reader, or perhaps flattering the reader with the implication that "we are above the common need for plot or character change or resolution." At its best, the naturalistic story or the plotless story may achieve a verisimilitude that pleases for its own sake, and the games one may play with fiction can be the greatest games in the world, but I would argue that the result is the substitution of an intellectual experience for one that traditionally has been emotional, that such storytelling arouses emotions without satisfying them, and, finally, that it does not give us what we really want from fiction. Writers may become bored with story and with plot, but readers left to their own devices do not. It is not fiction that is exhausted but some of its authors. "What most people need in fiction," Scholes has written," is something that satisfies their legitimate desire for the pleasures of storytelling, without making them feel ashamed of having some childish and antisocial impulse."

If we are to "reduce" (I use the word that others may want to apply) fiction to a formulaic pathway to "easy" satisfaction, where does the artistry begin? How do we distinguish good from bad? These terms, of course, are relative and can be applied to all levels of narrative, from the skill with which an author controls the readers' expectations and leads them to the pleasurable experience they seek; to the novelty, profundity, ingenuity, truthfulness, or marvelousness of the situation, complications, or resolution; to the fascination or believability of the characters; to the wisdom of the philosophy; to the colorfulness of the settings; to the vitality of the scenes; and to the skill of the writing itself. We have come back, you see, to all of those reasons for reading fiction that we found inadequate earlier, but now with an understanding that these are the components of fiction, not the experience itself. All successful fiction at whatever level of art can be reduced to simple statements of formula (how else could it be, since life itself is a formula of birth, development into adulthood, marriage, reproduction, struggle, and death?), and art, it seems to me, is not doing something differently but doing something better.

2

The Anatomy of a Short Story

Five classical terms describe the parts of a short story, and you must know them and know how these parts fit together before you can write readable short stories. The five parts are:

Situation

Fiction has been described as "interesting people in difficulties." The situation is the difficulty the interesting person is in. The description of the characters and the presentation of the situation are called exposition. The events of the story, called the plot, are brought about through the efforts of the main character, called the protagonist, to resolve the situation.

Complication

The situation moves the protagonist to action (if it does not, it is not a suitable situation; if the protagonist is incapable of being moved by it, he or she is not a suitable protagonist, at least for this situation). The efforts of the protagonist to resolve the situation create the complication, actually worsening the situation and making it unendurable; occasionally the situation gets worse through the actions of the antagonist or through natural processes. Complication also is called "the rising action," and sometimes is compared to the tying of the knot that is untied in the resolution.

Climax

Generally, the climax is the point of highest interest, where the reader responds most emotionally; more specifically, it is the turning point in the action—the point at which the rising action changes direction and becomes the falling action. This is the point at which the protagonist must do or die, succeed or fail; the pressures of the situation have reached their peak. Climax also is called crisis.

Resolution

After the climax comes the resolution, the resolving of the situation established early in the story, the solving of the problem. The situation should be resolved by the actions of the protagonist, not by an outside agency; and the situation resolved must be the situation that launches the story. The protagonist can fail or succeed or, in more sophisticated stories, achieve both failure and success, and the story can be a tragedy or a comedy, or something in between. The resolution also is called the falling action.

Anticlimax

Everything that follows the climax is called the anticlimax (the anti here means opposite of or reverse of, but also carries the connotation of disappointing or trivial or even unnecessary). For the best dramatic effect, the anticlimax should be as short as possible, or even be eliminated when the resolution occurs simultaneously with the climax.

Arranging the Short Story

The classical elements of the short story may not always arrive in such a neat arrangement, although this is the natural order (because it is the order in which the reader naturally becomes involved in the story through caring what happens to the characters). Sometimes the situation may be revealed as part of the complication, the climax, or even the resolution. In the old pulp action stories, the complication, or part of it, often came before the situation; such action was called "the narrative hook." In some cases (usually tours de force), the climax, or even the resolution, comes first. The more sophisticated the story, the more the parts of the story are likely to be out of order or hard to recognize, and the reader is compelled to suspend judgment (and work harder at putting the pieces together) until the situation is clarified, although sometimes it is only implied, or even omitted.

You should view all such alterations as deliberate risks deliberately assumed, since the emotional basis for the reading of fiction has been violated. In some cases, readers may not be sufficiently sophisticated to understand such experiments; such readers are sacrifices to the author's art. In some cases, the piece of fiction does not offer rewards sufficient to motivate readers to work hard enough to understand the experiment;

those readers will be lost, too. Only in those cases where the story will not respond, or will not respond as well, to the normal pattern of reader involvement is alteration justified. Your boredom with easy challenges is not enough.

Sometimes (though not as often as writers like to think), the reader is at fault, in that rewards are available for working harder both at learning how to read difficult fiction and at actually reading it. If sufficiently challenged and rewarded, readers will learn to read unusual forms and different patterns of fiction, though the process may take generations. Only writers who can afford to wait, and have something to impart that transcends natural reading patterns, should apply. And they shouldn't complain about being unread or misunderstood.

3

Why a Formula Is Not a Formula

The formula for writing fiction quoted to beginning writers has been put in various ways, but they all add up to the same basic notion about how to construct a story. Marion Zimmer Bradley said that early in her career an editor described the formula as "Joe gets his ass caught in a bear trap and tries like hell to get it out." That is substantially the same as John Ciardi's "character under stress," and both are much like the unattributed "interesting people in difficulties."

I remember reading an analysis by the Scott Meredith agency reading service of an unpublished author's story. The analysis included a statement of fiction's basic plot. Although I don't, in general, approve of literary agencies offering reading services and advise my students not to patronize them (a literary agency's function is to sell stories, not criticism, and to combine the functions is to risk confusing them), I found the advice sound. I made a copy of the analysis for my files, but like most such copies (and good intentions), I can't for the life of me remember where I put it. Damon Knight, however, worked for Scott Meredith and includes what he calls "the plot skeleton" in his Writers Digest book *Creating Short Fiction*. I offer it below:

1. a believable and sympathetic central character;
2. his urgent and difficult problem
3. his attempts to resolve the problem, which fail and make his situation more desperate;
4. the crisis, his last chance to win;
5. the successful resolution, brought about by means of the central character's own courage, ingenuity, etc.

Knight continues: "The reverse of this plot is the story in which the central character is the villain; the story ends with his defeat rather than with his victory."

Knight sets up the plot skeleton in order to knock it down. He says that nearly all successful short stories leave out the third element and the fifth, the third because it is too hard "to cram into a short story," the fifth, because it is too predictable. He also says that "it is not true . . . that every story has to have a plot skeleton; it is not even true that every story has to have a plot."

We can concede that every piece of "fictional prose" may not have a "plot skeleton" or even a plot, while debating whether every piece of "fictional prose" is a "story." Let us leave aside the arguments that the failures characters experience in some stories may be implicit rather than explicit and that some resolutions may be implied or simply postponed, that even some plots (and plot skeletons) may be implicit rather than explicit. If readers have reasons for reading fiction that differ from their reasons for reading other kinds of writing (reasons that I explored in chapter 1 "Why People Read Fiction"), they may experience disorientation or disappointment, sometimes subconsciously and usually difficult to define, when they encounter prose that looks like a story but frustrates the desires with which they turned to it—which is not to assert that people cannot learn to enjoy frustration, or to appreciate the art that plays with their expectations to provide a more "sophisticated" pleasure.

Here I wish to explain why a formula may not be a formula.

How can a formula not be a formula? *Webster's Second International* offers as its third definition of "formula": "a prescribed or set form; . . . a fixed or conventional method in which anything is to be done, arranged, or said;—often somewhat derogatory." The derogatory aspect stems, I suspect, from the belief that the word "formula" implies artificiality, or rigid adherence to rules that run against the demands of art, or even of common sense. If, however, we look at *Webster's* second definition of the word, we find: "a rule prescribing ingredients, with proportions, for the preparation of a compound; a recipe." Under that definition, a formula is the only way to make that particular compound or that particular cake. I hope to demonstrate that the fictional "formula" is natural rather than artificial; that it arises, as one might expect, out of common sense.

I am going to focus here on just a few aspects of the plot "formula" rather than the entire "skeleton." The reasons for some aspects of plot are obvious, even if they are not always honored. A resolution of the situation with which the story begins, for instance, may not need defense: If a situation is a promise, the resolution is its fulfillment—even though some resolutions may be implied rather than stated and some situations may be a mystery until they are resolved.

Most beginning writers, however, have difficulty understanding why characters must be placed under stress or why they must fail. Teachers of fiction writing, for instance, constantly are handed student stories in which characters of great or superhuman strength confront difficulties that offer no challenge to their abilities, or in which characters with debilitating weaknesses confront challenges with which they can never cope. The reason for the first kind of story may lie in the student's failure to understand that a story is not simply a series of interesting events, or even of problems solved; and the reason for the second kind of story, the one of weak characters facing overwhelming problems, that a story is not simply an account of personal stress.

But both kinds of writing problems more clearly relate to the student's failure to see that a story is about that moment in a character's life when he or she changes. After the story is over, the reader should feel that nothing in that character's life will ever be quite the same, that this is the decisive moment in that character's existence. In fact, a common flaw in student stories is that no one changes. Therefore a good question to ask a story is: Who changes?

Readers want to read stories about events that matter. The only events that matter are those that determine our survival—on our terms, whatever they are—which is why some critics maintain that the only proper subjects for fiction are love, war, and death. Perhaps, strictly speaking, love is not survival, even in the most general sense of racial survival, but if a story implies that the characters can survive without love then the story will lose its power to move us. The only lessons we can learn from fiction, then, involve how we must change in order to survive, and the only way fiction can offer these lessons is to show us characters changing in order to survive.

We do not ask, of course, that characters survive, that all endings are happy, only that characters are more capable of coping with their problems at the end than they were at the beginning; that even if they fail, they know—or we, as readers, know—why they failed and usually what they lacked that survival required of them. They weren't brave enough or wise enough, smart enough or honorable enough or tough enough; they didn't love enough or care enough. We learn from their failures.

How can we show characters changing? We begin with characters under stress, with interesting people in difficulties. Our characters cannot be able to solve their problems without changing because then they could solve their problems from the beginning; in effect, their problems are not serious enough. And if the problems are serious but still within the capabilities of the characters to solve without the necessity of change then the stories overlook more interesting moments: those moments in the characters' lives when they became capable of solving difficult problems, when, indeed, they changed. Thus Conan's hacking his way through an army of opponents is inherently less interesting than the time in his life when he developed the ability to handle such situations; at one point he wasn't, and then he changed— what made him change? That tells us something.

Any series of difficulties a character can handle without changing simply elaborates the obvious. We may enjoy such narratives at a simple, unthreatened, wish-fulfillment level—rather like watching an athletic team whose fortunes we care about scrimmaging against itself. We can enjoy the conflict and the skills displayed without concern about the outcome—but they cannot engage our deeper emotions.

If stories offer characters who cannot possibly cope with their problems, we have stories in which the characters cannot change, or if they change the change is for the worse; it does not make them more capable of coping. Fiction that shows us characters overwhelmed by their situations may have sociological value, but it falls short of our needs for story. We can sympathize with the unfortunate, we can even learn from their misfortunes, but we withhold our emotional involvement from them because we know it would bring us only pain without hope. Characters must be capable of changing if they are to involve us as we wish to be involved, and one of the responsibilities of the author when presenting a character is to reveal that he is capable of change.

If authors are to satisfy readers' needs for story, they must create situations sufficiently threatening, sufficiently serious, to require that characters change in order to cope with them. Such considerations, for instance, explain why situations must be matched with characters, and characters to situations. A situation that would require one kind of person to change might not move another. Too often in student stories characters are universal and situations are general. The minister with the temptation to sin or the criminal who must behave honorably, the coward who must act courageously or the brave man who must face his fears—they must change.

Finally, why must characters fail? The answer relates both to the fictional world and the real world. If characters could learn from anything but failure, the process would be too easy, and we would understand, subconsciously if not consciously, that they really could have done it from the beginning if the author had not put meaningless obstacles in their way. If characters can learn by being told what to do, or by reading the answer in a book, they have not really changed; the situation does not really test them. We often experience, as readers, the feeling of having been cheated when a character searches for an answer someone else knew all along, and when a character is told the answer we often wonder why the person who knew the answer didn't apply it to the problem himself or herself.

We also know that the only way we learn anything in the real world is by experience, which means by failure; if we are parents, we know that we cannot spare our children pain by warning them of pitfalls, just as we ourselves had to learn by making mistakes. Some theories hold that we can teach by rewarding success, and all teachers try to do that in one way or another, but many hard-to-define and difficult-to-duplicate processes may produce success; failure strikes us deeper and can be pinned down to one element or two. A good example is the average student story: Where it fails is easier to identify than where it succeeds, which is why most class discussions focus on what is wrong with a story rather than what is right. But that's okay: Failure, not success, is how we learn.

Failure, of course, makes us change. Not one failure. One failure may be excused as doing it wrong or doing parts of it wrong, or doing it for the wrong reasons or without sufficient confidence or faith. A second failure makes you doubt the method. A third should make you realize that only a new approach will succeed, that you lack wisdom or strength, courage or character. If failure has taught you that you must change, and the problem dictates that you must solve it or die, you will change if you have the capacity to do so.

Surely this is what we ask of fiction: that it provide us with involvement and example, with story and meaning, with caring and release. Is this formula, or is this life?

4

The Author's Strategy

Everyone has a strategy to help him or her get through the day: how to get started in the morning, how to keep going, how to cope with others, how to get work done, how to relax when the work is complete, how to get enough rest so that the next day can be productive or enjoyable. The author needs a strategy as well.

Often our strategies depend upon the strategies of others, our spouses, our parents, our children, our bosses and fellow employees, our teachers, our fellow students. The author's strategy depends upon understanding the strategy of the editor.

Editors seldom read manuscripts in the office any more, if they ever did. The office is where they do the business of publishing, where they negotiate with printers and artists and sales people and sometimes authors and their agents. The manuscripts they often take home with them to read after work. They read them on the train or at home before the cocktail hour or after dinner until bedtime. Any time they have left over they can use for themselves.

The editor's strategy, then, must be to say "no" fast. The sooner the editor can decide that a manuscript is unpublishable, the sooner he or she can get finished with the day's work and read something for pleasure or watch the evening news or even do his or her own writing. Or, more appropriately, get on to finding something in the pile of manuscripts that is worth publishing.

The editor seizes upon any clue to the fact that the author doesn't know what he or she is doing, doesn't know how to write a publishable story, or, at least, doesn't know how to write this story. The clue can be as obvious as an illegibly printed or handwritten manuscript or it can be an uninteresting title or a dull opening sentence, but usually it is a combination of characteristics. The editor may read a few sentences or even a page or two, but if nothing happens to make the editor hopeful that the story will be publishable, the editor will attach a rejection slip, insert the story into the return envelope, and get on to something more promising.

Knowing that, the strategy of the author must be: don't give the editor an excuse to say "no." This doesn't mean frantic prose or unrelenting action; it does mean that the author must be aware of what is going on in the writing and the story at all times. An established author has the innate authority of his or her previously successful stories; an unknown author must establish his or her authority within the story at hand. That implies an understanding of what it means to be a professional in terms of manuscript appearance and presentation; in terms of title and story beginning; in terms of skill in the use of language and sentence structure. It means having a good story and an awareness of how to tell it, getting the story started immediately and characteristically, and presenting it in terms of interesting people in difficulties learning how to cope; and connecting the events of the story to what the characters must learn if they are to cope. If the author has a good story to tell and good characters to whom the story happens, and tells it dramatically, undercutting future developments and reaching a satisfying resolution, without wasted words or scenes, the editor will read through to the end. If the editor has read that far, he or she has an investment in the story and will have a good reason to accept it for publication; or if, for some reason, the story cannot be accepted, the next one from that author will be read with the anticipation that this one may be publishable.

5

The Issue Is Character

What is character but the determinant of incident? What is incident but the illustration of character?
Henry James, "The Art of Fiction"

The test of a round character is whether it is capable of surprising in a convincing way.
E. M. Forster, *Aspects of the Novel*

In this world of social change, where radio and television psychologists and countless articles in magazines and newspapers encourage the popular belief that character is a problem treatable by counseling, therapy, or drugs, writers often turn for inspiration to the social illnesses of the day: alcoholism, drug abuse, battered wives and children, date rape, adultery, poverty, nuclear war. That's what the students in my fiction-writing classes do, and one of my challenges is to convince them that a case history is not a story. A case history is what I call a piece of fiction in which the issue is more important than the people it happens to.

These kinds of narratives are easy to identify, once you begin to watch for them, by the fact that their characters, like automobile parts, are infinitely replaceable. The characters exist only to exhibit the flawed behavior that best illustrates the social problem. It is not as easy, however, to figure out what to do about them.

Charles Dickens faced a similar dilemma in the early years of the Victorian era. That period, too, was marked by social change and even greater social evils, like debtor's prisons, workhouses for orphans, child abuse, child labor, slums even more deplorable than those today, public drunkenness, legal delays, and other problems created or exacerbated by a world being propelled by the Industrial Revolution from rural stability into urban insecurity. Freud, with his emphasis on emotional traumas in early life as a cause of later neuroses, and, by extension, of criminal and other antisocial behavior, would not arrive for some half-century yet, and Dickens and his contemporaries looked no further for an explanation of personal problems than basic character acted upon by social injustice. That may be the explanation why, in exposing the mal-

formed institutions of his times, Dickens's characters stick in the memory
as sturdy individuals trapped as they may be in the overwhelming social
evils of their times.

To cite one example, in *Oliver Twist* young Oliver is born to illustrate the evils of the workhouses of Dickens's times and such deplorable, vice-ridden slums of London as "Jacob's Island." The second paragraph begins:

> For a long time after it was ushered into this world of sorrow
> and trouble, by the parish surgeon, it remained a matter of
> considerable doubt whether the child would survive to bear
> any name at all, in which case it is somewhat more than
> probable that these memoirs would never have appeared, or,
> if they had, that being comprised within a couple of pages,
> they would have possessed the inestimable merit of being the
> most concise and faithful specimen of biography extant in the
> literature of any age or country.

What could be more of a case history than a child without a name,
whose undetermined sex requires the neuter pronoun? Nevertheless Oliver
emerges as an individual because Dickens endows him with incident
that illustrates his character as well as the convincing surprise that Forster
calls for. Forster, in *Aspects of the Novel*, expanded his comments on the
"round character": "If it never surprises, it is flat. If it does not convince, it is flat pretending to be round.

Oliver Twist may not quite offer the "convincing surprise" called
for by Forster, who considered Dickens's people nearly all flat, "and yet
there is this wonderful feeling of human depth," probably due to Dickens's
"immense vitality . . . that causes his characters to vibrate a little, so
that they borrow his life and appear to lead one of their own."

Forster reserved his illustration of round characters for "[all] the
principal characters in *War and Peace*, all the Dostoyevski characters
and some of Proust. . . ." He also points to Madame Bovary, to *Vanity
Fair*'s Becky Sharp, and to Tom Jones. He might also have cited the
characters in his own major novels, *A Room with a View*, *Howard's End*,
and *A Passage to India*, all of which have been filmed in recent years,
perhaps because we are just as interested as Forster was in the conflict
between those who live by convention and those who live by instinct.

Oliver's vitality, then, as well as his particularity, rescues *Oliver
Twist* from being mere case history. Dickens provided meaningful pres-

sure for reform by writing novels of character. Dickens avoided fiction's case-history trap by emphasizing the particular and avoiding the general. Certainly Oliver Twist and the other characters in Dickens's social-issue novels take on the aspects of real people because he provides the reader so many specifics about their lives and appearances and manners of talking, as well as evidences of their pasts, that we begin to see them as more real than the people we associate with in daily life. Why not? Often we know more about a Dickens character than we know about acquaintances.

The problems inexperienced writers face seldom respond to easy solutions, however, and the admonition "particularize" leads to such questions as "which particulars?" and "how much?" When students ask questions like that I like to refer them to some underlying theory of writing craft, to the fundamentals of story construction. Looking at story from the viewpoint of Marion Zimmer Bradley's "bear trap," we might say that characters are present in a story to extricate their posteriors from that bear trap. Some characters when caught in a bear trap would just sit there, suffering, until they die; others might struggle. But if we know that they are incapable of escaping or of learning from their experience we will view the trap as more important than the character.

To look at the matter the other way, a bear trap is constructed to capture a particular character's particularly sensitive anatomy, not to catch the first person who blunders into it. If fiction is interesting people in difficulty, writers can start with interesting people and match them up with appropriate difficulties, or start with the difficulties and invent interesting people to experience them. What matters is that the characters must be particularly stressed by those specific difficulties. Characters must act for their own reasons, not for the story's—and the author's—convenience; that principle could be extended to suggest that characters should exist in stories for their own reasons.

In order to change the case history into the issue-oriented story, authors need to choose characters who are not the typical alcoholics or wife beaters or polluters or warmongers; instead, authors should create characters who have reasons of their own to exhibit those characteristics, reasons that are peculiar to the individual—for whom they are especially meaningful or painful—and not common to the entire human species or even a sizable portion of it. Why, authors might ask themselves, is this situation a special problem for this person rather than for anyone?

The instinctive response of readers, although they may never be conscious of it, is to ask: "Why are you telling me about this person rather than about someone else?" If someone else can do just as well, then the author hasn't chosen the right character.

We live in an era when the highest critical praise is reserved for the psychological novel that Henry James championed in his 1884 essay "The Art of Fiction," but the most popular entertainment, visual as well as printed, revolves around ideas and issues. Look at the best-seller lists. But even idea- and issue-oriented fiction works not because the characters are universal but because they exemplify in their individuality the social flaws the author wishes to focus upon.

Beginning in the 1870s with Emile Zola, the naturalistic novelists dealt with the ways in which social problems shaped the people who were subject to them. In the early years of the century Frank Norris in *The Octopus* and *The Pit* and Upton Sinclair in *The Jungle* made their issues more dramatic by making their characters more special. In the 1920s Sinclair Lewis did the same thing with *Babbitt* and *Elmer Gantry*. In the 1940s and 1950s writers such as Richard Wright with *Native Son* and Ralph Ellison with *Invisible Man* made their cases against discrimination by making their characters individuals instead of types. Tom Wolfe, in *The Bonfire of the Vanities*, demonstrated that the same criteria of effectiveness in fiction holds just as true today. Authors like these succeeded, as writers succeed in all aspects of their craft, by seeing their stories more clearly and in more detail than their readers would if they were there. And when an author sees a character clearly, knows that character intimately, even though the experience of the character may illustrate a social problem, the character will come alive as an individual.

Too often characters exist only for the sake of the story at hand. I sometimes ask my students how their characters did in school, how they got along with their parents, what their favorite books are, and, most important, what events have changed or would change their lives. Most students can't answer. But writers have to know characters more intimately than they will be presented on the page. We must know what our characters did and wanted before their stories began—and what they'll do and want when their stories end. Then, while the experiences of the character may illustrate social problem, the character will also live as an individual.

I begin a new work by writing at least a few paragraphs about each major character—not only to describe the qualities they must possess to play their proper roles in the story, but also to determine what brought them to this narrative nexus and made them the people for whom these particular roles were meant. I specify "major characters" because fiction is filled with both flat and round characters, and both serve their purposes. Don't make a flat character round or flatten a round one. Unless the butler really did it, the butler should remain an opener of doors and a recipient of outer garments.

This emphasis on characterization may seem a bit odd, coming as it does from an author whose stories and novels have been published as science fiction, a genre that is not noted for its rounded characters. It isn't good enough to say my fiction is different from the rest, even if it were true, even if I wanted to. In fact science fiction is an idea-centered literature, and the characters are and must be subordinated to the idea if the idea is to be considered rationally. That may be why I am so sensitive to the necessity to make characters live as individuals rather than act out roles as types.

A few years ago I ran across Adam Smith's speculation that an Englishman might read in his morning paper that millions of Chinese had died in an earthquake and go on eating his breakfast, but if he were told that he would lose his little finger tomorrow, he wouldn't be able to work or sleep for worrying about it. What, I wondered, if there was some connection between the loss of a finger and the death of a million Chinese?

I tried to give the idea away to other writers without success. I finally wrote it myself, but only after I came up with a character who could make my far-fetched idea believable. I named him Benny Giroux. I gave him an abusive, alcoholic father who died early, a mother who protected him, and for whom he harbored a desperate love, a history of not doing well in school but a pride in his own logical mind, and a job as a dishwasher. I used all this background in the story because Benny had to believe what an ordinary person would not—that he could save other people's lives by cutting off pieces of himself. And finally, I gave him one last essential characteristic: altruism. It is this that makes his folly plausible at the same time that it redeems it, and, I hoped, redeemed for the reader the unpleasantness of a story about self-mutilation. The story was "Man of Parts," published in *Fantasy and Science Fiction* (August 1985).

A few years earlier I created a character whose reason for existence was to correct the evils of today's world so that the unlivable future from which he came would be avoided. I had suggested the idea to CBS as a possible television series. When I heard nothing more from those to whom I described it, I wrote up the idea as a story, "Child of the Sun," that was published in *Analog*. The following year it was anthologized in DAW Books *World's Best SF* and was then, ironically, optioned for a year by a production company at Universal. Eventually I got around to writing five more stories about the man who comes from the future to help us solve our problems and in the process tackles war, energy, dictatorship, terrorism, overpopulation, and pollution. Those stories also were published in *Analog*, and then the six "episodes" (I had not yet given up my illusion that they would make a good television series) were collected into a book titled *Crisis!* published in 1986 by Tor Books.

One answer to making characters believable in the face of overpowering issues is to draw them larger than life, like Superman or the Six-Million-Dollar Man. But I had told CBS that there were too many series about heroes; what television needed was not someone to solve our problems but to dramatize them so effectively that we would be forced to seek solutions for ourselves. So I made my time-traveling protagonist insignificant, not a man of action but a catalyst, someone who makes solutions possible by his presence, not by his heroism. In order to show him reacting to but not solving the problem at hand, I never got inside his head; I made the point of view that of a camera, as objective as possible. I even named my character Bill Johnson, the commonest name in my telephone directory. Nevertheless Bill Johnson became well known to *Analog* readers. [Stanley Schmidt, editor of *Analog*, had a writer named Bill Johnson, to whom he suggested he should write Jim Gunn stories.]

The answer to this almost insurmountable problem of keeping the character from disappearing into the problem was to make him unique. In the first place, his anonymity was a character trait; he had to be almost invisible if he were not to be noticed and remembered as he goes about his self-assigned tasks, lionized or exposed as a meddler, and prevented from acting on further problems. Second, he had a special talent: he saw glimpses of consequences, of the way situations would develop if no one acted. His visions of catastrophe were so graphic that he could not help involving himself (much as I hoped would happen to an audience watching such a series). Third, he had a special problem: every time he helped find a solution, he lost his memory and he had to leave messages to himself, telling him who he was and what he had done and what he was there to do.

Finally, I focused my camera on him as tightly as I could. The first story started like this:

> He opened his eyes. He was lying on a bed. The sheets and blankets were tangled as if he had been thrashing around in his sleep.
>
> He looked up at the ceiling. Cracks ran across the old plaster like a map of a country he did not recognize. On his left a window let a thin, wintry light through layers of dust. On the right was the rest of the room: shabby, dingy, ordinary. . . .

And a little bit later:

> The man swung his legs out of bed and sat up, rubbing the sleep out of his face with open hands. He appeared to be a young man, a good-looking man with brown, curly hair and dark eyes and a complexion that looked as if he had been out in the sun. He had a youthful innocence about him, a kind of newly born awareness and childlike interest in everything that made people want to talk to him, to tell him personal problems, secrets they might have shared with no one else.
>
> But after meeting him what people remembered most were his eyes. They seemed older than the rest of him. They looked at people and at things steadily, as if they were trying to understand, as if they were trying to make sense out of what they saw, as if they saw things other people could not see, as if they had seen too much. Or perhaps they were only the eyes of a man who often forgot and was trying to remember. . . .

I also involved him with a series of people whom he knew he would soon forget, so that he could never find personal happiness unless he gave up his mission. And in a final episode, I had him question his own sanity. Why should anyone believe the messages, filled with paranoid delusions that he was a man from the future returned to save the world, that he kept finding? He seeks help from a psychiatrist, even though as readers we know, having experienced the past that he cannot remember, that if he is ever cured an indispensable catalyst for the solution of humanity's problems will have vanished from the world. His pain is our hope for salvation.

He is capable not only of vision and of ingenuity but also like any rounded character, of surprising us in convincing ways.

Even in the most issue-oriented of fiction, authors can dramatize those issues more effectively—and create more memorable stories and novels—by creating characters who are the best possible representatives of their predicaments because they are involved in them, not for the author's reasons, but for their own.

6

Scene—The Smallest Dramatic Unit

Anyone who describes *the* way to write successful stories is oversimplifying. There is no one way; in fact, there may be as many ways as there are stories. Robert A. Heinlein preceded his 1947 essay "On the Writing of Speculative Fiction" with the following epigraph from Rudyard Kipling:

> There are nine-and-sixty ways
> Of constructing tribal lays
> And every single one of them is right!

And then Heinlein went on to describe what he called the three basic plots for the science-fiction human-interest story. They were, incidentally, "Boy-meets-girl, The Little Tailor, and the-man-who-learned-better."

The decision about how to tell a story begins (and often ends) with the author's decision about viewpoint. Percy Lubbock started the chapter on viewpoint in his 1921 study *The Craft of Fiction* (not to be confused with William C. Knott's nuts-and-bolts 1983 book) with the sentence: "The whole intricate question of method, in the craft of fiction, I take to be governed by the question of the point of view—the question of the relation in which the narrator stands to the story."

I recommend the entire chapter to the aspiring author (the entire book is a valuable study of literature, but not as relevant to the study of fiction writing). Lubbock discusses the various choices of viewpoint, the way they originated, and their virtues and drawbacks. He concludes, however, by recommending the more restricted viewpoint of the third person limited, which results in what Lubbock calls "true drama."

> In true drama nobody *reports* the scene; it *appears*, it is constituted by the aspect of the occasion and the talk and the conduct of the people. . . . [W]hen that point of view is held in the manner I have described, when it is open to the author to withdraw from it silently and to leave the actor to play his part, true drama—or something so like it that it passes for

true drama—is always possible; all the figures of the scene
are together in it, one no nearer than another. . . .

Lubbock concludes by remarking that the most undramatic presentation, omniscience, can be made to work, but "The voice is then confess-
edly and alone the author's; he imposes no limitation upon his freedom
to tell what he pleases and to regard his matter from a point of view that
is solely his own." Lubbock declares "that a story will never yield its
best to a writer who takes the easiest way with it. He curtails his privi-
leges and chooses a narrower method, and immediately the story responds. . . . The easy way is no way at all; the only way is that by which
the most is made of the story to be told, and the most was never made of
any story except by a choice and disciplined method."

The method of drama (or "true drama") allows the reader to observe the story directly as it unfolds, as if it were being played out in
front of his eyes like a performance on the stage. The stage offers no
opportunity for explanation or interpretation and certainly none for exposition. The actors enter and exit, speak their lines and perform their
actions, and from this, and only this, the audience (or the reader in the
case of fiction) is provided with the information necessary to come to its
own judgment about significance and meaning.

For this reason Hemingway, whose method was quintessentially dramatic, said that what he wanted to do was to show "the way things
were." Because he wanted to show "the way things were," his narratives contain no interpretation, since life itself ("the way things were")
provides no authoritative voice telling us what things mean. A reflection of reality was Hemingway's goal and it emerged from his view of
his (and humanity's) place in the universe—realistic, pragmatic, guided
by common sense. Other authors had different ways to look at the world
and told different kinds of stories about it. Arthur Mizener in *Modern
Short Stories* (Norton, 1962) described three kinds of attitudes toward
experience that led modern authors to produce three different kinds of
stories. He categorized them as "twentieth-century romanticism," "comedies of manners," and "subjectivism." Hemingway, James Thurber,
and Henry James, among others, wrote "comedies of manners," realistic narratives placed in communities whose carefully shaded behavior
provided readers with their only clues to meaning. Mizener's analyses
and the stories he reprints are worth study by the aspiring author as a
way of revealing how authors' philosophical orientations shape their

methods; aspiring authors can place themselves in one group or another and get some insight into why they choose one approach over another.

Hemingway, because of his desire to deal with "the ways things were," is a good guide to dramatic presentation—that is, the process that allows the reader to see directly what goes on and to draw his or her own conclusions. From this method comes the often quoted maxim "show, don't tell!" In another excellent analytical anthology, *The House of Fiction* (Scribner's, 1950), Caroline Gordon and Allen Tate appended valuable "Notes on Fictional Techniques," including sections on "Authority in Fiction," "The Four Methods" (viewpoint), "The Panorama and the Scene," "Discovery, Complication, Resolution, and Peripety," "Enveloping Action," "Tonal Unity," "Symbolism," and "Faults of the Amateur." The last, incidentally, they identify as "The Unwritten Story," "Lack of Proportion," "Neglect of the Reader," and "Dead Dialogue."

Here, however, we are concerned with "The Panorama and the Scene." Fiction, Gordon and Tate wrote, is made up of panorama and scenes. "The panorama, like the Greek chorus, affords the author the opportunity and the means for commenting on the individual happening and, again, like the Greek chorus, lends the characters dignity by relating them to humanity in general." But they go on to say that "the panorama, no matter which of its uses it is put to, stands always for the general. The scene represents the individual moment—a moment in time which can never be repeated."

Writers such as Hemingway and James set as their goal to present their narratives as much as possible in the form of scenes. James said that the fiction writer's chief concern is "the vivid image and the very [true] scene," and further that "processes, periods, intervals, stages, degrees, connexions, may be easily enough and barely enough named, may be unconvincingly staged, in fiction, to the deep discredit of the writer, but it remains the very deuce to *represent* them . . . even though the novelist who doesn't represent and represent 'all the time,' is lost . . . ."

The best description of the primacy of scene in science fiction was presented by A. E. van vogt in the same book, *Of Worlds Beyond* (Fantasy Press, 1947), in which Heinlein's essay was published. Van Vogt wrote about "Complication in the Science Fiction Story." He was the master of complication, and readers often arrived at the end of his novels still puzzled about some elements in the story.

That may have been one unintended consequence of van Vogt's methods, but they also produced marvelous scenes. Raymond Chandler in in the introduction to his collection of his *Black Mask* hard-boiled detective stories, *The Simple Art of Murder*, pointed out that the effective scene was the goal of the hard-boiled detective story. The good story was one that made good scenes. The rationale for what he called "the formal detective story," which he looked down upon as "spillikins in the parlor," was that the ending, when the detective gathered together the suspects, listed the clues, and revealed "who dunnit," justified everything that had gone before. The rationale for the hard-boiled detective story, Chandler said, was that the scene outranked the whole and that the good novel was one you would read even if the ending were missing. That's true enough of Chandler's detective stories, *The Big Sleep*, for instance.

"I write a story with a full and conscious knowledge of technique," van Vogt wrote in 1947. What was technique for him? "Think of [writing your excellent idea] in scenes of about 800 words. . . . Every scene has a purpose, which is stated near the beginning, usually by the third paragraph, and that purpose is either accomplished, or not accomplished, by the end of the scene. . . ."

Van Vogt got most of his theory from a writer named Gallishaw, who published "how-to-do-it" books on fiction writing in the 1930s when van Vogt was getting started. There were a number of those kinds of books around then, and a great deal of discussion among writers about formulas and the secret to writing stories that sold every time. Those were the days when ads in writer's magazines offered devices such as "Plotto" that did everything but write the story. That also was the period when pulp magazines and slick magazines crowded the news stands, and when writers such as Arthur J. Burks, Lester Dent, and Frederick Faust (who wrote under eighteen different pseudonyms, including Max Brand) made good livings by writing 10,000 words a day and selling it all, first draft, for as little as a penny a word.

All this seems pretty mechanical today. Times have changed, and the market for short fiction is a good example. It has dwindled to a detective-story magazine or two, a half-dozen science-fiction magazines (plus a rising number of on-line magazines, many devoted to science fiction, fantasy, or horror), and a handful of literary quarterlies (which pay mostly in copies). Nevertheless, writing in scenes still has something that helps writers organize their stories and present them in dramatic ways.

As a beginning, writers may benefit from thinking about the problem their protagonist must deal with and why he or she is unable to deal with it (if the character is capable of dealing with the problem, the story ends there). The story that unfolds from this "interesting character in difficulty" displays how the character acquires the capability of dealing with the problem (or an understanding of what it takes to deal with the problem even though the protagonist fails). This capability may be information (clues or data), strength of body or of character, resolution, wisdom, or a number of other qualities. Usually the protagonist's education comes through attempts to solve the problem that fail, and from these failures the protagonist learns (in fiction, as in life, we learn only through failure, or the lessons we learn through failure are clearer and more to be trusted—and certainly more dramatic—than the lessons we learn through success).

This learning process should be organized dramatically into a series of scenes, each one of which represents an attempt to solve the problem and a step on the way to changing the protagonist into someone who can deal with the problem (or fail definitively). To be effective each of these scenes should be three or four pages long (600-1000 words). Although this length seems arbitrary, a bit of experimentation will demonstrate that a scene of less than two and a half pages is not going to allow, in a dramatic form, a statement of the problem as it now stands, an effective effort to solve the problem, and a resolution of that effort. Similarly a scene that goes on for longer than four pages will benefit dramatically by being trimmed or divided. And a scene of only a paragraph or a few paragraphs ought to be rethought in dramatic terms.

In effect, then, a scene can be considered a miniature story, with a problem to be solved, an attempt to solve that problem, and a result of the attempt, all presented as a single dramatic unit. A collection of such scenes moves the story toward a final resolution that is the transformation of the protagonist. David Gerrold has said that at the end of the story the protagonist (and the reader) ought to feel that "after this nothing will ever be the same," and the most effective stories emerge from those moments in people's lives when everything changes. "Moments of sudden truth," they are sometimes called, or "epiphanies" (James Joyce defined it as "the moment when the whatness of things emerges from the vestment of its appearance")—they apply to rites of passage of all kinds, becoming an adult, falling in love, getting married, becoming a parent and its revelations, finding one's true vocation, discovering the secret of life or of happiness or of enduring pain or grief, facing the death of loved ones, of parents, of oneself. . . . In science fiction they usually concern the relationship of humanity to the universe. *The Encyclopedia of Science Fiction* called it "conceptual breakthrough," and one plot that led to this kind of epiphany was the one called by Heinlein "the-man-who-learned-better."

Even these can be dramatized, effectively, in the form of scenes. Let the stories, and the characters, speak for themselves. Try it. Later on, if you wish, you can speak to the reader directly, in your voice or in a voice adopted for the purpose.

As examples, take the series of six stories published separately in *Analog* and later collected as a kind of novel in the Tor publication *Crisis!* They dealt with a man named Bill Johnson (he tends not to be noticed—his desire is not to be noticed—so that I chose the most common name in my telephone book). Johnson does not know who he is until he finds a message that tells him he has come from the future to help prevent those contemporary problems that have led to a bleak tomorrow. He has one apparently unique ability, to foresee consequences, and a strong emotional impulse to intervene in those situations that threaten to turn out badly for humanity. He gets involved in one contemporary problem after another, but each time he does he forgets who he is and must leave himself a message.

I came up with the idea for a CBS series back in the 1960s, and when nothing happened wrote the first episode as a story, "Child of the Sun." Ironically, "Child of the Sun" was optioned by a production company at Universal, as a possible television series. When the option wasn't exercised after a year, I thought that decision-makers might have thought "Child of the Sun" was interesting but there weren't enough situations to make up a series. So I wrote five more of them, and even listed them on the contents page as "episodes." No one has yet taken the hint.

Nevertheless, the method of the *Crisis!* episodes is worth citing because I wrote the stories as filmic as possible. Each of the stories was done entirely in scenes, and each was told as if seen by a camera—with total objectivity, with no exposition, no dipping into anyone's thoughts or recollections. "Child of the Sun" begins:

> He opened his eyes. He was lying on a bed. The sheets and
> blankets were tangled as if he had been thrashing around in
> his sleep.

> He looked up at the ceiling. Cracks ran across the old plaster
> like a map of a country he did not recognize. . . .

Because the method is totally scenic, the purpose of the scene can never be explicit. Implied in the awakening of Bill Johnson, however, are such questions as who is this man and why are his perceptions important? On the second page, he finds a message on a cassette player that tells Johnson who he is and what he has done and where he is from and what he must do.

By the middle of the scene, Johnson picks up a newspaper and reads an article that moves him to action—packing a few belongings, saying goodbye to a middle-aged woman who manages the cheap apartment building where he was renting a kitchenette, getting on a bus, talking to fellow bus riders, and finally pulling out the clipping he had read in the newspaper earlier:

> ### CALIFORNIA GIRL ABDUCTED
>
> Death Valley, CA (AP)—The four-year-old daughter of Ellen McCleary, managing engineer of the Death Valley Solar Power Project, was reported missing today.
>
> McCleary returned from her afternoon duties at the Project to discover her housekeeper, Mrs. Fred Ross, bound and gagged behind her own bed and the McCleary girl, Shelly, gone from the home.
>
> Authorities at the Project and the local sheriff's office have refused to release any information about the possible abductor, but sources close to the Project suggest that oil interests have reason to desire the failure of the Project.
>
> McCleary was recently divorced from her husband of ten years, Stephen Webster. Webster's location is unknown.
>
> Authorities will neither confirm nor deny that the abductor left a message behind.

I'm not fond of using news stories, but it is integral to plot and Johnson's nature. In any case, this is a scene whose purpose, once the protagonist has been identified and the point of his presence in the situation has been revealed, is to involve the protagonist in a quest the purpose and significance of which we do not yet know, but as experienced readers (particularly of SF stories) we have confidence will be revealed to us before the story is over.

To take another example, let me offer a complete 800-word scene from the opening pages of "The Lens of Time" (*Analog*, October 1995):

Broadway swarmed with life like water in a stagnant pond. Scarlet and yellow omnibuses raced through the open parts of the street and locked wheels where it was narrower. At irregular intervals they stopped to discharge passengers. When the passengers stretched their hands through a hole in the roof to pay the conductor his ransom for release, he pulled a cord that opened the door and deposited them in a sea of slippery mud, to run a gauntlet of cart wheels and horses' hooves, before they could reach the relative safety of hotels such as the Astor House or the St. Nicholas. Railway cars holding as many as thirty persons and drawn by two or even four horses came down the side streets. All these among the carriages, the commercial wagons, and the foot traffic contributed to the clutter and the crush. Next to the buildings or leaning over into the gutters were boxes, buckets, lidless flour barrels, baskets, decayed tea chests, rusty iron pans, and earthenware jars full of ashes and vegetable refuse. All contributed their share of foul odors to that of the horse dung steaming in the ankle-deep mire of the street.

The man in the black cloak stood at the corner of 8th street and Broadway looking at the turmoil around him with the observant gaze of a scientist, absorbing the scene as a panorama before isolating the individual parts and analyzing them. What passed him was a polyglot mix of workmen and gentry, settled citizens and confused immigrants with their bundles of clothing hung over their backs. Some spoke American English, but many conversed in German and others in English transformed in Ireland into music.

In all that confusion of traffic and appearance and dress, no one paid any attention to the man in the black cloak. He picked his way down Broadway, staying close to the buildings to avoid being splashed by the onrushing vehicles and horses, and worked his way around heaps of refuse, until he reached Jones street. His eyes focused on a sign attached to a building on the west side. The sign read "Pfaff's" and stairs led down to a cellar entrance.

As the man in the black cloak opened the door his ears were assailed by the confused clamor of laughter and multilingual conversation, clattering dishes and clinking glasses, and voices shouting, and he breathed in the heady odor of lager beer and rich German food. The room was filled with wooden tables and chairs that extended to a modest bar against the wall, flanked by a swinging door leading to a kitchen. As the man in the black cloak stepped into the room, he could see that the room extended into an alcove under the sidewalk. There, at a huge table set with dishes and glasses, some twenty young men and a couple of women were talking with great animation. All but one were fashionably dressed.

The man in the black cloak seated himself at an unoccupied table nearby and ordered a glass of wine before he turned to watching the table of revelers in the alcove. Occasionally he could overhear a scrap of conversation or song, but mostly the competition for attention created only a hubbub of noise. From time to time someone left, lingeringly, as if tearing himself from loved ones, and sometimes one or more persons arrived to a chorus of welcomes and clasps of fellowship.

Finally a man arose unsteadily from near the head of the table, and with many long farewells, made his way toward the door. He had a young face, although at the moment it was flushed and the eyes were a bit glazed. He had a broad forehead from which his long brown hair had already started to recede, a substantial nose that had been broken at least once, and a receding chin that he partially concealed by a bushy, swooping mustache. As he passed, the man in the black cloak arose from his chair and said, "Mr. O'Brien?"

"You have my name, sir," the other said, a touch of Ireland in his voice. "But you have the advantage of me."

"You are Fitz-James O'Brien, the noted poet, playwright, and author?" the man in the cloak continued.

"The same," O'Brien replied with a hint of impatience.

"Let me apologize for accosting you thus," the man in the cloak said, "but my name is T. J. Whelpley. I am a physician, and a writer, though not by any means of your stature and renown, and I have been waiting to speak to you on a matter of some urgency."

"And what would that be, Dr. Whelpley?"

"Will you come to my rooms, Mr. O'Brien, so that I can show you something interesting and we can talk at leisure?"

"Do you have any beer?" O'Brien asked.

"I have some reasonably good claret."

"Claret will do," O'Brien said. "I was going to my room to work on a new poem, but, to tell the truth, it was only duty that called me and not Calliope or Erato. Lead on, my dear Dr. Whelpley."

You don't have to recognize the scene—New York City in the 1850s or the research that produced the authentic details of what lower Manhattan looked and sounded and smelled like then [but you might wish to refer to this scene when the time comes to focus on description]—and you don't have to know that Fitz-James O'Brien wrote a classic science-fiction short story "The Diamond Lens" or that Dr. Whelpley introduced him to the microscope and acted as his consultant on the story that made O'Brien's reputation. You don't even have to know that O'Brien volunteered his services to the Union army shortly after the Civil War began, and that he died of septic poisoning from an untreated gunshot wound in 1862, at the age of thirty-four. It would increase your appreciation of the story if you knew those things; some of this information is dramatized or suggested in the remainder of the story. Most important, however, is the fact that the scene itself raises questions about the purpose of the man in the black cloak in this nineteenth-century New York setting and by the end of the scene that purpose is accomplished by persuading the poet O'Brien to come to his rooms for an important purpose. What that purpose is, and why it is important, ought to keep the reader interested in reading further.

While nothing dramatic happens in the scene [the story's purpose is to dramatize a moment in history, using self-referential SF materials, when the American public had a choice between the promise of burgeoning science and the heady passions that would led to war], the method is essentially scenic and dramatic.

7

A Local Habitation and a Name

The poet's eye, in a fine frenzy rolling,
Doth glance from heaven to earth, from earth to heaven;
And as imagination bodies forth
The forms of things unknown, the poet's pen
Turns them to shapes, and gives to airy nothing
A local habitation and a name.

William Shakespeare

Readers buy into a story for a variety of reasons, but one that is in the author's control is the feeling of reality created by a firm sense of time and place. After the portrayal of credible characters, the next task an author must perform is to identify for the reader where events happen. The first step is for the author to imagine the scene in detail, to experience it through every sense, so that the art of presenting it to the reader is the art of describing what one sees, hears, smells, touches, and tastes.

A mistake often made by beginning authors is the telling of a story at the level of story, recapitulating situations and interactions from what writers have read; it is natural that writers start that way—writers emerge out of readers, and their first instinct is to create what they have most enjoyed. But no reader really wants second-hand Stephen King or third-hand *Star Trek*. The only kind of writing that is worth doing—and readers sense this even though they may not behave like it sometimes—is what only the individual author can write, and that means that authors must write out of their own unique existence and experience. They must internalize every aspect of their stories, which means to totally re-imagine everything.

In the kinds of stories that emerge out of the love of reading, events happen without being solidly grounded or adequately re-imagined. In order for the reader to care, the author must care, must write from the heart, must see and feel everything as if it were really happening. When the process is done well, the author should feel that he or she can walk around inside the scene and know where objects are located even if they are not part of the story.

According to Caroline Gordon, Honoré de Balzac discovered that a character did not exist in fiction until that character had interacted with another character, and Gustave Flaubert discovered that nothing exists in fiction until it has been located in time and place with an appeal to at least three senses. In *Madame Bovary*, the physician Charles Bovary is summoned late at night to a farm eighteen miles away to set a broken leg. It is the occasion upon which he meets Emma, the patient's daughter, and Flaubert describes the scene in this fashion:

> Towards four o'clock in the morning, Charles, well wrapped up in his cloak, set out for the Bertaux. Still sleepy from the warmth of his bed, he let himself be lulled by the quiet trot of his horse. When it stopped of its own accord in front of those holes surrounded with thorns that are dug on the margin of furrows, Charles awoke with a start, suddenly remembered the broken leg, and tried to call to mind all the fractures he knew. The rain had stopped, day was breaking, and on the branches of the leafless trees birds roosted motionless, their little feathers bristling in the cold morning wind. The flat country stretched as far as eye could see, and the tufts of trees round the farm at long intervals seemed like dark violet stains on the vast grey surface, that on the horizon faded into the gloom of the sky. Charles from time to time opened his eyes, his mind grew weary, and sleep coming upon him, he soon fell into a doze wherein his recent sensations blending with memories, he became conscious of a double self, at once student and married man, lying in his bed as but now, and crossing the operation theatre as of old. The warm smell of poultices mingled in his brain with the fresh odor of dew; he heard the iron rings rattling along the curtain-rods of the bed and saw his wife sleeping.

And a little later:

> The horse slipped on the wet grass; Charles had to stoop to pass under the branches. The watchdogs in their kennels barked, dragging at their chains. As he entered the Bertaux the horse took fright and stumbled.
>
> It was a substantial-looking farm. In the stables, over the top of the open doors, one could see great cart-horses quietly feeding from new racks. Right along the outbuildings extended a large dunghill, from which manure liquid oozed, while amidst

fowls and turkeys five or six peacocks, a luxury in Chaucois farmyards, were foraging on top of it. The sheepfold was long, the barn high, with walls smooth as your hand. Under the cart-shed were two large carts and four ploughs, with their whips, shafts and harnesses complete, whose fleeces of blue wool were getting soiled by the fine dust that fell from the granaries. The courtyard sloped upwards, planted with trees set out symmetrically, and the chattering noise of a flock of geese were heard near the pond.

These passages may provide more details about a nineteenth-century French farm than many readers are interested in knowing (like the school girl's review of a book about penguins), but, after reading them, no one can deny the feeling that this place existed, indeed still exists in every reader's mind when the passage is read. The reason it provides a sense of reality is that Flaubert was describing something that he himself had experienced, or had imagined a scene so intensely that it was the same as experience. And he reported it to the reader by describing not only the way it looked but also the way it sounded (horse trotting, iron rings rattling, dogs barking, chains dragging, horses feeding, geese chattering), the way it smelled (warm poultices, dew, manure liquid), and the way it felt (warm sleepiness, smooth barn walls, dusty wool). The sense of taste isn't evoked here, although it is in the following scene, but certainly taste, too, is effective in creating a feeling of verisimilitude, and if something is eaten or is drunk without the taste being reported to the reader, unless the character involved is distracted from tasting, the reader is not going to believe that eating or drinking really took place. Sometimes, as Proust reported in *Remembrance of Things Past*, taste can be the most powerful sense.

The reader's awareness that reality impinges itself upon all the senses lies behind the need to imagine and to describe in rich detail. In the real world no place exists without dimensions and without furniture, of one kind or another; no place exists that does not have characteristic sounds and smells and touch and sometimes tastes—unless, of course, the character has been deprived of one or more of these sensations, individually or by special circumstances, and in these cases the deprivation itself ought to be noted. If, for instance, a character enters a room that is totally dark, the reader would be informed, but it is equally true that if a character enters a place that is totally soundless, that too is exceptional. The same is true of places that are without odor or touch. But often, in describing a setting, anything other than how it looks is omitted, and the impression it leaves is that the character is in a place that does not have odor or sound or touch.

Flaubert's pace and exhaustive detail are not for everybody or for every kind of story, but they reveal what a sense of place is capable of achieving. Settings in which the actions of the story take place are essential.

In the scene from "The Lens of Time" in "Scene—The Smallest Dramatic Unit" I gave an example of my attempt to evoke New York City of the 1850s. But description is possible, even desirable, in scenes in places that have never existed—the future, for instance. When I first learned about Flaubert's "discovery," I was in the midst of writing a series of stories about the next steps in humanity's explorations of space. That was back in 1957. I had published "The Cave of Night," "Hoax," and "The Big Wheel." For Caroline Gordon's Writers Workshop I wrote "Powder Keg" (and would later write "Space Is a Lonely Place" and publish them all as *Station in Space* in 1958), and I included the following description, which was intended to make an experience real to the reader that was at that time still imaginary, spaceflight.

> They walked across the pitted, concrete landing field toward the skyscraper-tall three-stage rocket, broad-finned at the bottom, its wings even broader at the top. . . .
>
> As they climbed up concrete steps onto the takeoff platform, the ship had grown so tall that it seemed about to topple over on them. They approached the giant hammerhead crane beside the shuttle. Grant's footsteps clicked behind them.
>
> There was a smell of old fire to the platform mingled with the sharp odor of acid and the mingled stench of old chemicals and oil. . . .
>
> After the interminable drone of the check-off, the lifting of the shuttle took him by surprise. Kars gave no warning on the intercom; there was suddenly more than half a ton of lead sitting on his chest, squeezing the breath out of his body, refusing to let him draw in more.
>
> His head was turned slightly to the side, forced deep into the cushions, and he could not move it. Outside the night flamed red and yellow and white, until he had to shut his eyes against the brilliance. The ship trembled and shuddered and shook, and the roaring of the rocket motors was everywhere, pervading every tortured cell of his body. . . .

The reality that began a couple of years later turned many of these descriptions into fantasy (and turned *Station in Space* immediately into alternate history). I got the look of the rocket (I had to imagine the other sensory details) from an issue of *Collier's* devoted to the possibility of a space station and a trip to Mars, written by Willy Ley and Wernher von Braun and illustrated by Chesley Bonestell. It was later published as a lavishly illustrated book, *The Conquest of Space*. Research is an asset not only to imagining in detail but also in getting the basic facts right; a reader's confidence is easy to forfeit and a loss of confidence in one aspect of a story often extends to every other aspect, whereas validation at the basic level of reality often lends credence to everything that is invented.

Setting can be established in various ways, from the descriptions otherwise detached from the events of the story that often are provided by the omniscient author to the subjective impressions of the first-person narrator. Flaubert's settings are somewhere in the middle—although they are not Charles Bovary's observations, they are presented to the reader in the way in which Bovary (or anyone approaching the farm) would have encountered them. The setting in "Powder Keg" is a bit more impressionistic—although not first-person, they are presented as Captain Phillips's perceptions.

The author's challenge is to create dramatic pictures in the reader's mind, and better pictures are created when the author takes the time and trouble to re-create the pictures from the words on the page. That is the essential part of revision—being able to read the words on the page without supplementing them with the author's vision or intent. For the purpose of stimulating the reader to produce those pictures, two strategic approaches are possible: beginning with a dominant impression and moving to the details in the order in which they would be observed, or laying out the scene according to some other orderly principle. The key to success is order, and the avoidance of chaos or fuzziness.

One way to achieve unity and clarity is for the author to ask: if I were there, how would the details of this setting appear to me? But how an author goes about this is dictated by viewpoint and strategy. The ability to do it well can be improved by craft, which is knowing how to do something and being aware of what one is doing when one is doing it. Whichever method the author chooses, the best setting is one that the reader does not have to struggle to re-create. Whatever draws a reader out of a story to a consciousness of the story being told works against the story's success (unless, of course, the story is meta-fiction, or self-reflexive fiction, in which the story-telling process is the point of the story).

Finally, we should recognize that the demands of verisimilitude in setting vary with the kind of story. Comedy and farce require less attention to setting than naturalistic fiction, and adventure fiction, romances, gothics, and every other kind of fiction have their own emphases. Even settings in fantasy range from airy insubstantiality to dark Lovecraftian details. Some stories require the reader's belief that they are happening, have happened, or could happen; others require a suspension of disbelief. In every case, however, the author is wise to consider giving the places where his story takes place "a local habitation and a name."

8

Speaking Well in Print

Dialogue in fiction is easy to write but difficult to write well. Readers like it. It looks good on the page, opening the uniform gray of clotted text to the pleasant vistas of attractive designs and easy reading. But readers are quick to be turned off by dialogue that doesn't sound the way people talk or talk that doesn't move the story forward. For this and other reasons dialogue is a trap for the unwary.

Dialogue, like adjectives and adverbs, ought to force itself into a story. I recommend to student writers that they try to write their stories without any dialogue and then include only what they absolutely cannot do without. Generally, when people speak to each other the story stops, and whatever story movement even the best dialogue provides is slow compared to the movement provided by people actually doing something.

We know that to be true in life itself. Mostly when people are talking, nothing is getting done, and the longest dialogue communicates the least. If you think about the moments when you were mostly deeply involved in story, it was when the characters were actively trying to resolve their difficulties.

Nevertheless, most stories demand that two or more people confront each other and attempt to draw from each other the information or response that is necessary for resolution, or a step toward the change that is necessary for resolution. The mechanism usually is conversation, although other methods of communication are possible and often more dramatic: a raised eyebrow, a grimace, a frown, a gesture, a blow to a table or wall or another character. . . .

The key to good dialogue is a good ear. A good ear means that the author has listened to people talk and has heard the way they talk as well as understood the message embedded in their talk. Most people don't hear; most people don't even listen. They're too busy thinking about what they will say next. A good ear also means that the author has spoken his or her own written dialogue and proven that it is speakable and colloquial and appropriate. An experienced author can hear dialogue just by looking at it on the page.

Ford Madox Ford once used the fact that people don't listen to each other as a key to writing believable conversation. Two people he said ought to talk *past* each other rather than to each other. That certainly is a way to write *believable* conversation, but it isn't the way to write *effective* conversation unless the effectiveness desired is verisimilitude. That is where good conversation ought to start—in reflecting real speech—but it is not where conversation ought to end. Generally conversation ought to get somewhere as well as be natural.

In that respect, a second key to good dialogue is conciseness. In dialogue less is more. A good talker can go on for a quarter of an hour and say very little; a person of few words must choose them well, and even a grunt or an exclamation can speak volumes. Moreover, when people talk in the real world they generally speak in single sentences or even in partial sentences, and then the other person interjects a response or a comment or changes the subject.

A third key to good dialogue is the realization that the eye is more powerful than the ear. The word that people read carries more weight than the word people hear. A verbal contract isn't worth the paper it's written on. A sign is a more important prohibition than a spoken caution. And it is a fact of life that we become accustomed to language that we would find obtrusive or offensive if it were written; locker-room obscenities tend to get tuned out, but they cannot be tuned out on the page. That is why authors need to reflect, in their stories, not real conversation but the illusion of real conversation. Authors should reduce colloquialisms and vulgarisms and dialect and mannerisms to a level that, when read, will give the same impact as when heard. Some writers have estimated this as one-seventh of what is heard, but this is only a rough guide.

Once an author has determined that two people must confront each other and must speak, certain rules for good dialogue come into play. The first, as reflected above, is that dialogue must give the illusion of real speech. The second is that dialogue must be in character. It is not only the way that people speak, it is the way a specific character speaks, even though he or she does not speak like other people. In fact, since every person's speech is different, reflecting that difference in speech improves a story: not only does the character determine the speech, the speech characterizes the speaker.

The fourth rule is that dialogue must get somewhere and be about something. Like everything else in a story (and the key to good revision is cutting out everything in a story that isn't essential) dialogue must be necessary. For that reason, the parts of conversations that are normal in everyday life but add nothing to a story need to be left out. This includes the "hello's, how are you's, how's your family's, what's happening's," and other chit-chat that acknowledge somebody's entrance or existence or human relationships or simply smooth the rough spots of life. When the telephone rings, for instance, it should involve essential information or an important interruption, and the meaningless exchanges ought to be paraphrased, if they are included at all. For example:

> Sally picked up the telephone. After a few words she put it down, slowly. "John's dead!" she said.

A series of hellos, goodbyes, and other words and phrases without content would dilute drama. But that is not the worst sin in dialogue; the worst sin is using dialogue to disguise exposition. Exposition, which can be defined as the information a reader needs to understand the situation, is undramatic, but the expository "lump" is even lumpier in conversation, not only because it is awkward and rings false (the characters already know the information to be imparted; the phrase "as you know," or its equivalent, is a clue that what follows or precedes it is exposition), but because exposition takes far longer in conversation.

Mechanics

Good dialogue not only is difficult to write; the mechanics also often trip otherwise effective writers. Attributions, for instance. When someone speaks in a story, the reader wants to know who is speaking and should not be kept in doubt (unless the identity of the speaker is concealed for drama). Attribution ought to either precede the speech or follow close enough after the beginning of the speech that the reader can ascertain the speaker in a glance. Because attribution is less dramatic than the speech itself, this means that the usual form is a short statement followed by an attribution, or if the statement is longer than a line, the attribution often comes after the first natural phrase. Thus:

"Get your hands up!" he said.

But: "Get your hands up," he said, "or I'll make sure you never deal cards with those hands again!"

Two mistakes that writers sometimes make in their attributions: they separate the attribution from the statement by a period, or they capitalize the first letter of the attribution. Like this:

"Okay, you got me." he said.

Or: "Okay, you got me." He said.

The attribution is part of the sentence and ordinarily is separated from the statement by a comma (or a question mark or exclamation mark where appropriate). This applies to attributions that precede statements as well:

He said, "Okay, you got me."

Sometimes, although it's a bit old-fashioned, the attribution that precedes a statement is followed by a colon:

He said: "Okay, you got me."

Another mistake that writers sometimes make is to seek variations for the verb "said," such as "spoke," "stated," "uttered," "intoned," "muttered," "murmured," etc. It is permissible to use "asked" (but "queried" is a bit too formal, like most Latinate synonyms) or even a verb that includes the manner of speaking such as "shouted" or "screamed," and even "muttered" or "murmured" are possible in this context, although often what is spoken in these contexts are difficult to murmur, and often a speech is "hissed" that has no "s's." But the unforgivable error is to use a verb in attribution that is not a form of speech:

"Get your hands up!" he smirked.

Or: "Get your hands up!" he smiled. Or grinned. Or frowned. Or grimaced.

When a character's actions or expressions are important, such information should be provided after the attribution:

"Get your hands up!" he said and smiled.

Or: "Get your hands up!" he said, gesturing with his automatic.

In the first example, the "smile" should follow the action of "saying" rather than being coordinated with a comma, because it is difficult to say "Get your hands up" while smiling. Try it.

Whenever writers get into this kind of effort to spice up conversations, they run the risk of distracting the reader, sometimes with unconscious humor (and, of course, such mal- attributions have been and can be used for comic effect). In general, writers should simply repeat "said," which tends to fade out, visually. Seeking alternatives leads the author into what James Blish called "book-saidisms."

Sometimes no attribution is necessary; indeed, the best principle is to reduce attribution to the minimum necessary for clarity. If the person who is speaking is understood, as when speakers alternate brief statements, the attribution is unnecessary. This is particularly true in a rapid exchange of very short remarks, sometimes single words, when attribution not only is unnecessary, if opposing sides have been established, but would destroy the pace. Attribution also can be omitted when speech follows or precedes a statement about the character:

He raised his automatic. "Get your hands up!"

Or: "Get your hands up!" He raised his automatic.

Or even: "Get your hands up!" He smiled.

If you must "smile" something, make it an action independent of speech.

No attribution is necessary when a speech is in the same paragraph because the reader understands that the person involved in the rest of the paragraph is speaking. For the same reason, the author must be careful not to mix actions of characters within a single paragraph when unattributed speech is involved, and usually even when it is not (although sometimes action and reaction, or response, cannot be separated).

Another caution about punctuation (which can be applied to other aspects of the story in addition to dialogue) is the placement of question marks and exclamation marks. Commas and periods always go inside the closing quote marks, but question marks and exclamation marks can go either inside or outside, depending upon the meaning of the sentence. If the quoted material is the question or exclamation, the punctuation goes inside; if the sentence of which the quote is a part is the question or exclamation (and the quoted material is not) the punctuation goes outside the closing quotes. And note: single quote marks are used *only* inside double quotes and *never*, as they sometimes seem to be, to differentiate short quotes (such as single words) from longer quotes; writers often get this confused, because the British only use double quotes inside single quotes. They also put commas and periods outside closing quotes.

If dialogue continues into a second or third paragraph (ordinarily to be avoided, but sometimes someone is telling a long story or making a speech), the closing quote is omitted from the final statement of the first paragraph, and a quotation mark begins the next paragraph, to indicate to the reader that the speech continues past the previous paragraph and into the next.

Writing good dialogue is a skill to be cultivated. For some readers, good dialogue is what differentiates good books from ordinary books; and for some, good dialogue will justify the reading of any piece of fiction.

9

Suspense in Fiction

There are two kinds of suspense in fiction: one involves information that the author deliberately withholds from the reader; the other involves events that are unknown because they have not yet happened or have not yet been discovered.

For this reason viewpoint is as important as the information or the event. An omniscient author's viewpoint does not work well with the suspense story, because all information—including that which the reader most wants to know—is withheld until the author chooses to reveal it. The suspense story responds best to a limited viewpoint; one reason the detective story, for instance, is usually told from the first-person viewpoint is because information is withheld more naturally when the detective who is narrating the story has not yet discovered it, and has no way of knowing what it is until he comes across it. And yet, even first-person narration is told after the fact, and the narrator, with conscious artfulness, is withholding information. The only reason first-person narration works well and omniscient narration works at all with the suspense story is because readers do not press too hard upon authors' conventions in the suspense story. But how many times have you, as a reader, clenched your teeth in anger as a chapter ended with the detective saying, "Now I knew who had committed the crime."

Even worse is the omniscient commentary in what has become known as the Mary Roberts Rinehart school of suspense, "Had she but known what dire consequences. . . !"

Only third-person limited narration, therefore, can be truly effective in telling the suspense story. The objection to withheld information, in case it is not obvious, is that the reader's impatience becomes directed at the author and not the narrative. As Percy Lubbock pointed out in his chapter on viewpoint in *The Craft of Fiction* (1923), "the story may be told so vivaciously that the presence of the minstrel is forgotten. . . . If the spell is weakened at any moment, the listener is recalled from the scene to the mere author before him. . . ."

Suspense about events (what will happen next?) differs in another significant way from suspense about information (who dunit? what will make sense out of the data already presented?). Ordinarily we think of the suspense story as dealing primarily with the second kind of suspense: what is happening to Rosemary? what does her baby look like? The first kind of suspense is usually associated with the adventure story. But because few stories are pure examples of their type—there always is some adventure in the suspense story and some suspense in the adventure story—readers usually find both kinds of suspense: in addition to the questions raised above, what will Rosemary do? and what will the satanists do to her? In the formal, English detective story, the suspense usually is about information; the hard-boiled American detective story usually involves action. Raymond Chandler once said that a good detective story is one you would read even if the last page were missing.

The questions authors need to ask themselves when considering suspense stories is how to make events come unexpectedly so that readers will become excited about what will happen next and how to plant questions in readers' minds that will only be answered by information or events that will come later.

My one conscious effort at creating "the event" kind of suspense was modeled after A. E. van Vogt, whom I had always considered the master of this kind of suspense in science fiction. Van Vogt's article on "Complication in the Science Fiction Story" (*Of Worlds Beyond*, 1947, reprinted more recently by Advent Press) is still worth reading, with its description of the 800-word scene and so forth. But what I noticed about van Vogt's fiction was that something unexpected always happened at the end of a scene, with implications that would be explored in the next scene, and so on. When I wrote a short novel that appeared in its magazine form as "Name Your Pleasure" and as Part II of my novel *The Joy Makers*, I tried to work in van Vogt's unexpectedness at the end of every scene. James Blish called van Vogt's technique "the extensively recomplicated story" and claimed that Charles Harness did it better than anyone. In its crudest form, this is the cliff-hanger technique used in so many adventure serials and soap operas, of which Edgar Rice Burroughs was the master, sometimes alternating chapters about separated characters so that readers had to read two chapters to get the characters off their respective cliffs. Burroughs even ended at least two novels (*A Princess of Mars* and particularly *The Gods of Mars*) with cliff-hangers.

There are dangers in this kind of approach to suspense, however. The unexpected event cannot be totally unexpected. It must be appropriate in light of what has gone before and what will come after. Otherwise one sacrifices coherence for suspense (van Vogt often was accused of leaving too many questions unanswered). And the cliff-hanger eventually seems artificial and manipulative.

Ideally, as Poul Anderson has pointed out, one should say about any turn of events in a story, "How surprising! But how natural! Why didn't I see it coming?" The secret, if there is one, is to tell readers what is going to happen but in such a way that readers don't know they have been told until afterward. The late Caroline Gordon once said that in any well-constructed story the ending should be implicit in the first sentence; as an example, I like to cite Hemingway's *The Old Man and the Sea*, "He was an old man who fished alone in a skiff in the Gulf Stream and he had gone eighty-four days now without catching a fish." In my story, "The Cave of Night" (first part of *Station in Space*), for instance, I threw away a comment early in the narrative that a situation like the Floyd Collins incident or the Kathy Fiscus incident "could probably be constructed artificially, but if the world ever discovered the fraud, it would never forgive." At the end of the story, it turns out that the man trapped in space is a fraud, but the fraud turns out to be a greater tragedy for the individual. Obviously this kind of clue planting (James called it "undercutting") varies in effectiveness with the sophistication of the reader; the more sophisticated readers will pick up clues sooner and recognize them for what they are, but those kinds of readers are likely to be pleased by the author's skill and their own shrewdness. Sometimes, of course, clues can be planted so covertly that only a Joyce scholar can ferret out the meaning, and these may do little good as foreshadowing.

The story that uses information as its source of suspense must be sure that readers know what the question is: Where is the purloined letter? who is committing the murders in the Rue Morgue? How did the murderer get out of the locked room? What really happened that night at Manderly? But the writer of this kind of suspense bears a burden as well: the answer must match the question in ingenuity and drama. If the reader comes up with a better answer than the author, or even if the author's answer is pedestrian or otherwise unrewarded, the reader is going to be disappointed. That is why suspense stories, like detective stories, often are written backward, starting with the answer and working back to the question.

Finally, of course, suspense isn't everything. Satisfaction is everything. The story needs to be suspenseful enough to keep readers reading, but that can be accomplished in a number of ways—the best way may be to get readers involved in caring about the characters. If readers care about the characters and want them to get out of their predicament, readers will continue to read even if they know that the characters are doomed, or know that they will find a solution.

10

Getting the Words Right

Ernest Hemingway once gave an interview to the *Paris Review*. It was reprinted in *Writers at Work*, *The Paris Review Interviews*, *Second Series* (1963).

Interviewer: How much rewriting do you do?

Hemingway: It depends. I rewrote the ending to *Farewell to Arms*, the last page of it, thirty-nine times before I was satisfied.

Interviewer: Was there some technical problem there? What was it that had stumped you?

Hemingway: Getting the words right.

When everything else has been taken care of in a piece of fiction, the last thing that must be got right is the words. As a matter of fact, if the words are right the other things may not matter. Sometimes, if the story is engrossing or the adventure is exciting or the romance is enthralling or the pathos is heartrending, the rightness of the words may not matter. But the right words can redeem a banal plot, round out the flattest character, bring the most vaguely perceived place into vivid view and turn the dullest series of events into scintillating action; they even can make a reader forget that the story has no point, or believe that there is a point that the author has chosen to conceal.

Unless authors are blessed with a unique ear for language or gifted with a special turn of phrase, they come late to the realization of the importance of the right word. And yet they know that the true wordsmiths in science fiction and fantasy, like Sturgeon and Lafferty and Bradbury, can create marvels out of dross. At some point in the creation of a story, usually in the revision such as Hemingway refers to, the words must be cleaned and polished and set neatly row by row.

The language that isn't quite right grates on the ears and jangles the nerves. The words that are exact and precise soothe the spirit and clarify and enrich the story. The right words are more than avoiding the wrong words. Writers who wish to be master of their craft must develop a sensitivity to language, a critical dissatisfaction with imprecision and infelicity, and a dedication to a search for the right word and the telling phrase long after the ordinary writer has settled for something about right. Ask any master writer to describe the most difficult part of his craft, and he will reply, "Getting the words right."

Oh, yes. The last words of *A Farewell to Arms* are:

He went down the hall. I went to the door of the room.

"You can't come in now," one of the nurses said.

"Yes I can," I said.

"You can't come in yet."

"You get out," I said. "The other one too."

But after I got them out and shut the door and turned off the light it wasn't any good. It was like saying good-bye to a statue. After a while I went out and left the hospital and walked back to the hotel in the rain.

11

How to Be a Good Critiquer and Still Remain Friends

For those of you new to the art of critiquing other people's fiction, a few words of advice:

The value of the critique is only partially to provide feedback for the author; perhaps the most important part is to develop critical skills that can be applied to your own work. Being considerate of other people's feelings about what they have created is not simply a practical application of the Golden Rule—that is, if you aren't cruel about the other person's story, they may not be cruel about yours when your turn comes—it is practice in being even-handed in appraising your own work, neither evaluating it too highly nor hating it too much.

A critique should begin by evaluating the intent. The New Criticism thought this was a fallacy—the intentional fallacy—but unless you understand what the author was trying to do, you will be unable to evaluate how well the work succeeds. Every story has some ideal form at which it is aiming—this might be called the Platonic theory of fiction—and the ultimate goal of the critiquer is to discern what the ideal form is and to help the author see it and how to achieve it. Sometimes that is as difficult for the critiquer as for the author, but it is an essential part of helping the author and improving the skills and understanding of the critiquer.

The critiquer should try to see what is good about a story before suggesting ways to improve what does not work as well. But this and the preceding does not imply that the critiquer should hold the story to some lesser standard because the author is not a professional writer. Hemingway said that writing a novel is getting into the ring with Mr. Tolstoy, and writing an SF story is getting into the ring with all those writers who get their stories published. The only meaningful success for a story is publication, and all stories should be measured against that standard: What would it take to make the story publishable? Being considerate of the author's feelings is tactful and tactically desirable—authors accept criticism better when they aren't angry or hurt. But the greatest insult one can offer an author is not to take the author's work seriously and hold it to the highest standards.

The author should understand that not everybody reads stories identically. Everyone brings a different set of experiences and expectations to the reading process, which results in a series of readings that impinge tangentially upon the story itself—this is part of what is known as "reader-response criticism." The author's job is to put the various viewpoints into context—if the spread of opinions is great, the work may need tightening, the expectations it arouses, more careful consideration. As for the rest, the author should take what is useful and apply it, and store the rest away for possible later consideration. After all, the final decisions about the form and substance of the story are the author's.

In general, critiquers should avoid commenting about mechanical mistakes—punctuation, spelling, even diction or sentence structure except when that gets in the way of communication. A general remark ("the mechanics kept pulling me away from the story," for instance) is sufficient. Focus on the general response.

Everybody should comment on every story but be succinct. Be analytical; don't ramble. Try to get to the heart of your reactions, because this is the art that you wish to cultivate for your own work—the ability to figure out quickly what works for you and what doesn't. You may question individual sentences or even paragraphs that raise questions the story doesn't answer, but concentrate your attention most on the overall impression. That overall impression, your understanding of what the author is trying to do and how well the author has accomplished it, ought to be directed toward what would be necessary to make the story publishable.

Finally, remember that the hardest task writers have is to know when they have written well and when they have written badly. Most writers have creative desires and abilities or they would not be writers; but they often aren't good critics, which takes another set of talents entirely. That is what we learn in workshops, as much through critiquing other people's stories as in having our own critiqued.

Goethe's recommendations for critics is a good standard for a workshop:

(1) What did the author intend to do?
(2) How well did he or she do it?
(3) (last and least important) Was it a good thing to do?

Part 2

Writing Science Fiction

12

The Origins of Science Fiction

Before we can talk about science fiction, we need to establish what we are talking about. SF, as I will call it from now on, has had many definitions, none of them truly satisfactory, and even the name itself has detractors. But perhaps I can justify its appropriateness, since the name seems to stick better than any other. Science fiction is the fictional exploration of the unknown. The "science" part refers to the nature of the exploration. "Science" means "knowledge." The fictional exploration is into ways of "knowing."

Humanity has tried many strategies for knowing: transcendence, mysticism, revelation, psychic powers of all kinds, drugs, prayer. . . . Science is the strategy invented by Western Civilization beginning about the time of the Renaissance and accelerated by the Industrial Revolution and the Age of Enlightenment. The science strategy involves rational investigation and the development of theories supported by reproducible results. This is the strategy incorporated in SF, and the others are excluded.

But we need a definition a bit more precise. The one I have been using for SF lately is "the literature of discontinuity." Traditional fiction is the literature of continuity: it deals with people we know in the world we are familiar with operating by rules we understand.

A distinguished writer and critic of SF, Algis Budrys, tells a story about the second person on Earth. As he rises to look at the wonders lying all about him, he feels a tap on his shoulder, and a voice from the first person on Earth says, "Let me just acquaint you with my rules." The third person on Earth gets a similar tap, but the voice says, "Let me acquaint you with *the* rules."

Traditional fiction is concerned with the attempt by the characters to discover what the rules are and the story describes how they learn about them and how to live with them. SF, on the other hand, begins with the assumption that the rules may not make sense, are incomplete, or are inappropriate for this new situation. SF is about new situations, which is why I call it "the literature of discontinuity." Fantasy also is the literature of discontinuity, however. Although SF and fantasy have some basic similarities, we need to distinguish between them because we read them differently.

Fantasy presents its readers with a world in which one of the "rules" has been altered arbitrarily: let us assume, the writer of fantasy says, that little girls can fall down a rabbit hole into wonderland, or that some people can transform themselves into bats and drink blood and live forever, or that a fairy world where magic works lies just next door or all around us unperceived. Just discard your skepticism for a bit and let the fantasy weave its spell around a world where our wishes or our fears can come true.

The premise of SF is not the same; it asks the reader only to assume that the world has been changed by an unusual but natural event. The reader must suspend disbelief only to the extent of granting the writer a plausible assumption. I distinguish between the literatures of discontinuity, therefore, by calling fantasy "the literature of difference" and SF "the literature of change."

Fantasy has been around since the beginnings of storytelling; SF, only since the early to mid nineteenth century. That is because humanity has long believed in the possibility of unseen powers and mysterious forces, but it has only believed in the existence of man-made change since the Industrial and Scientific Revolutions. Up to that point the only changes humanity experienced were the changes of the seasons and the disasters of drought, flood, disease, revolution, and war.

Wind power and water power brought about a kind of mini-Industrial Revolution as early as the twelfth and thirteenth centuries, but it was aborted by years of bad weather, the Black Plague, and the Hundred Years War. Chemical power—the burning of coal to produce steam and the harnessing of that steam to perform useful work—launched a process that has not ended yet: scientific discovery and technological application have combined to produce continuing change not only in the way people live but the way they think about themselves and their relationship to the universe.

In the Middle Ages, for instance, people, whatever their station, considered themselves a part of creation. To understand it, they had only to consult revelation or its interpreters; once they discovered the divine plan their responsibility was to accommodate themselves to it. In the Age of Science, people consider themselves a part of nature, and, most important, the part capable of understanding the rest. That becomes their responsibility: to understand the universe and their place in it. To understand it, they must discover how it works and develop theories to explain why it works in that fashion and not in some other; in comparison with the universe, they have become minuscule, but the power to understand gives them the power to go anywhere and to do anything.

The realization that life was changing, that cities were growing as people walked off the farms and into the factories, that distances were shrinking as railroad engines and steamships took the place of wagons and sailing craft, that scientists were unveiling the mysteries of the human body, the movements of the planets and the stars, new forms of energy, and the properties of matter in various combinations—all these led certain writers in the nineteenth century to consider how change had affected humanity in the past and might be a continuing force in human affairs. Those speculations, when turned into stories, created what we have since come to call science fiction: the literature of change.

Some scholars consider Mary Shelley's 1818 *Frankenstein* the first SF novel; others believe that Edgar Allan Poe and Nathaniel Hawthorne wrote stories in this tradition in the 1830s and 1840s. Certainly these were the first attempts to cope with the idea of human change. Still, these writers, and their immediate successors, did not establish the new genre; that was left for the French master, Jules Verne, whose first SF *voyage extraordinaire, Journey to the Center of the Earth*, was published in 1864, and whose novels of technological improvement and fabulous journeys would transport his readers twice a year until his death in 1905.

A decade before Verne's death, H. G. Wells began publishing his scientific romances, beginning with a series of stories in 1894 and continuing with a succession of brilliant novels—from *The Time Machine* in 1895 to *The First Men in the Moon* in 1901. Between those two were published *The War of the Worlds*, *The Invisible Man*, *The Island of Dr. Moreau*, and *When the Sleeper Wakes*. To the Vernian tradition of exploration and adventure was added the Wellsian tradition of ideas and social comment; Verne and Wells continue as the twin sources of almost all SF.

Society's increasing dependence on machines demanded new and better-educated workers, and all across the industrialized world primary education became compulsory and secondary education, a growing option. That educational revolution, in turn, created a new class of readers, and new magazines were published to occupy the increasing leisure hours of workers and their sons (women's minds were considered too fragile for such reading): first dime novels, then boys' magazines, then the new pulp magazines that started with the creation of *Argosy* in 1896, which advertised 192 pages of fiction for a dime. *Argosy* and its companions and competitors offered adventure stories of all kinds, but readers soon began expressing a preference for one variety of story over another, and the category magazines got going with *Detective Story Monthly* in 1915, followed by *Western Story Magazine* in 1919.

The twin traditions of Verne and Wells merged in 1926 with the creation of the first science-fiction magazine, *Amazing Stories*. Publisher Hugo Gernsback, an emigré from Luxembourg fascinated by invention, an inventor himself and a publisher of such popular-science magazines as *Modern Electrics* and *Science and Invention*, said that he was going to publish "a charming romance of science intermingled with scientific fact and prophetic vision." He called it "scientifiction," and he reprinted most of Verne and Wells and a good deal of Poe as well.

In 1929 Gernsback lost control of *Amazing Stories* and founded several other magazines that eventually were combined into *Wonder Stories*. In the first of these he coined the word "science fiction," a word that has stuck better than any of the alternatives that have been suggested, such as "speculative fiction" or "science fantasy." Another competitor sprang up in 1930, *Astounding Stories of Super Science*. The Clayton chain of pulp magazines decided to add it to the thirteen magazines it was publishing in part because they were printing the covers on a sheet big enough for sixteen, and the SF cover was virtually free. Such were the reasons that controlled the destinies of magazines, authors, and genres. But the Clayton chain failed in 1933, the third year of the depression, *Astounding* was taken over by Street & Smith, and came under the editorship of John W. Campbell in 1937.

True to his popular-science background, Gernsback believed that SF should promote understanding of science and technology through fiction, that SF should be a sort of candy-coating for a pill of information; one reader even suggested that the scientific information in the story should be marked so that the reader could identify it more easily. The original *Astounding Stories* editor, Harry Bates, wanted a pulp-adventure story set against a pseudo-scientific background instead of battlefields or exotic far-off lands. Campbell asked for well-written stories placed in science-important settings—a story, he said, that "could be published in a magazine in the 25th century."

In these magazines of the 1920s and 1930s the readers and writers of SF interacted to develop ideas and conventions and images. Isolated in large part from the rest of literature, the genre went through an intense growth, nurtured by what has been called the SF "ghetto," creating a fandom, breeding new writers out of fans, building stories on top of stories. Out of this hothouse atmosphere sprang such authors as Isaac Asimov, Robert A. Heinlein, Theodore Sturgeon, A. E. van Vogt, and what has come to be called "the golden age of science fiction."

World War II changed SF as well. Not only was it the first major conflict whose course was determined by science and technology, it validated those persistent, and often ridiculed SF concepts, the rocketship and the atom bomb. In the late 1940s and early 1950s, as a consequence, SF proliferated in new magazines, anthologies, and hardcover and softcover novels. One of those magazines, *The Magazine of Science Fiction and Fantasy*, emphasized literary quality; another, *Galaxy*, stressed sophisticated narrative, including satire, and it focused on social response to change. Later, in the 1960s, the English magazine *New Worlds* would produce an avant-garde fiction, utilizing the stylistic innovations of the mainstream, focusing on the helpless victims of change and sometimes displaying attitudes that were anti-science and even anti-science fiction.

All of these traditions still are displayed in SF, and all have been integrated into the genre, even the most recent, called "cyberpunk," which looks toward a gritty near-future world of vast new powers produced by drugs, computers, and international corporations from the perspectives of a rebellious underclass struggling to survive.

Today the walls of the SF ghetto have fallen. The magazines that once encompassed the entire territory have lost much of their influence. They still exist—unlike the other pulp magazines—but the SF book has become more important. Immediately after World War II, a handful of books were published each year; by the mid-1950s this had climbed to about 100; by the early 1970s, after a decline in the late 1950s and early 1960s, to a couple of hundred; and by the 1990s, to 2,000 SF and fantasy books a year. In the late 1990s SF and fantasy comprise the leading genre with the possible exception of the romance; one of every four or five books of fiction published is SF or fantasy; eight of the ten most popular films of all time, and thirteen of the top twenty, are science fiction or fantasy; and SF and fantasy books appear regularly on the *New York Times* best-seller lists.

What was once a minority literature, mostly consumed by the isolated adolescent male, has become a majority literature read occasionally by almost everybody, at least almost everybody born since 1950, and intensely by a substantial body of male and female high school and college students. Why they should be young may not be a surprise: the young have more time for reading, and more appetite for adventure, even for romantic escape; but even more important may be the fact that they have not yet clearly established for themselves the nature of the consensus that makes up the adult reality, and they have not accepted it as the only possible consensus, nor have they completed the series of compromises that integrate the self with the community.

In other words, they represent the state of mind with which readers must approach science fiction. A few readers carry this skeptical, questioning attitude into their adult lives and remain SF readers; their numbers seem to be growing along with the baby-boom generation. The isolated adolescent boy who was the SF reader of the 1930s has become a majority, and some of the adolescents who grew up after SF reading became acceptable have kept their speculative turns of mind after most of their contemporaries have given them up. Even the SF writers are getting older; Isaac Asimov and Robert Heinlein have died but Frederik Pohl and Arthur C. Clarke are in their eighties, and Jack Williamson is in his nineties; and all are still as productive as ever.

Asimov once identified a further, and perhaps more important, reason for the increasing readership of science fiction. "We live," he has said, "in a science-fiction world. It is the world we were writing about in the 1930s and 1940s." It is a world of space shuttles, planetary probes, intercontinental ballistic missiles, nuclear power, supersonic air travel, robots, computers, post-industrial societies, and unrelenting change. It is a high-tech world created by scientific research in which the losers of World War II became, for a while at least, the winners in the postwar technological competition, and in which scientific breakthroughs—thermonuclear fusion, say, or room-temperature superconductivity—will determine the future of the world and the development of space habitats or extraterrestrial colonies may determine the future of the human species.

In a science-fiction world, if you don't read SF not only are you not with it; you may not be behaving rationally. Traditional fiction may concern itself with a variety of adjustments to things-as-they-are, but it refuses, it must refuse if it is not to become SF, to incorporate one basic truth about the world: things-as-they-are is not things-as-they-will-be. Science fiction, which long has been accused of being escapist litera-ture, is the only fiction that is realistic; and any fiction that does not include in its basic description of the world that it is in the process of changing to something else is fantasy.

Perhaps we should be glad, then, that young people are reading SF. They are not simply indulging in wild flights of escapist adventure. There may be some of this in their SF reading, to be sure, but why not? Adolescence is the time for dreams of swashbuckling and derring-do. But SF has a serious side; even at its most adventurous, it involves an assumption of change and of adjustment to that change, and many of the changes to which SF characters must adjust are the changes that human-ity must face today or tomorrow. When Asimov was a boy people criti-cized him for reading escapist literature, but he points out he was escap-ing into pollution, overpopulation, war, plague, aliens, and worlds driven by science and technology.

Today we can see these problems looming ahead of us much more clearly, and we can deal with them realistically if we work at doing so. If our young people are reading about them, they may be able to deal with them more rationally. SF, John Campbell once said, allows us to practice in a no-practice area. Moreover, people who have grown up reading about conditions different from those in which they live and about characters who have interacted with those conditions and coped with them are less likely to feel helpless when the world changes around them. "Future shock," Alvin Toffler wrote in his book with that title, is the disease brought about by the premature arrival of the future. But for the SF reader, the future doesn't arrive soon enough. Science fiction, Toffler wrote, is the sovereign remedy for future shock, and he urged the teaching of science-fiction courses in primary schools.

Finally, youngsters who read SF are learning in the most painless—and therefore the most effective—way that the future will be different. They are learning, as the best universities try to teach them, that there is no use mastering a body of skills or a body of knowledge and expecting it to last for a lifetime; much more important is mastering the art of learning and the habit of flexibility. George Santayana has said that those who ignore history are destined to repeat it; we might paraphrase this to state that those who ignore the future are destined to be its victims.

We cannot stop the future from happening, but sometimes we can choose among futures by understanding the consequences of action and inaction, by the extrapolative thinking that science fiction encourages, and we can make the future more palatable by building into ourselves the ability to adjust. The future will be different? Then there is opportunity for improvement. If things are not as good as they can be, the existence of change means that we can make them better.

I'm not saying that science fiction will give us the future, only that it gives us glimpses of possible futures. It could only be created when man-made change became a fact of everyday life, and it could only come to full flower in a world like today.

The motto of the Mystery Writers of America is that "crime does not pay—enough." The motto of the Science Fiction Writers of America is that "the future isn't what it used to be." If we think about it in as many ways as possible—including the speculative fiction that allows the author to show people coping with change—we can make the future as good as the past, or even better.

13

Toward a Definition of Science Fiction

The most important, and most divisive, issue in science fiction is definition. I wrote about it in terms of its historical development in the preceding chapter, but I am brought back to it once more by an article in one of those fascinating developments in science fiction, the fanzine. The article, "Science Fiction by the Numbers," written by Robert Sabella, was published in the winter 1985 issue of Richard Geis's *Science Fiction Review*.

My involvement with definition may have begun with my original discovery of science fiction and my realization that this literature was different from every other kind. I got deeper into the question when I wrote a master's thesis on modern science fiction in 1951 and even more involved when I started work on *Alternate Worlds* in 1970. My most pressing concerns, however, developed from my fifteen-year involvement in teaching science fiction and the editing of the anthology *The Road to Science Fiction* for my class. Much of my work in the field, it turns out, has been an attempt to grope into an understanding of what science fiction is, how it got to be that way, and how it differs from other kinds of literature.

The article in *Science Fiction Review* quoted my definition from *Alternate Worlds*, "a fantastic event or development considered rationally." That was an attempt to come up with a brief definition. But, as Mr. Sabella illustrated with his definition, brevity means lack of precision. What my definition suggested was that fantasy and science fiction belong to the same general category of fiction—that is, the fictional world represented is not the world of the here and now or even the there and then, but the fantastic world of unfamiliar events or developments. By "rational" the definition suggests (but does not explain) the difference between fantasy and science fiction.

A longer and more precise definition is attempted in my four-volume anthology, *The Road to Science Fiction*:

> Science fiction is the branch of literature that deals with the effects of change on people in the real world as it can be projected into the past, the future, or to distant places. It

> often concerns itself with scientific or technological change,
> and it usually involves matters whose importance is greater
> than the individual or the community; often civilization or
> the race itself is in danger.

But even this definition is not comprehensive, and I must confess to some waffling here with words like "often" and "usually." Perhaps real definition requires for completeness the entire four volumes of *The Road to Science Fiction*, with its examples. My semester-long course actually is a quest for definition that my students and I pursue by means of historical development, thematic analysis, comparison and contrast, and examples.

But let's have another go at what I consider to be the key critical question in the field. I remember an excellent debate between Damon Knight and me in my classroom in which Damon maintained there was no significant difference between fantasy and science fiction, and I insisted there was. An immediate complication: do the words we use have the same meanings for us both? If Damon considers everything irrelevant except the fantastic element (or that part of the fiction that is contrary to things as we know them), I never will convince him that there is a meaningful difference.

The problem of definition also is complicated by the fact that science fiction is not an ordinary kind of genre. Unlike the mystery, the western, the Gothic, the love story, or the adventure story, to cite a few of the popular genres, science fiction has no typical action or place. Readers do not recognize it, as they recognize other genres, because of some critical event (such as a crime and its detection) or its setting (the mythical west during the period 1865–1900). As a consequence, science fiction can incorporate other genres: we can have a science-fiction mystery, a science-fiction western, a science-fiction Gothic, a science-fiction love story or, most likely of all, a science-fiction adventure story.

The first step toward definition, then, must be the elimination of those aspects of the fiction that are not unique to science fiction—the aspects of the mystery, the western, the Gothic, the love story, and the adventure story, or even those elements of traditional fiction that do not relate to the changed situation, such as sex or extraneous characterization—before we can begin to recognize what is left as being irreducibly science fiction. Sometimes, of course, nothing is left, and we may conclude that the piece in question was not science fiction at all. If there is something left, that something, I have observed, is change. Some significant element of the situation is different from the world with which we are familiar, and the characters cannot respond to the situation in customary ways, that is, without recognizing that a changed situation requires analysis and a different response. Or if the characters attempt to respond traditionally, without recognizing the need for a different response, they fail, or they fail for the rest of us, the human species.

It may be useful here to make a comparison with what was called "new wave" SF, which seemed like science fiction and was usually published in science-fiction magazines, but to many long-time science-fiction readers did not seem to have "the right stuff." In the usual "new wave" story the situation was different, but the characters responded to the situation in traditional ways, or, if in new ways, in ways that were inappropriate or had no likelihood of coping with the situations. Thus the characters in those stories usually failed to cope with their situations, but their failure was attributed to the catastrophic scope of their situations or its incomprehensibility or to universal defects in human nature, not to individual lack of knowledge, wisdom, character, or effort.

The situations of traditional fiction are those of the everyday world, including the everyday world of history. The broad area of fantastic literature is characterized by situations in which a significant element is different from the everyday.

As a mid-term examination I used to give my students an opportunity to choose a brief definition among the following and write an essay upon it: Science fiction is a literature of (1) ideas; (2) change; (3) anticipation; (4) the human species. These are not particularly effective as definitions, although I think there is something to be said for (2) and (4), but they offer students the opportunity to develop and defend their own ideas. I bring it up now, however, because I added another choice: (5) discontinuity.

Traditional fiction, it might be said, is the literature of continuity. Whatever the situation, it is continuous with everyday experience, and the decisions that must be made by the characters are decisions based upon prior experience, upon tradition. The moment characters in any kind of fiction encounter new situations or attempt new solutions to traditional situations, the story begins to feel like science fiction. Science-fiction readers respond to these situations, and traditional critics reject them for a variety of reasons, but mostly because science fiction, as I discussed in the preceding chapter, is the literature of discontinuity. Historical fiction that deals with moments of change, of discontinuity, often have appeals to readers similar to those of science fiction, which may explain why stories of prehistoric man, like those of Waterloo, London, Wells, and Golding, usually are considered science fiction.

One immediate objection might be raised to describing science fiction as the literature of discontinuity: perhaps the term is appropriate to the "what if," speculative, kind of story, in which the basis of the story is the element of the new and different. But what about the "if this goes on," extrapolative kind of story such as Pohl and Kornbluth's *The Space Merchants*? I would suggest that we only recognize the work as science fiction if the extrapolation produces a significant enough accumulation of change that it is, in actuality, discontinuous. If the extrapolation is minor, is not sufficiently discontinuous, like *Seven Days in May*, for instance, or even *Dr. Strangelove*, then it doesn't feel quite like science fiction to us.

But we must then further differentiate science fiction and fantasy, which is also the literature of discontinuity, though often, to be sure, it is only discontinuous at certain moments or at certain periods of the day or night, and sometimes the discontinuity has alternative explanations. Mr. Sabella's suggestion, "A story is science fiction if it accepts *every* axiom of the real world plus one or more imaginary axioms," is on the right track, but I would like to approach it in another way.

The place I like to start is the reading experience, where, I believe, all criticism begins: First we read something and respond to it, and then we ask ourselves why we responded in that way. It seems to me that we read fantasy and science fiction differently, that is, we ask the text different kinds of questions. The kinds of questions we ask determines how we read it; if we ask the wrong kinds of questions, we will be unable to read the fiction properly. This, incidentally, is what we mean by "genre": our previous reading experience in literature with similar characteristics not only leads us to particular expectations about a particular piece when we encounter those characteristics but also prepares us to ask the right questions, the questions to which it will respond.

Few of us analyze our generic experiences; we respond intuitively. And most readers respond intuitively (and differently) to fantasy and science fiction. If they do not they end up confused and sometimes disappointed, because the fiction does not respond to their questions.

If the difference between fantastic literature and the literature of everyday experience lies in the changed situation, the difference between fantasy and science fiction lies in the fact that fantasy takes place in a world in which the rules of everyday experience do not apply, and science fiction in the world of everyday experience extended. That is, fantasy creates its own world and its own laws; science fiction accepts the real world and its laws. We could not live in the real world if we operated by the assumptions of the fantasy world; but the assumptions of the science-fiction world are compatible with our own. We can believe in the existence of aliens somewhere else in the universe, or that time machines or faster-than-light spaceships eventually may be developed, and still function without real-life problems; but if we behave in our everyday life as if werewolves, vampires, and doorways into other worlds exist, our lives will be difficult, even if we remain outside institutional walls.

When we read science fiction, we recognize that it applies to the real world, and we ask it real questions. The first one is: How did we get there from here? If the question is irrelevant or whimsical, then the fiction is fantasy. On the other hand, if we insist that the fantasy answer our real-world questions, we cannot read it. For instance, if we insist on knowing where the hole is located that Alice uses to get to Wonderland or how she can fall interminably without killing herself, or how one can get through a mirror into the world beyond, we cannot read *Alice in Wonderland* or *Through the Looking Glass*, and part of our experience in growing up is learning how to distinguish fantasy from reality. We all, as children, may have cherished the notion that, like Alice, we might one day find the mirror that we could pass through into a brighter, better, or more exciting world, but we learn not to act upon it.

As a consequence, a reader instinctively (and a critic analytically) looks for the author's instructions on how to read a work. Usually a writer offers them early (unless the writer's strategy depends on reader uncertainty, a risk that writers should assume only for a suitable payoff, and whose risk, and payoff, a critic should assess); most fantasies begin fantastically. When a character falls down a rabbit hole or passes through a mirror, the writer is telling the reader: Don't ask realistic questions.

In the science-fiction story, on the other hand, realistic questions are essential for full understanding and enjoyment; the reader is supposed to compare the fictional world to the real world and find it not only better or worse, or simply different, but be able to ascertain what made it better or worse or different. If the reader doesn't ask hard questions of *Mission of Gravity*, say, or *The Left Hand of Darkness*, and reads them instead as fantasy (or as adventure), the reader misses most of the significance of those novels. The point of those novels, substantially different in subject and theme though both occur on alien planets, lies not only in their differences from our world and our society but also their resemblances to our experiences. And part of the pleasure we derive from them and our ability to learn from them comes from our recognition that the same laws of nature and assumptions about behavior apply to us in the same way they apply to the characters in them.

Science fiction, then, is the literature of change. Change is its subject matter and its method. Fantasy might be defined as the literature of difference. Fantasy occurs in a world not congruent with ours or incongruent in some significant way. Science fiction occurs in the world of everyday experience extended into the unknown.

The fact that some element of a science-fiction story may violate existing scientific theories, the time machine, say, or the faster-than-light spaceship, does not necessarily control our decision about whether to read the work as fantasy or science fiction. What is not possible in our state of knowledge may be possible in a hundred years or a thousand or a million. The presence of a time machine or a faster-than-light spaceship does not make a work fantasy if we are supposed to consider them realistically, that is, if we are supposed to ask hard questions about them and their consequences. The reason authors, such as H. G. Wells in *The Time Machine*, go to so much effort to make their time machines believable is to instruct the reader thereby how to read their stories, to put them into the proper realistic frames of mind about the pasts or the futures they visit. A time machine could be used in a fantasy, of course, but if it is to be read as a fantasy the author should describe it in fanciful, that is, unrealistic, terms, and warn the reader not to ask realistic questions.

Fantasy and science fiction belong to the same broad category of fiction that deals with events other than those that occur, or have occurred, in the everyday world. But they belong to distinctly different methods of looking at those worlds: fantasy is non-realistic; science fiction is realistic. Fantasy creates its own universe with its own laws; science fiction exists in our universe with its shared laws. Fantasy is a private vision that one accepts for the sake of the vision; science fiction is a public vision that must meet every test of reality. The basis of fantasy is psychological truth; nothing else matters. The basis of science fiction is the real world. Does the story respond to hard questions? Nothing else matters.

We misread fantasy and science fiction if we apply the reading protocols of one to the other. Borderline cases create the most serious difficulties. In my classes, I used to describe fantasy and science fiction as existing along a spectrum of explanation: the more explanation in a fantasy story the more like science fiction it seems; the more unrationalized assumptions in the science-fiction story, the more like fantasy it seems. And, I would say, when they met in the middle they were virtually indistinguishable, and we even call them, sometimes, "science fantasy."

I no longer find that satisfying. At that time, I think, I had not yet come to my realization that the science-fiction genre, because it has no characteristic action or place, is a kind of super-genre, capable of incorporating the others. Most of the difficult cases become easier to analyze if first the elements of other genres are peeled away. In the case of Edgar Rice Burroughs's John Carter stories, for instance, we have a small residue of evolutionary notions and cultural criticism. In A. E. van Vogt's Null-A novels, we have a larger residue of ideas that we are supposed to consider in the light of the real world: the ability of a new system of logic to liberate the rational mind as well as to develop super powers, and the effect of these on political structures on Earth and Venus and later as they extend into the galaxy.

The critical decision as to whether these works, and others like them, are better read as science fiction or fantasy is controlled by our feelings about whether we get more out of the works by subjecting them to hard questions or to none. On this basis, I would suggest that the Burroughs's John Carter novels will be destroyed by hard questions and are best read as fantasy, and that van Vogt's Null-A novels ask for intellectual scrutiny even though their adventure plots sometimes frustrate our attempts to make sense of them.

The differences between the literature of continuity and the literature of discontinuity, and in the literature of discontinuity between the literature of change and the literature of difference, are real and significant. Applying to one the critical standards appropriate to another comes from a failure to recognize those differences and results in misreading and misunderstanding. A case in point is James Thurber's "The Macbeth Murder Mystery," in which an inveterate murder mystery reader, trapped without his favorite reading material on an island resort, misreads Shakespeare. Examples could be multiplied.

Traditional critics, when they have condescended to consider science fiction, have found it inadequate when measured against traditional standards. Robert Scholes wrote in his introductions to the Oxford series of author studies, "as long as the dominant criteria are believed to hold for all fiction, science fiction will be found inferior: deficient in psychological depth, in verbal nuance, and in plausibility of event. What is needed is a criticism serious in its standards and its concern for literary value but willing to take seriously a literature based on ideas, types, and events beyond ordinary experience."

Science fiction's recent popularity has made it a more tempting target: Exposure is easier than explanation; ridicule is wittier than analysis. But science fiction and fantasy never will receive meaningful criticism until the qualities that make them special are understood and an appropriate set of critical standards is developed for them.

14

The Worldview of Science Fiction

Fred Pohl recalls that British writer John T. Philliphent once wrote to him that he had discovered what set science-fiction writers apart was that they used the science-fiction method—but he died before he could say what the science-fiction method was. So we are left groping for what distinguishes SF from other kinds of fiction and, like the blind men fumbling around the elephant, we find ourselves dealing with one aspect or another but never quite encompassing the whole beast. Fred goes on to speculate that what his friend had come up with had something to do with the way in which SF writers look at the universe. There may be something to this.

Certainly SF, like science itself, is based on the assumption that the universe is knowable even though the greatest part of it may be unknown and may be destined to remain mysterious for the life of any of us, or, indeed, the life of all of us, by which I mean the human species. The knowable universe has no room for the supernatural, or those experiences that by their very nature can never be "known." To bring experiences of the transcendent or the ineffable into the natural world is to destroy one or the other. Thus we have a basic distinction between fantasy and science fiction and even, though it is not immediately apparent, between mainstream fiction and science fiction.

I would like to suggest, however, that the worldview of science fiction can be narrowed even further. The relationship between science fiction and Darwin's *The Origin of the Species* long has been apparent. We know, of course, that modern science fiction began with H. G. Wells. Wells seems contemporary and everything before Wells seems quaintly historical, Mary Shelley, Poe, even Verne. *The War of the Worlds* can be updated, but *Frankenstein* or *From the Earth to the Moon* can only be produced as period pieces.

Shelley and Poe and Verne were influenced by blossoming science and an awareness that the world was being changed by it and by its child, technology, but Wells had the benefit of the publication of *The Origin of Species* in 1859. At an obvious level, Darwin's theories of evolution were the most important elements in Thomas H. Huxley's career in biology, and his relationship with Darwin and the defense of his theories in debates across the English countryside are well known. Almost as well known is the fact that the young Wells spent his first year of college studying biology under Huxley and recalled it as a shaping influence, and the fact, as Jack Williamson demonstrated in his doctoral dissertation published as *H. G. Wells: Critic of Progress*, that the early (and most important) portion of Wells's SF writing was a coming to terms with evolution. Not quite so apparent is the fact that Darwin's theories underlay what we now point at as science fiction.

I've always felt that naturalism and SF have a lot in common—that SF, say, is fantastic naturalism, or naturalized fantasy, or simply that which hasn't happened yet, that we know of, treated naturalistically. Maybe it goes farther than that.

C. Hugh Holman, in *A Handbook to Literature*, defines naturalism as "a movement in the novel in the later nineteenth and early twentieth centuries in France, America, and England," and

> in its simplest sense . . . the application of the principles of scientific determinism to fiction. . . . The fundamental view of man which the naturalist takes is of an animal in the natural world, responding to environmental forces and internal stresses and drive, over none of which he has control and none of which he fully understands. It tends to differ from realism, not in its attempt to be accurate in the portrayal of its materials but in the selection and organization of those materials, selecting not the commonplace but the representative and so arranging the materials that the structure of the novel reveals the pattern of ideas—in this case, scientific theory—which forms the author's view of the nature of experience. In this sense, naturalism shares with romanticism a belief that the actual is important not in itself but in what it can reveal about the nature of a larger reality; it differs sharply from romanticism, however, in finding that reality not in transcendent ideas or absolute ideals but in the scientific laws which can be perceived through the action of individual instances. This distinction may be illustrated in this way. Given a block of wood and a force pushing upon it, producing in it a certain acceleration: Realism will tend to concentrate its attention on the accurate description of that particular block, that special force, and that definite acceleration; Romanticism will tend to see in the entire operation an illustration or symbol or suggestion of a philosophical truth and will so represent the block, the force,

and the acceleration—often with complete fidelity to fact—
that the idea or ideal that it bodies forth is the center of the
interest; and naturalism will tend to see in the operation a clue
or a key to the scientific law which undergirds it and to be
interested in the relationship between the force, the block,
and the produced acceleration and will so represent the operation that Newton's second law of motion (even on occasion in
its mathematical expression—$F = ma$) is demonstrated or proved
by this representative instance of its universal occurrence in
nature. In this sense naturalism is the novelist's response to
the revolution in thought that modern science has produced.
From Newton it gains a sense of mechanistic determinism;
from Darwin (the greatest single force operative upon it) it
gains a sense of biological determinism and the inclusive metaphor of the lawless jungle which it has used perhaps more
often than any other; from Marx it gains a view of history as
a battleground of vast economic and social forces; from Freud
it gains a view of the determinism of the inner and subcon-
scious self; from Taine it gains a view of literature as a product of deterministic forces; from Comte it gains of view of
social and environmental determinism. . . .

Most of Holman's description of naturalism could be applied to science
fiction with only a few reservations. The reason for this is partly because both are the products of modern science and in particular of the
theory of evolution. Darwin produced naturalism and science fiction
applied naturalism to the fantastic. In other words, science fiction takes
the unusual, the remarkable event that has not happened, and presents it
as part of the natural world. More important, the naturalistic story treats
human beings as part of the natural world, as a product of their environment, and their failures and successes (primarily their failures) as a
result of their environment rather than their characters or decisions, but
as captured in that moment like fossils embedded in limestone. Science
fiction, on the other hand, treats human beings as a species that has
evolved as a result of environment but, and this is the crucial distinction
from naturalism, as a species upon whom the evolutionary process is
still at work.

Science fiction, then, deals with people as if they were creatures as
adaptable as the protoplasm from which they emerged. Change the conditions and humanity will change. The first premise of SF is that humanity is adaptable. To that premise, however, science fiction added

another that naturalism never had: Although humanity is as much a product of its environment as the other animals, it possesses a quality that the other animals lack—the intellectual ability to recognize its origins and the processes at work upon it, and even, sometimes, to choose a course other than that instilled by its environment. In naturalism such recognition at best leads to sense of tragic loss.

One of the best statements of this SF worldview is contained in Isaac Asimov's *The Caves of Steel* and *The Naked Sun*—his 1950s Robot Novels. In *The Caves of Steel* people have become so accustomed to enclosure that they all suffer from agoraphobia; for them even the possibility of going outside the roofed city is unthinkable. The murder mystery that drives the action of *The Caves of Steel* is based upon the agoraphobia of its citizens, and a major factor in its solution is Lije Bailey's ability to think the unthinkable.

Moreover, a subplot of the Robot Novels involves the plans of some Spacers to push the short-lived, disease-ridden, agoraphobic Terrans into expanding into what will later become the Galactic Empire, but that depends upon Terrans conquering their agoraphobia and being able to set off in spaceships for distant suns. Bailey not only fights his own fears of open spaces in *The Naked Sun* but he organizes a group to help others do the same.

These two basic principles, it seems to me, create that difficult-to-define something by which we identify science fiction, and if it doesn't involve them we may feel that it is *like* SF but it doesn't quite have the right stuff. At least that is true of American SF. New Wave SF, for instance, tended to describe the environmental aspect of human behavior but, like naturalism, stopped at that. Or, rather, it assumed that people are moved more by obsession than rational choice, and that crippled their ability to cope with change. J. G. Ballard's stories and novels are good examples, with their characters paralyzed by change rather than adapting to it or moved to action by it. A good deal of non-English-language SF does not have the second premise (the ability to act other than the way one is conditioned to behave), either, and when I was researching stories to include in *The Road to Science Fiction #6: Around the World* I found a great many stories that involved the naturalistic recognition of humanity's evolutionary past but not as many that dealt with the human ability to recognize that fact and rise above it.

This is not to say that there is anything inherently right or wrong about belief in the power of rationality over conditioning. Most of the time people do behave as if they were programmed, but occasionally they act as if they had free will. American SF has focused on the few problem solvers who have done the most to change life and society, and thereby, according to American SF, to change people themselves. Other SF, Forster's "The Machine Stops," say, as opposed to Campbell's "Twilight," may have based its beliefs about people on the more common kind of behavior.

In "The Machine Stops," for instance, humanity has been reduced to total dependence on the machine and not only does not recognize that fact (except for one aberrant individual) but does not even notice when the machine begins to fail. In "Twilight" humanity has lost its curiosity because of the lack of competition, not because of the machine, but at the end a visitor to that far-distant future instructs a machine to create a curious machine, making it the inheritor of humanity's mission to ask questions of the universe.

Mainstream fiction seems to do without Darwin entirely. As a matter of fact, in a mainstream story the origins of humanity, if they enter at all, are more likely to be biblical than evolutionary. If evolution enters, the story is transformed into science fiction.

Mainstream fiction's preoccupation with the present reflects an apparent desire to freeze reality in its current state, and a belief that everything that has happened or is likely to happen is of little importance except as it reflects upon the present. Mainstream's preoccupation with the reactions and reflections of individuals who have little influence in their own times and no historical influence suggests that reality is less important than the way people feel about it. To put it another way, the concentration by mainstream fiction on social interactions seems to incorporate the conviction that the most important, if not the only important, aspect of existence is the ways in which people relate to each other.

Science fiction, on the other hand, incorporates a belief that the most important aspect of existence is a search for humanity's origins, its purpose, and its ultimate fate. Mainstream fiction may seem more "real" because it reflects the reality that most people deal with in their everyday existence: the social world and our interactions with it and our feelings about it. But is the evolution of humanity less real because it is less quotidian?

The shape of mainstream fiction is dictated by its belief in what is important. It is dense with character not because that is what "good fiction" concerns itself with but because that is what mainstream fiction is about. Science fiction, which has often been criticized because of the thinness of its characterization, is similarly the result of SF beliefs. When one is concerned about the way in which people are the products of their environments and how one can free oneself to act in ways other than those to which one has been conditioned, the feelings of the characters about their situations, or even aspects of individual character or reactions to the general predicament, seem of little moment.

Similarly, mainstream fiction has minimized or discarded plot as "mere incident," while plot remains at the heart of science fiction. This suggests that for the mainstream what happens does not really matter; nothing new is going to occur, and the only proper concern is how character should react to repetition. Science fiction, on the other hand, exists in a world of change, and the focus is on external events: What is the change and how are humans (or aliens) going to respond to it?

15

Where Do You Get Those Crazy Ideas?

Science fiction is often called a literature of ideas. No one should be surprised, then, to learn that the most important part of writing a science-fiction story is getting a good idea; nor that the question laymen always ask science-fiction writers is "Where do you get those crazy ideas?"

That's us—the people with the crazy ideas. It's no use saying, "You mean crazy ideas like atomic energy, space travel, overpopulation, pollution, automation, catastrophes, holocausts, technological change, evolution, and all the other limitless possibilities in a universe which may be infinite and possibly eternal?" It doesn't even do any good to ask, "How can you keep from having crazy ideas when you are living in a world that is changing while you look at it? How can you avoid wondering what will happen next when life is one surprise after another? How can you avoid speculating about the direction change is heading and where it will take us and how this will affect the way people live and feel and behave?"

So I just shrug and say, "Oh, crazy ideas come easy when you're in the business."

This business—crazy ideas—has become the last frontier of the short-story writer. Anyone who wants to begin writing by selling short stories, which is much the easiest way to begin, had better try to write science fiction because that's about the only market left. There may be a couple of detective magazines still and a western magazine or two, but the biggest market for short fiction in this country still is the half-dozen or so science-fiction magazines, the dozen or so semi-professional magazines, the dozen on-line magazines, and the occasional original science-fiction anthology. And the market for non-category stories exists only in the little magazines that pay little or nothing. Even in the field of the novel, science fiction has passed the western and the mystery.

Moreover, science fiction always has been peculiarly receptive to the beginning writer.

If people persist in asking where I get my crazy ideas, I usually dig deeper into what some authorities call creativity and I call a habit. Noticing the fictional possibilities in the flow of information that comes into my head has become a pattern of behavior. "What a great idea for a story!" is the typical reaction.

Ideas, of course, are not unique to science fiction. Every story, of any kind, demands an idea, though it may be less specific, less speculative. Students in my fiction writing classes with some experience in writing generalize their complaint. "I can't come up with anything to write about," they say. That's another way of asking, "How do you get an idea?"

That's such a preposterous complaint that I usually begin by saying to them the same thing I say to the laymen: "How do you avoid getting ideas?" I have card files stuffed with ideas for stories, and desk drawers jammed with story ideas jotted down on odd scraps of paper. I'll never have time to get to all of them, not even to ten per cent of them. The problem for every real writer is not getting ideas but finding the time to write.

I admit that this answer is a bit unfair. It wasn't always this way with me. I tell my students about the second time I turned to freelance writing. It was more serious this time: now I had a wife and a child. I wasn't experimenting but trying to make a career of it. I returned from a trip to New York City where I had been talking to editors; I had a couple of story ideas and a panicky feeling that I might never have another. That was the moment when I began jotting down every idea that occurred to me. Soon I had a stack of them and I never panicked again—about that.

That leads me to a point I should make early: write ideas down. A few words are enough. The idea that comes to you at an odd moment, as you are reading or watching something happen outside your window or listening to a lecture or lying awake in bed at night or dreaming, the idea that seems so magnificent and unforgettable will vanish within hours, even minutes, never to be recalled unless it is written down. All of them will not seem as wonderful when reread; many golden ideas turn into lead with the passage of time; but some will retain that magic ability to re-create excitement every time the author touches them. Those are the ones with the basic quality every idea for fiction should have: they impel the writer toward the typewriter to turn them into story. Excitement, a glow in the stomach, a fire in the head—that's how a writer recognizes a good idea.

But where does he or she get the idea in the first place? Since an author is a writer, he or she reads—no one who isn't in love with reading should consider writing as a career or even an avocation—and he or she gets ideas as he or she reads. It doesn't matter whether it is fiction or nonfiction, a newspaper, a magazine, or a book.

In science fiction, speculation about new developments in the hard or soft sciences is the source of many story concepts. Once this kind of speculation was more prevalent in the general magazines such as *Scientific American*, *Time*, *Newsweek*, *Saturday Review*, or *Psychology Today*; the scientific journals were likely to leave the speculation to others. This is changing as science becomes more aware of its responsibilities and more willing to consider the consequences of its discoveries. An experienced science-fiction writer can build his own speculative world on a bare description of some discovery, but most of us can benefit from the informed projections of other, more experienced minds.

Once scientists were not much good at speculation. To know too much about a subject inhibits the ability to think wild thoughts. But recent discoveries have shaken up the conservatives who used to feel that they knew not only most of what was known but at least the general nature of what could be known about their disciplines. New and unexpected breakthroughs in astronomy and physics, chemistry, biology, and other sciences have loosened the chains of reality that bound the scientific imagination. Today the craziest ideas are being thought by astrophysicists such as Freeman Dyson and the late Carl Sagan.

Larry Niven got the basic idea for *Ringworld* from speculations by Dyson that a truly advanced civilization would be able to use all the energy radiated by its sun; it would be able to reconstruct the planets of that sun into a sphere completely enclosing the sun. The inhabitants could live on the inside of the sphere and not only enjoy all the sun's energy but a vastly increased living area. Dyson's point was that such civilizations would be invisible in the visual spectrum but would radiate the sun's energy as heat in the infrared; thus, we might be able to detect advanced civilizations by picking up strong infrared where we could see no star.

The concept of the gigantic living space captured Niven's imagination. He changed it, however, into a gigantic ring—a slice from Dyson's sphere—a million miles wide and entirely encircling the sun.

My novel *The Listeners* was inspired by reading Walter Sullivan's *We Are Not Alone*, a historical survey of efforts to communicate with other worlds and an account of speculation by astronomers, beginning in the late fifties, about the possibility of picking up communications from other intelligent creatures in the universe.

A writer can even get ideas from encyclopedias, almanacs, or statistical reports. I was reading an article about "Feeling" in the *Encyclopedia Britannica* (it isn't in the current editions, so don't look for it); it developed into an analysis of the various ways to be happy and ended with the final sentence, "But the true science of applied hedonics is not yet born." That statement expanded into my novel *The Joy Makers*.

I got the idea for a fantasy story called "The Beautiful Brew" from a Virgil Partch cartoon that showed two men looking at a mug of beer on which the foam had shaped itself into the bust and head of a girl. The caption was something like: "That guy really puts a head on a glass of beer."

Other people's stories also can be a rich source of ideas. The first few paragraphs of a popular story are intended to intrigue the reader, to draw him into the story; in addition, they suggest what the story is going to be about, and in the best-crafted stories they tell the reader what is going to happen, how the story is going to end, but in such a way the reader doesn't understand. Often, then, after reading the first few paragraphs of a story I find myself thinking ahead; sometimes I'm wrong about how the story will develop, but then I have a story idea of my own.

Or, as it often happens in science fiction, writers may find themselves disagreeing with the author's solution to a basic concept and use the author's situation to reach a different resolution, sometimes exactly the opposite, as Robert Heinlein's *Starship Troopers* inspired Gordon Dickson to write *Naked to the Stars*, Harry Harrison to write *Bill, the Galactic Hero*, and Joe Haldeman to write *The Forever War*.

A writer may also take the emotional impact of a story and translate it into other situations, as I tried to do with the ending of Graham Greene's *The Heart of the Matter* in an otherwise totally dissimilar story called "The Power and the Glory."

Sometimes a writer may approach the problem of idea from the angle of story, that is, from the interrelationships of people. A human problem often can be intensified in a science-fiction situation; or, it can be considered more dispassionately in a cooler environment than our hot contemporary scene with all its instant preconceptions and prejudices.

Thus a story of lovers may achieve new levels of emotion if they are separated by time rather than distance, as in Heinlein's *The Door into Summer*; or if one is a human being and the other is an android, as in Lester del Rey's "Helen O'Loy" or J. T. McIntosh's "Made in U.S.A."

The generation gap may become more significant if parents are discovered plotting against their children, as in my story "The Old Folks," or if the son is a superman, as in Henry Kuttner's "Absalom"; and the problems of parenthood can be dramatized more effectively if the infant is an omnipotent superman, as in Kuttner's "When the Bough Breaks."

Possibilities such as these can occur to a writer while he is reading other kinds of literature, or while glancing over the feature and human interest stories that appear in every issue of the daily newspaper. Such capsule stories about real human beings suggest to the writer what he can never satisfactorily invent: the fantastic variety of situations into which men and women can involve themselves, and the fantastic variety in which men and women exist.

Finally, the writer can get ideas from observation—by watching people, by listening to conversations, by absorbing the anecdotes of friends or relations—or, best of all, from personal experience, which is the writer's unique source of inspiration. It is all he ever has in the end, even in science fiction. One of my best-known stories, "The Misogynist," was based on my own experience with women. On an index card one day in 1950 I jotted down three words: "Women are aliens." Six months later, when I had come up with a viewpoint character and a way of handling the narration, I had a unique story.

Science fiction has a great deal of concept sharing. It is a close community of writers, even of readers, and one writer will construct his story on another writer's premises or extrapolations. "Science fiction builds upon science fiction," Donald A. Wollheim wrote in his personal history of science fiction, *The Universe Makers*. Simply rewriting an old idea is worse than nothing; a writer must bring to his story some new vision, some different twist, which will reinvigorate the concept. Science fiction demands novelty; that is both its distinction as a category and its problem for the writer.

Novelty is not always easy. In my illustrated history of science fiction, *Alternate Worlds*, I encompass all the themes of science fiction in fourteen phrases: (1) far traveling; (2) the wonders of science; (3) man and the machine; (4) progress; (5) man and his society; (6) man and the future; (7) war; (8) cataclysm; (9) man and his environment; (10) superpowers; (11) superman; (12) man and alien; (13) man and religion; and (14) miscellaneous glimpses of the future or the past. Within these broad categories, however, lie an infinity of unique perceptions about the human species and its possibilities.

Science fiction is "origin of species fiction" wrote English critic Edmund Crispin, and almost all of the concepts of science fiction have racial implications for the human species. Trivial topics have little success. Novelty and meaning, meaning and novelty—a new idea, a different perspective, significance. The demands that science fiction makes on writers drains them—sometimes drives them into writer's blocks.

And yet a writer who is good enough can pick up an old idea and make it as good as new. Heinlein did it with a 1951 novel called *The Puppet Masters*, which took the old theme of invasion by alien monsters, made them parasites, and created an effective new novel. In his collection of novellas, *Born with the Dead*, Robert Silverberg made brilliant new use of three old ideas: the revivification of the dead, the sun stopped in the heavens, and euthanasia.

Originality, however, is safest for the beginning writer. If he should be so incautious or so unaware as to submit a story about flying saucers, visitors from other worlds who turn out to be our ancestors, World War III, or even time travel, he is likely to receive in the return mail only a printed rejection slip, or at best a note reading, "Heinlein did it better." Young writers naturally begin with imitation; they get turned toward writing because they love reading and admire the work of particular writers. But the novice must break with the past; he or she must do his or her own thing rather than pale or inept reworkings. The new writer is wise to avoid ideas that end with classic revelations: the alien castaways on earth who turn out to be Adam and Eve, the catastrophe that turns out to have destroyed Atlantis, the character sent to Earth (or out of the future) to save it from destruction who turns out to be Christ or Mohammed or Buddha. David Gerrold wrote *The Man Who Folded Himself*, Michael Moorcock wrote *Behold the Man*, and most of us have tried our hand at old themes and done them badly or well, but the beginning writer should leave that for his more experienced, later incarnation. Harlan Ellison could take the old theme of the omnipotent computer that rebels against its human masters, that becomes a tyrannical God, and make it new again in "I Have No Mouth and I Must Scream"; that is no job for a novice.

The beginning writer should try to find a new perception. John Campbell, the long-time editor of the magazine that was born as *Astounding* and became *Analog*, wrote in 1947: "The reader wants the author to do one of two basic things—and prefers the author who does both. The author's function is to imagine for the reader, of course—but he must either (a) imagine in greater detail than the reader has, or (b) imagine something the reader hasn't thought of. Ideally, the author imagines something new, in greater detail."

Get a fresh idea. That demands a considerable familiarity with science fiction, of course, in order to identify what has been done before. A good place to start is the *Science Fiction Hall of Fame*, Volumes I and II, but there are other good anthologies, such as my own *The Road to Science Fiction*. A hopeful writer of science fiction should have read everything he could find, short stories, novels, magazines, books. Then he may be ready to distinguish the old from the new, the bad from the good.

Once the writer has a fresh idea, he should explore its implications; he should imagine it in depth, the way Hal Clement imagined the "whirligig world" of extremely high gravity where his *Mission of Gravity* took place; or Frederik Pohl and Cyril Kornbluth imagined the world controlled by advertising agencies that they created in *The Space Merchants*. Then the writer must imagine people trapped in that world, up against things, forced to do things they don't want to do or can't do, trying to adjust or trying to change the conditions.

In Tom Godwin's touchstone story "The Cold Equations," the pilot of an emergency delivery ship is forced to eject an innocent girl stowaway into airless space because otherwise the ship would crash and its essential cargo be lost. Where did he get that crazy idea? Perhaps by considering the traditional story in which women and children are saved first, no matter what the cost.

In John W. Campbell's novelette "Who Goes There?" a group of Antarctic scientists discover buried deep in the ice an alien monster that has the power to absorb any protoplasm and imitate it perfectly. Where did Campbell get the idea? He had written "The Brain Stealers of Mars" a few years before, which concerned the ability of Martian creatures to read minds and turn themselves into confusing duplicates. Campbell returned to the idea in "Who Goes There?" with a different setting and one small alteration: the imitated protoplasm must first be eaten.

Robert Heinlein's "Universe" begins with the idea of a spaceship that is a world in itself. Murray Leinster had described one in his "Proxima Centauri," but Heinlein added the facts that the ship must travel for generations to reach its goal and that a mutiny had destroyed awareness of mission and meaning until the survivors consider the ship to be the entire universe and their remembered history as parable.

In "A Martian Odyssey" Stanley Weinbaum asked whether aliens had to be unfriendly, and if an intelligent alien could not learn to communicate quickly with a reasonably intelligent human.

We know where Isaac Asimov got the idea for "Nightfall," the classic story in which a world is surrounded by six suns and a moon so that night falls only once every 2,050 years, and when it does the inhabitants of that world go mad and burn their civilizations to make light. John Campbell challenged Asimov with a quotation from Emerson (Asimov used it as an epigraph to his story): "If the stars should appear one night in a thousand years, how would men believe and adore, and preserve for many generations the remembrance of the city of God!"

Murray Leinster took the old idea of "First Contact" with aliens and pointed out that it need not be a deadly encounter, no matter how much is at stake, even racial survival, if a trade-off can be conceived that is more profitable than conflict.

We might speculate that Arthur Clarke got the idea for "The Nine Billion Names of God" when he learned that Tibetan monks are trying to enumerate all the names of God as they spin their prayer wheels; when they have done so, the world will end. In Clarke's story they obtain a computer to do the job in 100 days instead of 15,000 years.

In 1941 Lester del Rey asked himself what would happen if something went wrong in an atomic factory; his answer was "Nerves." Cyril Kornbluth noted in 1951 that successful people were limiting their families, unsuccessful ones were not; he foresaw "The Marching Morons." In 1947 Jack Williamson wondered what a perfect machine would do to humanity, and visualized it doing everything so much better that mankind was left "With Folded Hands."

Horace Gold, founding editor of *Galaxy*, suggested to Fred Pohl that the problems of poverty might some day be supplanted by the problems of affluence; if you were poor you would have to consume more, if you were rich you could afford to live simply. When Pohl solved the fictional problems he wrote "The Midas Plague."

Not all stories can be reduced to this kind of simple summary, just as all ideas cannot be traced to a single source. Many stories are either more complex or dependent upon mood or description or style. But somewhere there is an idea lurking behind the finished product, even if it is only an idea for a setting where something important or exciting must happen, or a character to whom something must happen, or a situation that places a character under stress.

Fiction, John Ciardi once said, is character under stress. It doesn't matter whether you start with the character and develop the stress that will peculiarly test that character, or if you start with the stress and invent a character who will be peculiarly tested by it.

My own definition of a short story is: "a short piece of prose narrative about a human problem which is complicated by events and resolved satisfactorily." The problem must be *human*, or, in stories with protagonists who are animals or aliens, problems that we can imagine as human, with which we can identify; otherwise, readers are uninvolved and uninterested. There must be a *problem*, or it is only a sketch or a description or an essay. To use the term "short story" for slice-of-life pieces only confuses matters, for then we must find another name for the narrative in which a problem occurs that a protagonist must solve.

Moreover, the two kinds of writing have different impacts upon the reader. The problem must be *complicated*—made more difficult, more urgent— by *events*, happenings, and not just reflection, because this process intensifies our concern about the person with the problem and builds up to a final pay-off of satisfaction. The problem must be *resolved*, or we feel that the writer has promised us something the author did not deliver; and it must be resolved *satisfactorily*—that is, the problem posed must be the one resolved, and the resolution must satisfy the promises the rest of the story has made.

The beginning writer will start with no idea, no problem, no sympathetic character; the events of his narrative will be haphazard rather than directed at complicating the story's problem, if there are any events; and if he has a resolution, it will not resolve the problem posed, or in a way that is cheap, easy, or out of character.

How, then, does the beginning writer recognize a good idea when it comes to him? First of all by its originality, second by the excitement it engenders in him to get to a typewriter or word processor, third by its ability to attract good characters, to collect places where the idea must happen, to lead somewhere, to put characters under stress, to force characters to act, and finally to resolve itself.

A good idea becomes good fiction when it states itself in terms of human conflict; up to that time it is merely an interesting observation, such as "women are aliens," or "the advertising agencies are taking over the world," or "only persons willing to perform military service should be permitted to vote."

A person with a file drawer full of good ideas is not yet a writer; he or she must turn those ideas into stories. That requires some uncommon attributes. We hear, for instance, that writers are sensitive. Some are; some aren't. But every good writer is conscious of sensory stimuli. He is visually alert and aware of sounds and smells and tastes and the feel of things. He puts these things into his stories, when they are appropriate, when he is striving for verisimilitude, because he knows that no place exists in reality or in fiction without appearance, without sound and smell, and some, without taste or feel.

In addition, the writer must have certain skills, not only in the use of words but in the techniques of fiction. He or she should know the difference between summary and drama, what Carolyn Gordon and Allen Tate call the panorama and the scene. Panorama is the broad view generally encountered in a summary of events or in exposition; it is sometimes necessary but usually nondramatic. Scene is the closeup; it shows things happening before the reader's eyes; it is drama, and everything else is only preparation for it. Often the beginning writer summarizes everything, and ends up with a scenario. The experienced writer visualizes the action of the story happening in front of him like a stage play, and reports it to the reader as it happens. He writes in scenes. As Henry James urged, he doesn't tell, he shows.

The writer gets involved. Harlan Ellison says that when he is writing a story he paces around and acts out all the parts. I find myself gesturing and speaking bits of dialogue. Anyone passing by must think us strange indeed.

It helps a beginning writer to see the action of the story as a struggle between a sympathetic character and his or her opposition, whether it is another character or a natural obstacle or conditions. Usually a character must accomplish something or take an action that is important to him. His coping, or being unable to cope, with the situation is what creates reader interest. The sophistication of the story emerges through the ingenuity of the situation, the cleverness of the resolution, the verisimilitude of the details, the subtlety of the presentation, the appropriateness and the wit of the language, and the validity of the observations of life and character.

I stress sympathy in character because too many beginning writers present characters who are at best passive and at worst unlikable or incompetent or uncaring or dull. We cannot become interested in them because we know from the beginning that they don't want anything we want, or if they do then they won't get it and the resolution will be obvious or omitted or invalid. I don't mean, of course, that they must be "nice" people or even "good" people; however, they must be people whose problems we can imagine being involved in no matter how outlandish, and whose responses to those problems we can understand. We can even use a character we dislike, whom we want to see fail, but he must be threatening someone we care about.

I also stress the importance of the action the character must take. Too often beginning writers set a task that is unimportant, often easily accomplished, for the characters; they don't care much about it, and the reader cares nothing at all.

Reader involvement is the only way to create a successful story. Writers establish an implicit contract with every person they can induce to read their story: you invest your money and your time, and I will entertain you in a certain way; I will show you a person whose situation will intrigue you, and I will show you that person coping or failing to cope with that problem in a way that will provide you with a pleasant suspense and a final satisfaction that is your reward for reading.

One reason fiction has been dying is that too many readers have been disappointed too often. They have become disillusioned by the breaking of the contract.

All of this doesn't mean formula writing; or, it means formula only insofar as life itself is a formula. Our main business in life is success, however we measure it; sometimes success is just survival, sometimes getting what we want or love and avoiding what we dislike or hate; sometimes it is finding what is important and real in life. But it all begins with birth and progresses through various stages until death ends it, and the various combinations are limited in broad outline. They move naturally—in a formula, if you will—through growing up, into adulthood and responsibility, to independence and the effort to get an appropriate share of the world's goods, to romance and the problems with love that does not endure, to the deterioration of the body and the mind that extends through middle age into senility. In between we have various subthemes such as the difficulties of communication, the search for meaning, and the battle between tradition and change. A formula is something that, like human experience, is infinitely repeated.

Heinlein has said that there are only three basic human-interest plots: (1) boy meets girl, the romance; (2) the little tailor, the character who rises from low to high estate mostly by solving problems; (3) the person who learns better, the character who believes one thing about himself or his world and learns that he has been wrong.

Plots can be sliced in other ways, depending upon the element one chooses to emphasize. One is the story of the child developing into an adult, the rite of passage; another, the revelation of the true nature of life or oneself, the story of sudden truth. And most stories involve several plot types: a romance within a problem story, for instance, and possibly the man who learns better as well.

What distinguishes a story from a sketch is that in a story something changes. Usually someone changes; but sometimes it is only his circumstances, as in the case of many adventure heroes, Conan or James Bond or Kimball Kinnison. But even in the most adventurous of stories usually the protagonist has been changed by his of her experience, if only to the extent of satisfying, for the moment, their desire for adventure.

Final recommendations for the beginning writer:

(1) Begin with a worthwhile idea, preferably one that is fresh and new but at least one that hasn't been exhausted.

(2) Create characters who can ideally dramatize your idea; make them suffer; make their suffering move them to action.

(3) Plan out a scheme of action—a plot—that will present all the scenes necessary to show the characters working out their problem or problems.

(4) Omit everything that doesn't advance the plot. This doesn't mean description or essential exposition, but it does include unnecessary scenes or casual conversation or pointless characters. Everything must work; everything must contribute. Ask yourself: if I leave this out will it matter; if the answer is no, leave it out.

(5) Start your story in the middle of things, as Homer began *The Iliad*. This is the point where the problem of the story is stated; where characters are shown in the grip of the situation. Then, if you must, backtrack to exposition. Exposition is dead material, however, and is best integrated into the action of the story.

(6) Avoid clichés in plot, characterization, and phrasing. This is difficult for the beginning writer, because every writer begins as a reader in love with someone else's ideas. Learning to avoid the trite is half the task of learning to write.

(7) Write in scenes; visualize them completely; bring in other sensory detail when possible.

(8) Dramatize everything you can; try to eliminate everything that isn't dramatic.

(9) Like a sculptor who creates a statue out of a block of stone by chipping away everything that isn't statue, remove everything from what you have written that isn't story.

(10) Revise.

(11) Submit what you have written for publication. Heinlein said this a long time ago; it's still true. You must aim at publication.

And if you find a new way to get crazy ideas, please let me know.

16

Heroes, Heroines, Villains
The Characters in Science Fiction

Fiction is fashioned from the stuff of people's lives, and yet the characters in science fiction seldom are fully realized people; often they turn out to be stand-ins for an attitude, a creed, a society, a way of life, or even the human race. This is the dilemma in which science fiction has found itself from its beginnings, and it is the reason why science fiction has so often been dismissed as sub-literary.

The traditional critical view of science-fiction considers its characters cardboard, its events ridiculous, its diction pedestrian, its style undistinguished; and, therefore, it has no claims on serious critical consideration.

I do not intend to venture here into the full range of responses to that critical dismissal nor into the reasons why some critics have been taking a new look at science fiction nor why science fiction recently has become the subject of many college courses.

Chapter 5 was concerned with character in traditional fiction. What I am concerned with here is why science-fiction characters are less than fully realized individuals and why this must be so; for if we are to understand the problems of characterization in science fiction, we must understand why science fiction has needs different from other fiction.

In 1927 E. M. Forster wrote a major consideration of the craft of fiction writing called *Aspects of the Novel* and introduced the division of characters into "flat" and "round." Flat characters have a single characteristic that does not change throughout the work—Mrs. Micawber was Forster's example. She can be summed up, he said, in the statement, "I never will desert Mr. Micawber." Round characters have several characteristics, some of which may be (or seem) contradictory—in the end they are like people, unpredictable, but in a convincing way.

We should not defend science-fiction characters by pointing out how far mainstream characters depart from that ideal: all characters are selected to fulfill the necessities of plot, no characters are truly unpredictable, none are truly rounded, and the best are a selection of traits. For there is a difference between science-fiction characters and the characters in traditional fiction. The characters in the former are, indeed, less rounded and more typical. The critic who fails to recognize this is going to miss the point of science fiction, but the writer who fails to understand it is going to wonder why his stories are misunderstood.

"What is character but the determinant of incident," Henry James wrote, "and what is incident but the illustration of character." Whether a writer begins with an intriguing situation for which he or she invents characters not only capable of doing those things that must be done in the story but of being uniquely tested by the situation, or whether a writer begins with a fascinating character for whom he or she invents a situation in which that character will be revealed or exposed, the result is substantially the same. Plot and character must meet and fit exactly.

"Each character is created in order, and only in order, that he or she may supply the required action," Elizabeth Bowen wrote in her *Notes on Writing a Novel*. Those who maintain otherwise are capable of deceiving themselves.

All fiction intends to entertain. Beyond this basic concern, the purposes of fiction vary, and the differences between stories are created largely by the differences between their purposes.

Traditional fiction is primarily concerned with character. It reveals character by focusing on its development, its critical moments of awareness or awakening, its recognition of itself. It reveals character through its interaction with life and life's processes. Traditional fiction intends for us to marvel at the complexity of human nature or the variousness of human behavior; it seeks to elicit the nod of agreement at the revelation of the human animal or of life, or the shock of recognition at, in Hemingway's phrase, "the way it was."

This has been the main body of what we call serious literature since Gustave Flaubert invented modern fiction in the mid-nineteenth century, an invention that subsequently was improved and extended by Henry James and James Joyce. And yet their intense concern for one person's epiphany is not the entirety of traditional fiction. Although Flaubert is sometimes called a naturalist, the literary tradition of which he was a founder does not include the kind of naturalism fathered by Zola, which subordinates character to environment; nor does it include much of what seems even more fashionable today: surrealism and what Robert Scholes has called fabulism. In these latter two, at least, character is reduced to a kind of blind need in the midst of terror, confusion, or noncausality, and it is life and the author's imagination that are fascinating in their complexity.

One other category among many—the *roman à thèse*, or thesis story—
has been a literary mode for generations, and in the thesis story character always is subordinated to the thesis, or point, to be defended. In its
construction the science-fiction story often is a special case of the thesis
story—that is, when it is a story of idea. Science fiction, of course,
includes other kinds of stories—stories of mood, character, adventure,
romance—but none of these could sustain science fiction as a genre; it
must stand or fall with the story of idea.

That a science-fiction story ought to have a rounded character, then,
is not at all certain; rounded characters might well detract from the
effectiveness of many science fiction stories. C. S. Lewis pointed out in
his essay "On Science Fiction":

> Every good writer knows that the more unusual the scenes
> and events of his story are, the slighter, the more ordinary,
> the more typical his persons should be. Hence Gulliver is a
> commonplace little man and Alice a commonplace little girl.
> If they had been more remarkable they would have wrecked
> their books.

In traditional fiction the characters not only are the reasons for the story
(in the sense that their complexity is what the story is about and if that
aspect were taken away there would be no story) but their resemblance
to people in real life itself gives an essential feeling of reality to the
story; in Forster's phrase, it "harmonizes the human race with the other
aspects of [the author's] work." Other aspects contribute to that feeling
of reality—the setting, the events, the language, the dialogue—but the
verisimilitude of the characters is a major factor in its acceptance.

In the science-fiction story, on the other hand, the situation is far
from our ordinary experience. Verisimilitude is not the issue but rather,
as in the theater, the suspension of disbelief. But unlike fantasy, where
the suspension of that disbelief is sufficient, science fiction provides
reasons for suspension; the fantastic must be rationalized. In this uneasy
marriage between fantasy and rationality, various devices have been used
to hold the marriage together, ranging from simple explanations to all
the tricks of naturalism, depending upon the position the story occupies
in the spectrum between fantasy and rationality.

H. G. Wells attempted to naturalize his fantastic stories by using
ordinary people and an enveloping fog of commonplaces, tricking the
reader, he said, "into an unwary concession to some plausible assump-

tion" that allows the author to "get on with his story while the illusion holds." Robert Heinlein provided a wealth of everyday detail about his future worlds and from this built up a convincing picture of a different social or technological situation. Realistic characters should help obtain that suspension of disbelief, that unwary concession.

They do. But only to the extent that they look like people and act and talk the way people in those circumstances would act and talk. At the same time they must be able to perform appropriately in a situation that departs in small or great part from the normal. The larger the departure from the normal the greater the emphasis will be on that which departs—the background, the ambience of the story—and the less important will verisimilitude in characterization become. In many stories we might search the world around and never find a real person capable of performing the necessary actions or responding in the necessary way.

At an even more basic level, no one reads science fiction to become better acquainted with real people; the strangeness of the situation is the drawing power of science fiction. The characters exist to react to those circumstances, show how those changed circumstances would (or will) affect people, show how they will bring out the best in people (in romantic science fiction) or the worst, show how they will change man into a god or a beast, into superman or subhuman. The characters are surrogates for the reader or for the human race.

Much of science fiction is "origin-of-species" fiction, as Edmund Crispin called it, concerned with man "as just one of a horde of different animals sharing the same earth," and with his survival as a species and sometimes with the survival of his cultural and ethical values. "In the act of dredging such people [as Madame Bovary or Strether or Leopold Bloom] out from the stupendous mass of their fellows in which they lie submerged their creators, however brilliant, convict themselves of disproportion: it is as if a bacteriologist were to become fixated not just on a particular group of bacteria but on one isolated bacterium," Crispin wrote in a 1963 *Times Literary Supplement*.

Moreover, we want science-fiction characters to be typical, in terms both of literary theory and story reality. The actions of idiosyncratic individuals reveal only the varieties of human behavior; the actions of types reveal the characteristics of the group represented, up to and including the human race. And as human beings reading about times of decision that concern the fate of the human race, we hope to be represented well and fairly, perhaps by those who rise to the highest standards of conduct we hold up for ourselves, certainly not by those who cannot achieve what we accomplish every day. It may not be significant that an idealized human succeeds; but, it is meaningless that an inferior human fails.

In science fiction's brief history, various styles of characters have come into and out of favor. Partly their popularity has been a product of the times or of the literary tradition from which no author is completely free; partly the choice of characters has been determined by the individual temperaments and interests of the authors.

Mary Shelley is considered by Brian Aldiss and others the first science-fiction writer, on the basis of her 1818 novel *Frankenstein*. For my tastes the novel is overly influenced by the Gothic novel and the romantic tradition; it reflects the fears of science but none of its promise. At its worst *Frankenstein*, true to its traditions, can descend to the "no-good-can-come-of-this" school of writing.

Frankenstein is an aristocrat driven by hubris and morbid curiosity to create artificial life, a blasphemous act for which he is inevitably punished. He became the prototype for a character who would persist throughout much later science fiction and down to present times in films and comic magazines, a character vulgarly called "the mad scientist," whether he is in fact certifiable or not, but more accurately called the overreacher. He is often careless. He takes unnecessary risks out of an unseemly haste. In fact, he often seems compulsive, acting not out of rational motives but frequently against his best interests. His monster, on the other hand, became another type character: the demonic force unleashed that inevitably must return to destroy the character who released it.

The next two major figures in science fiction are Edgar Allan Poe and Nathaniel Hawthorne. They too were the inheritors of the spirit of romanticism, and their characters tended to be somewhat like Frankenstein: overreachers or obsessed by an idea or a desire, like the scientist Aylmer, who kills his wife in Hawthorne's "The Birthmark" in an effort to remove her one blemish; or Rappaccini (or for that matter Giovanni, who is moved by a compulsion we find more acceptable, love), who in an attempt to protect his daughter from the world's evil makes her poisonous to the world; or like Valdemar in Poe's "The Case of M. Valdemar," who has himself hypnotized as he is dying in order to cheat death.

Poe's vision of the strange world around him included other kinds of heroes. Some of them were curious observers of the world, such as the letter-writing heroine of "Mellonta Tauta" or the shrewd (but not quite shrewd enough) Scheherazade of "The Thousand and Second Tale of Scheherazade," who tells the king a story so real that the murderous monarch cannot believe it. But most of them were men of overexquisite sensibilities trapped in a world on the edge of madness, such as Bedloe in "A Tale of the Ragged Mountains." He was described by Poe as "in the highest degree sensitive, excitable, enthusiastic. His imagination was singularly vigorous and creative; and no doubt it derived additional force from the habitual use of morphine, which he swallowed in great quantities." Another example is the narrator of "Ms. Found in a Bottle," who is moved to an ocean voyage by nothing more than "a kind of nervous restlessness which haunted me as a fiend."

Jules Verne seems to me the first real science-fiction writer in that he devoted most of his career to this kind of writing and he made a fortune at it. Moreover, he seemed to be as much concerned with the authenticity of the science in his stories as he was with the stories themselves. He understood the questing spirit of the new science, and his major interest was in reflecting it. This shows up in the primary concern in his novels for their backgrounds and paraphernalia. For him the journey was the thing; not for nothing were his novels known as *voyages extraordinaires*.

Verne's heroes, after the feverishly romantic figures created by Shelley, Hawthorne, and Poe, were like open windows in a sickroom. They were usually frank and outgoing seekers after truth; their characters were sometimes leavened with eccentricities that sometimes made them comic, like Professor Lidenbrock in *A Journey to the Center of the Earth*. They were men of strong purpose who thought little of difficulties and discomfort; they let nothing stand in their way, whether it be the hazards of a descent through uncertain caves into the center of the earth, a voyage around the world at the 38th parallel of latitude, or a cannon-shell trip to the moon. They were explorers, scientists, and adventurers, and they were capable of handling any emergencies that occurred or of coping with any strange circumstances in which they found themselves.

Occasionally—and paradoxically in his best work—Verne dealt with a more complex character like the enigmatic Captain Nemo, whose motives for ramming ships in the open seas were obscure; "I have done with society," he said, "for reasons which I alone can understand." Another more complex character was Robur of *Robur the Conqueror* and particularly of the later book, *The Master of the World*, although here he may be more the mad scientist.

By the time H. G. Wells began to write his "single-sitting stories" for the *Pall Mall Budget*, romanticism had given way to realism under the influence of Newton's mechanics, Darwin's evolution, Marx's dialectical view of history, Comte's view of society, and Taine's view of literature; and the easy optimism of the nineteenth century about the promise of science had become a victim of the debates over Darwinism and the growing problems of industrialization. After his first novel about an inventor known only as The Time Traveller and his third, about a scientist who invented a chemical that produced invisibility, Wells wrote mostly about ordinary citizens facing unusual circumstances with no more than ordinary fortitude or ingenuity, as in the everyday characters of *The War of the Worlds*, the Bert Smallways of *The War in the Air*, the matter-of-fact explorer of "Aepyornis Island," even the surprised shop clerk who became "The Man Who Could Work Miracles."

With Wells science fiction became less fanciful, more possible, and his use of ordinary characters, particularly as viewpoints on the fantastic events of his stories, provided a critical foundation for the development of modern science fiction. At least one stream of science fiction had left the exotic landscapes of romanticism for the commonplaces of realism and the brutality of naturalism. Fantasy about people like us, speaking our language, acting as we might act: in this strange tension science fiction grew to maturity.

Its development was influenced by social factors such as the universal education acts that provided a newly literate audience in English-speaking countries for stories of fantasy and adventure, and the growth of cheap magazines, aided by such technological developments as the Linotype and pulp paper, to provide them.

The romantic writers of the early pulp magazines—men like George Allan England, Edgar Rice Burroughs, and A. Merritt—were more Vernian than Wellsian; their heroes were larger than life. They were strong, romantic, Victorian, and always ready for adventure; and their adventures were on a scale suitable to test their muscles and their courage, if not always their intellects. They faced a ruined world without dismay, went off to Mars by astral projection, descended into the middle of the earth by mechanical mole, followed a shining creature into a vast cavity in the earth once occupied by the moon, and through it all, in the most hopeless of situations, their motto remained, "I still live."

Hugo Gernsback approached the pulps by a different route; he came by way of the developing popular science magazines, particularly those dealing with the new technologies of radio and electronics, and he believed that science fiction existed to forecast the future for the impatient, to create more scientists, or to candy-coat a pill of information. He had it worked out to a formula for the science-fiction magazine *Amazing Stories* he founded in 1926: "The ideal proportion of a scientifiction story should be seventy-five per cent literature interwoven with twenty-five per cent science." The heroes of his own scientific adventures, such as the 1911 serial *Ralph 124C 41+*, were little more than spokesmen for his lectures about technology and the world of the future. They were magnificent when it came to whipping up a new invention such as radar, but their discussions of science always seemed to puncture the excitement of the narrative.

Edward Elmer Smith, on the other hand, specialized in great, jet-thrust adventures through the solar system and later the galaxy by scientist-adventurers somewhat reminiscent of the romantic heroes of the pulps, but Smith's characters were more likely to solve their problems with a formula or a bus bar than with a sword, although upon occasion a space axe came in handy. Later in his career Smith dealt in supermen, rather than simply speculating about the abilities of the best human minds. Smith developed his own super characters, such as the Grey Lensman and his children, and he raised questions about the kind of abilities a superman might have. Smith generally opted for goodness, intelligence, and strength, including strength of character; in his epics they needed it all, for they opposed the blackest villains in science fiction and what they held back was evil itself.

Only a few years later A. E. van Vogt would suggest a different kind of superman, not just a superior human but a mutant superior in only one or two senses or abilities, such as telepathy, multiple brains, or third eyes.

Meanwhile John W. Campbell, who rivaled Smith in creating scientific miracle workers for his own space epics, in the persona of Don A. Stuart returned to Wells's common man and neutral observer in such stories as "Twilight" and "Night," although in stories such as "Who Goes There?" and *The Moon Is Hell* he represented scientists in difficult situations working with a proper spirit of calm scientific detachment. As editor of *Astounding Science Fiction* he encouraged writers to depict scientists with an effort at verisimilitude, to show them as if they were part of a legitimate scientific culture. The characters in the stories he printed tended to be those who won their positions by merit—

meritocracy seemed to be the kind of government he favored—or villains steeped in prejudice or hereditary privilege whose regime the meritocrats pull down.

With Isaac Asimov the science-fiction character becomes as truly logical as if he were bound by the three laws of robotics. More than most science fiction up to that time, Asimov stories turned upon points of logic rather than the courage or emotional attitudes of the characters. His protagonists and antagonists alike were motivated by what they consider logical within their framework of knowledge and expectations. With Asimov we see the final development of the idea story that finds its ultimate expression in a story such as Tom Godwin's "The Cold Equations," whose characters are determined by equations as cold as those that dictate the conclusion.

Most of Robert Heinlein's work seemed to be concerned with right choices and how people are led to make them or to accept them. His characters, therefore, tend to be men who know how things are done, how society operates, how people work; as others have pointed out, the most common pattern of his novels is the tutoring of a young man by a wise man who knows how. (Incompetence in the Heinlein universe is worse than evil; you can protect yourself against the bad people but not against the incompetent.) In 1947 Heinlein wrote that for many years he thought there were only two basic "human-interest" plots in SF—"boy-meets-girl" and "the Little Tailor"—but L. Ron Hubbard pointed out a third: the-man-who-learned-better. Heinlein used this theme of education, of learning better, in one novel after another.

In traditional literature this kind of story has been called the apprenticeship novel; Voltaire's *Candide* is the best-known example and Goethe's *Wilhelm Meister* is the archetype. The apprenticeship novel requires for its main characters a wise man who wishes to teach (sometimes replaced by the lessons of life itself) and a young man who not only is capable of learning but is motivated to learn by hunger or repression or danger or desire to assume his rightful place.

After the golden years of the forties and the first dramatic impact of writers such as Asimov, Heinlein, and van Vogt, editors and their magazines began to shape the direction of science fiction and its characters. In 1949 Tony Boucher and J. Francis McComas were the founding editors of the *Magazine of Fantasy and Science Fiction*; in 1950, Horace Gold occupied the same position with *Galaxy. Fantasy and Science Fiction* emphasized fantasy, literary values, and out of these a greater concern for the interior lives of the characters and their relative importance within their stories. *Galaxy* concentrated on social science fiction and Gold asked for heroes who were losers as well as winners, jerks as well as jocks. In order to make this kind of story hold reader interest, the writers had to convince the reader of the reality of the characters. Galaxy also featured satire; satire requires characters who are types.

The tendency throughout the fifties and sixties was toward greater realism and more roundness in characterization as the stories themselves tended to be more realistic, less concerned with problems of science (real scientific breakthroughs or even new technological developments became increasingly hard to find during this period) and more concerned with problems of people. In the late sixties and early seventies surprising developments in biology, biochemistry, and astronomy brought back some of the old fascination with science in writers such as Larry Niven and Jerry Pournelle, not to mention a long-time craftsman such as Poul Anderson. And in the eighties, Gregory Benford and William Gibson broke new ground, Benford by portraying scientists as real people involved with human problems as well as science, and Gibson by his depiction of street people responding to dehumanizing technology by scorning its values while learning how to use it for their own purposes.

Ray Bradbury anticipated much of the later concern for the interior life of characters with his downbeat stories acted out by technological illiterates. His characters not only make mistakes but are in general neither as bright nor as well intentioned as their readers. Bradbury's characters are common to most of the literature of his time; the Bradbury hero is anti-hero. His characters are as helpless in the grasp of social circumstance as the spaceship crew in the hands of the Martians in "Mars Is Heaven."

What distinguished Bradbury in the science-fiction field was not only his unusual flair for language but his anti-heroes and his anti-science plots. What distinguished his fiction from the traditional fiction of his time were his images—elements of horror, spaceships even if they are made of tin cans, other worlds even if they are created out of the author's head—and their personal emotional quality.

What appear to be rounded characters may be only characters different from those in vogue; sometimes their characteristics have been reversed. The anti-hero, for instance, may be just as stereotyped as the hero, but for a time he seems fresh and new and, since life has more losers than winners, perhaps more realistic. When Bradbury's adults and children exchange roles—his children are complex and often sinister, his adults are naive and innocent—the result is as striking as if Bradbury had invented an entire new species.

The so-called "New Wave," beginning about 1965, brought avant-garde concerns and techniques to science fiction. In another essay I said that what made the New Wave seem different was its adoption of the literary tradition of subjectivism, as well as its concern for style, offbeat subjects, and a sophistication in plot development that sometimes approached obscurity. Another way to look at the New Wave is to consider the differences between the Aristotelian and the Platonic views of reality. The former sees the world as an object that exists independently of the observer and can be externally verified; the latter sees the world as illusion and fundamentally unknowable. The Aristotelian view has generally prevailed in Western culture and Western literature; but the Platonic, which has become associated with Eastern thought and fiction, has recently come into vogue. One might compare this trend with the rise in popularity of Eastern philosophy and mysticism.

The New Wave incorporated much that is common to the line of contemporary fiction that began with Kafka. Insofar as it goes all the way to world-as-illusion, its characters are just as stereotyped as those of pulp science fiction, a fact that is not as obvious because the motivations of the characters, if any, are seldom revealed. They usually do not act; they are acted upon. Instead of motivations they have compulsions. Since they live in a capricious world, where cause and effect are irrelevant, their emotions run a gamut of anger, bitterness, resentment, confusion, and resignation. In the situations in which these characters are trapped, Burroughs's courageous man, Asimov's logical man, or Heinlein's competent man would be counterproductive. The New Wave story demands an anti-hero more like Poe's man of exquisite sensibilities. Beyond that, we can reaffirm our earlier generality: the plot—and the vision of the world that produced it—creates the people who live there.

Science fiction is filled with memorable heroes: the obsessed Dr. Frankenstein; Ardan, Verne's adventurous Frenchman who volunteers to ride to the moon in Barbicane's cannonshell, Edgar Rice Burroughs's and A. Merritt's romantic and unconquerable warriors; Edward Elmer Smith's gray-uniformed superman battling an entire galaxy; Van Vogt's paranoid supermen; Heinlein's wise old men and competent young ones.

It has not provided the same quality of villains; science fiction has nothing to rival the comic-strip villainy of Flash Gordon's Ming the

Merciless, not even the total evil of Smith's Eddorians and the waves of blackness through which Kimball Kinnison must fight his way to the victory of good. Science fiction developed its view of life while naturalism was the dominant mode of literature. Even if it had not, Darwinism and the developments of sociology and Freudian psychology would have made villainy ridiculous. In naturalism the enemy is environment and lack of understanding. Even the earliest pulp romantic heroes struggled against environment rather than evil-hearted men; what they fought was ignorance, inertia, onrushing fate, nature, space, the tides of history, or the universe itself. With opponents like these, who needs villains?

The heroines of science fiction have been even less distinguished. Joanna Russ complains, with some justice, that science fiction has not done right by its women, that they are represented almost entirely in typical feminine roles as prizes, incentives, supports, or motivations but seldom as individuals with their own humanity. Certainly there are major female characters in science fiction, from Haggard's She to Weinbaum's Black Flame and Alexei Panshin's Mia Havero, but they are the exceptions. The same truth, however, is evident in traditional fiction. Fiction, of all kinds, has been historically a man's game, and men's concerns and images have dominated its pages. With its predominantly male authorship and readership, with its scientific and technological orientation, science fiction may surprise by what it has done for its women rather than what it has not. The increasing number of women who have been attracted to the field in the past few decades, both as authors and readers, has liberated the women trapped in a landscape of phallic symbols, and memorable heroines are beginning to appear in significant numbers.

The writer of science fiction has all of the traditions and characters of his predecessors available to him. At this moment stories are being written in the styles of Verne, Wells, or Burroughs and of Campbell, Asimov, or Heinlein. Each tradition differs in some significant way from the others, and each demands a particular kind of character to make it work.

Situation and character go together. Where they do not complement each other, the story fails; the only major exception is humor. John Ciardi has defined a story as character under stress—another way of saying that characters and stress are uniquely appropriate to each other, that there is one ideal character for every stress, one ideal stress for every character.

This is immediately perceived as true in particular cases. In the science-fiction lecture film Poul Anderson did for the University of Kansas series, he pointed out that *Hamlet* works only because the prince is introspective, sensitive, and equivocating, that if he had been a man of action he would immediately have avenged his father's death. The writer at work, however, may be tempted to make his characters neutral—or neutered—as kind of blank figures on which readers can project their own motivations and desires. But everyman is nobody, and this is not the way to build reader identification. Readers identify with characters because they seem real.

In Harlan Ellison's "I Have No Mouth and I Must Scream," the blob of humanity whose predicament inspires the title would not make a story if he did not feel he had to scream. His mouthlessness is the ultimate condition which makes his situation unbearable. His eternal torment is his punishment for liberating his fellow victims from the tortures of a vengeful computer-god.

Traven, the central character in J. G. Ballard's "The Terminal Beach," is unmotivated. He is driven by a compulsion he doesn't understand to wander among strange concrete structures left on H-bombed Eniwetok. But he had to be a particular kind of compulsive wanderer, a man who remembers, reflects, imagines, and dreams. And the strangely acquiescent prisoner in Tom Disch's "The Squirrel Cage" must be the kind of person who speculates about his situation and has the imagination to conceive all sorts of fanciful explanations and at the end accept his fate.

The kind of eventless, motiveless narrative in "The Terminal Beach" and "The Squirrel Cage" is about as far as story can be pushed, but curious experimenters still try to achieve reality with bored, incurious characters in a dull, repetitive world. Their accomplishment is a bored reader. The ultimate absurdity is a fiction nobody reads.

Even in the science-fiction idea story, the principle of "character under stress" holds true. In Tom Godwin's "The Cold Equations," the girl who stows away on the Emergency Delivery Ship must be innocent and naive as well as ignorant of the fact that every ounce of weight has been carefully calculated to enable the ship to just reach its destination, and the pilot must be humanly concerned about the girl's fate but not romantic. If he views the situation as a mechanical problem to be solved mechanically, Godwin has no story; if the pilot cannot accept the verdict of the cold equations and, like John Carter, will not save himself if the girl must die, he and the girl would die together and their precious cargo would be lost. Or Godwin could have found a sentimental conclusion—the pilot rigs an automatic landing system or teaches the girl which buttons to push before he walks out into space. Or he could have made it false to the situation by discovering something aboard ship that could be ripped out.

The situation dictates the characters, just as the characters, by what they are, create the situation. And at some point, if the story is to come alive, the characters must assume a life of their own and begin to shape or reshape events (plot) around them. Elizabeth Bowen went on to say in *Notes on Writing a Novel* that rather than being "created" the character "is recognized [by the novelist] by the signs he or she gives of unique capacity to act in a certain way, which 'certain way' fulfills a need of the plot." And since preexisting characters, once recognized, have lives that extend both before and after the incidents of the story itself, these characteristics, when perceived, may make the plot seem overrigid, arbitrary, and the novelist must adjudicate. Ultimately everything must be relevant to each and every other part of the story.

The science-fiction tendency is to make the characters the creatures of the plot; in mainstream fiction, characters tend to create their own plots. Plots are tyrants and want to turn characters into puppets; on the other hand, not all characters are good plotters. The best advice to writers in any genre is to preserve its strengths and shore up its weaknesses. In science fiction this would amount to making the characters as round as they can be without detracting from the actions they must take. The characters in science fiction need not be as flat as they have been. Even though roundness in character creates its own expectations in the reader's mind, the writer need not be led into obscurity or irrelevancies by his desire to make his characters more believable. Kimball Kinnison would not have been any less a superman if he had entertained a few doubts, nor would John Carter have been less a figure of romance if he had admitted the possibility of defeat.

Even though it may have tendrils in its hair or gills in its neck, humanity is the one subject of science fiction. What delights and surprises us in a novel such as Hal Clement's *Mission of Gravity* is our kinship with his fifteen-inch, many-legged Mesklinites.

Part 3

The Writers of Science Fiction

17

H. G. Wells
The Man Who Invented Tomorrow

The year was 1902. The occasion was a meeting of the Royal Institution. The speaker was a short, intense, thirty-six-year-old man who had attained considerable success already as an author of articles, stories, and novels. In his high-pitched voice, which has been described as something between a squeak and a falsetto, he was telling his audience about something new in human affairs: the future.

The speaker was H. G. Wells. For eight years he had been writing what he called "scientific romances," which later generations would call "science fiction." He had written his last true science-fiction novel and would write only a few more science-fiction short stories—he had turned to more direct and less entertaining forms of preaching—but in these few years he had established the ideas, methods, and theories that would shape the writing of science fiction after the creation of the science-fiction magazine in 1926.

Jack Williamson, the science-fiction author (and scholar) whose work has been published over eight decades, has said that the most important aspect of *Amazing Stories* was that it brought back into public awareness the science-fiction novels and short stories of Wells. Other writers—Mary Shelley, Poe, Verne—preceded Wells, but Wells was unique, and his unique views and methods made him, to Williamson and others, the father of modern science fiction.

Herbert George Wells was born in 1866 in Bromley, Kent, the fourth child of a gardener and a lady's maid who had met when both worked at an estate called Up Park. They had been married eleven years when "Bertie," as he was called, was born, and for those eleven years they had tried to make a living out of a crockery shop named Atlas House. It was a living scarcely distinguishable from poverty; they were able to survive only because of Joseph Wells's career as a professional cricketer and from the sale of cricket equipment in the shop. But it was the burial ground of their hopes.

In such dismal circumstances Bertie came along, unwanted, ignored by his father, who was away from home a great deal, and fussed over by his mother, whose fear of failure reflected the English apprehension that success was only a thin crust separating citizens from the volcano beneath. In Sarah Wells's early Victorian world the most important thing for her children was "getting on," and getting on meant having a solid trade to which one was apprenticed early.

Wells attributed his escape from this life and his mother's plans for him to two broken legs. The first happened to Bertie at the age of seven shortly after his mother proposed that he start helping out in Atlas House. Wells called it "one of the luckiest events of my life" and because of it, he wrote, "I am alive today and writing this autobiography instead of being a worn-out, dismissed and already dead shop assistant." During the weeks he was laid up on the parlor sofa, he was deluged by books brought home by his father and sent to him by neighbors.

The second broken leg, four years later, was his father's. Joe Wells broke his thigh falling off a ladder. The accident finished his career as a cricket player. Shortly afterward, at the age of fifty-seven, Sarah Wells was given the opportunity to return as housekeeper to the estate at which she had worked before she was married. She left her husband in possession of Atlas House and her son Bertie apprenticed to a draper. His mother, Wells recollected, thought "that to wear a black coat and tie behind a counter was the best of all possible lots attainable by man—at any rate by man at our social level." Within a month, however, he had proved unsuitable because of his carelessness and inattentiveness, and he was let go.

Wells's mother made two more attempts to apprentice her reluctant son, once as a chemist and again as a draper, the latter for two years before he pleaded to be released from the remaining two years to become an assistant teacher in a middle-class school. In between his apprenticeships Bertie had proved a remarkable student, and he had spent a winter at Up Park coming into contact with such books as *Gulliver's Travels* and Plato's *Republic*, and learning an appreciation for wealth and leisure and gentility.

Desperation, even thoughts of suicide, were behind his battle for freedom. Education was the only hope for a youngster of his class to rise in the world. The year was 1884, fourteen years after the passage of the Elementary Education Act of 1870 that began the education of working-class children, half of whom earlier had had no schooling at all. Wells, however, never attended the National Schools; his mother scrimped to send him to a series of private academies, village schools, and grammar schools, poorly taught though they were.

In his new position Wells taught during the day and studied in the evening, preparing himself to pass a series of examinations in physiography, geology, physiology, chemistry, and mathematics. The government, in an effort to train more science teachers, had offered instructors four pounds for each student who achieved an advanced pass in a subject, and the young Wells earned his teacher more than Wells had been paid for his year's work.

In fact, Wells did so well that he was invited to apply for a scholarship at the Normal School of Science in South Kensington. At the age of eighteen, Wells began a formative period of college studies. For the first year he studied biology and zoology under Thomas H. Huxley, the champion of Darwinism in England, who had founded the Normal School only five years before as a center for science teaching.

In spite of his frequent defense of Darwin's theories, Huxley was not a blind believer in the blessings of natural selection. He gave a famous lecture at Oxford on "Evolution and Ethics" in which he said:

> Social progress means a checking of the cosmic process at every step and the substitution for it of another, which may be called the ethical process; the end of which is not the survival of those who may happen to be the fittest . . . but of those who are ethically the best.

The conflict between these two processes lay at the heart of much that Wells was to write.

Huxley was a great teacher, and for the rest of his life Wells carried that year with him as "a nucleus" around which he "arranged a spacious array of facts." The second year Wells studied physics under an indifferent professor named Guthrie, and Wells's interest faded. The third and final year he studied geology under a Professor Judd and failed his final.

Perhaps more important than his classwork to his later career were his extracurricular activities. He was a faithful member of the Debating Society, attended meetings of the Fabian Society, listened excitedly to the speeches and debates of some of the great men of his time, and, with some friends, founded the *Science Schools Journal*. He was the first editor and he wrote several pieces for it that evidenced an early interest and skill in speculation. One was an article on "The Past and Present of the Human Race" (which was revised and published in the *Pall Mall Budget* in 1893 as "The Man of the Year Million"); in it he imagined a

time when distant descendants of mankind would be great brains floating in tubs of nutritive fluids, when humanity would live by chemicals
and sunlight alone on a planet where it had destroyed all other plants
and animals (*cf.* John W. Campbell's 1934 story "Twilight"), and when
humanity's heirs would be driven underground by the cooling of the sun
and earth to live in galleries linked to the surface by ventilating shafts
(*cf.* E. M. Forster's 1909 story "The Machine Stops"). He also wrote
for the *Journal* some science-fiction stories, including one about time
travel called "The Chronic Argonauts."

His failure in the third-year final had destroyed his hopes for a scientific career; instead, he took a teaching job in Wales. He was rescued
from that by a kidney injury, suffered in a game of English football, and,
while recovering from that, a diagnosis of tuberculosis. After an extended period of convalescence and a few odd jobs in London, Wells
took on another teaching position at a private academy, got his bachelor
of science degree by examination, and accepted a new position at University Correspondence College. There he wrote a textbook on biology
and co-authored another on physiography.

This renewal of his interest in writing was given further impetus
during a month's recuperation after a flare-up of his illness, and he
wrote an article entitled "The Rediscovery of the Unique" that was
accepted by the *Fortnightly Review*. A commitment to a career as an
author, however, had to wait until after his marriage to his cousin Isabel
(which was so disappointing that he was unfaithful with his wife's friend
within a few weeks) and a recurrence of his tuberculosis that convinced
him he would not be able to continue as a teacher.

A passage in a novel by J. M. Barrie entitled *When a Man's Single*
gave him an idea about articles that brought him quick success as a
freelance journalist; a character comments that saleable materials can
be fashioned out of the ordinary things of life such as pipes, umbrellas,
and flower-pots. In 1893 Wells sold at least thirty articles, primarily to
the *Pall Mall Gazette*. Soon editors began to ask him to do book reviews
and drama criticism.

By the end of the year, however, Wells had parted with his wife
(whom he supported and remained on good terms with until her death at
the age of sixty-four) and had run off with a young student named
Catherine Robbins, whom he came to call Jane. Within two years they
were married, after his divorce from Isabel, and Jane remained his faithful
wife for the rest of her life, forgiving his frequent infidelities, both the

casual kind and those that lasted for years and were viewed by many as scandalous.

In 1894 Lewis Hind, the editor of the *Pall Mall Budget*, suggested that Wells use his knowledge of science to write a series of stories for which he would be paid five guineas each (a guinea was a pound plus a shilling). "The Stolen Bacillus" soon was on the editor's desk and five more followed before the year was over. The big opportunity came, however, when William Ernest Henley, editor of the *National Observer* (and author of "Invictus"), asked Wells for a series of articles. Wells dug up what he called his "peculiar treasure," "The Chronic Argonauts," and revised it as seven articles that were published in 1894. Although the *National Observer* was sold and Henley was fired, he immediately became editor of a new monthly, *The New Review*, and he asked Wells to revise his "Time Traveller" articles as a serial. He also persuaded publisher William Heineman to take the story as a book.

The result was "The Time Machine." As Henley had suggested and Wells suspected, it was to make his reputation. While he was waiting for it to be published, he worked on *The Wonderful Visit*, a satirical book based on Ruskin's remark that if an angel were to appear on earth someone would be sure to shoot it; and he sketched out the first draft of *The Island of Dr. Moreau*. He was working rapidly, trying to support his parents and his ex-wife as well as his own household, and words flowed from his pen.

In March 1895 the *Review of Reviews* said, "H. G. Wells is a man of genius." Magazines pestered him for articles, reviews, and criticism. Soon, however, health forced him to move back to the country and depend on the writing of fiction rather than articles. But he was doing well financially and, as his mother had always wanted, "getting on."

In his new home in Woking, Wells took up cycling and, as he did with many of his interests, worked that into a picaresque novel called *The Wheels of Chance*. His early science-fiction stories were collected into another 1895 book entitled *The Stolen Bacillus and Other Incidents*. He continued to write short stories, many of them not science fiction, and another volume, *The Plattner Story and Others*, came out in 1897. More important for his career, *The Island of Dr. Moreau* was published in 1896, *The Invisible Man* in 1897, *The War of the Worlds* in 1898, *When the Sleeper Wakes* in 1899 (*Tales of Space and Time* was published the same year), and *The First Men in the Moon* in 1901.

In those half-dozen years he had moved twice, first to a rented villa in Worcester Park and then to a house, called "Spade House" because of the design worked into doors and windows, he had built for himself at Folkestone. In both locations he came into contact with other writers and was welcomed into the literary world. George Bernard Shaw became a lifelong friend, as did Arnold Bennett and Joseph Conrad. Friendships with George Gissing and Stephen Crane were cut off by their early deaths.

After reading *The Invisible Man*, Conrad wrote:

> I am always powerfully impressed by your work. Impressed is *the* word, O Realist of the Fantastic! . . . If you want to know what impresses me it is to see how you contrive to give over humanity to the clutches of the Impossible and yet manage to keep it down (or up) to its humanity, to its flesh, blood, sorrow, folly. *That is the achievement!*

Ford Madox Ford, another friend though they later had serious disagreements, called Wells "The Dean of our Profession," and said, "It did not take us long to recognize that here was Genius. Authentic, real Genius. And delightful at that." The senior citizen of the group, Henry James, also was an admirer; he wrote of *Tales of Space and Time* that "you fill me with wonder and admiration. . . . Your spirit is huge, your fascination irresistible, your resources infinite." Eventually they would quarrel. Wells gave a talk in 1911 to *The Times* Book Club on "The Scope of the Novel" and James published two articles in 1914 in *The Times Literary Supplement* on "The Young Generation" of writers, including Wells. In 1915 Wells published *Boon*, a formless novel that contained a bitter satire of James. But earlier James could still speak of being filled with "wonder and admiration" for Wells's early stories and scientific romances, of reading *The First Men in the Moon* "*à petite doses* as one sips (I suppose) old Tokay," and of allowing *Twelve Stories and a Dream* "to melt, lollipopwise, upon my imaginative tongue."

Between *When the Sleeper Wakes* and *The First Men in the Moon* came a novel that would represent a significant change in Wells's work and aspirations. It was *Love and Mr. Lewisham*, published in 1900, and it was the first of a series of novels about contemporary life and manners that drew heavily upon Wells's own experiences. Arnold Bennett wrote to express his regret that Wells had abandoned imaginative romances, and Wells demanded, in return, "Why the hell have you joined the conspiracy to restrict me to one particular type of story? I want to write novels and before God I *will* write novels. They are the proper stuff for my everyday work, a methodical careful distillation of one's thoughts and sentiments and experiences and impressions."

After 1901 Wells abandoned science fiction except for those stories collected in 1903 in *Twelve Stories and a Dream* and in 1911 in *The Country of the Blind and Other Stories*. The rest of his writing career would be devoted to his autobiographical novels, such as *Kipps* (1905), *Tono-Bungay* (1909), *Ann Veronica* (1909), *The History of Mr. Polly* (1910), *The New Machiavelli* (1911), and *Mr. Britling Sees It Through* (1916); to propaganda pieces that often seemed like science fiction, such as *The Food of the Gods* (1904), *A Modern Utopia* (1905), *In the Days of the Comet* (1906), *The War in the Air* (1908), *The World Set Free* (1914), *Men Like Gods* (1923), *Star-Begotten* (1937), and *The Holy Terror* (1939); and various kinds of discursive fiction and nonfiction, in particular his encyclopedic work that made him so much money, *The Outline of History* (1920), which was followed a decade later by *The Science of Life* (1930) and *The Work, Wealth and Happiness of Mankind* (1932).

Some critics have attributed the change in Well's writing to the turn of the century (and the end of Queen Victoria's long reign in 1901) and the casting away of the *fin de siècle* mood that had dominated the literature of the late nineteenth century. Bernard Bergonzi writes:

> Wells, at the beginning of his career, was a genuine and original imaginative artist, who wrote several books of considerable literary importance, before dissipating his talents in directions which now seem more or less irrelevant. In considering these works, it will be necessary to modify the customary view of Wells as an optimist, a utopian and a passionate believer in human progress. The dominant note of his early years was rather a kind of fatalistic pessimism, combined with intellectual skepticism, and it is this which the early romances reflect. It is, one need hardly add, a typical *fin de siècle* note.

But there are other reasons for Well's change. The author of the scientific romances had written hard and fast for half-a-dozen years in order to make a name and some financial security for himself and for those who depended upon him; he may have written himself out in that direction. Moreover, he was moving in new circles, making new friends, seeing the possibilities of affecting the direction of events in real life. In 1903 he joined the Fabian Society and soon tried, unsuccessfully, to turn it into more than a genteel debating society. He became acquainted with politicians and newspaper publishers, even joining elite discussion groups that included future war ministers and lord chancellors, foreign secretaries and directors of the London School of Economics, as well as Bertrand Russell and Sidney Webb.

He also made a celebrated renunciation of literary art. In his autobiography (1934), he pointed out what he saw as distinguishing his intentions from those of Conrad and James. They looked upon the novel as a form of art; Wells saw it as a means to an end. He wanted his writing to be appraised "as a system of ideas"; they wanted ideas to enter, if at all, only as an integral part of the artistic whole. He wanted to write about himself, his reactions to what had happened to him and what had happened and was happening in the world; they wanted the writer kept out of it.

The literary approach, Wells finally decided:

> would have taken more time that I could afford. . . . I had a great many things to say and. . . if I could say one of them in such a way as to get my point over to the reader I did not worry much about finish. The fastidious critic might object, but the general reader to whom I addressed myself cared no more for finish and fundamental veracity about the secondary things of behavior than I. . . . I was disposed to regard the novel as about as much an art form as a market place or a boulevard.

Wells also may have realized that if he allowed himself to be compared to Conrad and Wells, or even Bennett and Galsworthy, by their standards he would always be found wanting (science-fiction writers would have similar complaints in later years). In his 1911 lecture on "The Scope of the Novel," Wells tried to set up new standards. Fiction should not be trivially entertaining or, on the other hand, subject to "fierce pedantries" of technique. He called for "a laxer, more spacious form of novel-writing: that would be "irresponsible and free" and "aggressive." He insisted that the author should be allowed to "discuss, point out, plead and display" and to enter the novel himself if this would help the reader understand the ideas.

> The novel is the only medium through which we can discuss the great majority of the problems which are being raised in such bristling multitude by our contemporary social development. . . . In this tremendous work of human reconciliation and elucidation, it seems to me it is the novel that must attempt most and achieve most. . . . Before we are done, we will have all life within the scope of the novel.

"In the end," Wells summed up in his autobiography, "I revolted altogether and refused to play their games. 'I am a journalist,' I declared, 'I refuse to play the artist! If sometimes I am an artist it is a freak of the gods. I am a journalist all the time and what I write goes now—and will presently die.'"

Certainly what Wells wrote after 1901 had to go then—and most of it is dead, with the exceptions of *The Outline of History,* which still sells, and the social, autobiographical novels, *Kipps* and *Tono-Bungay*, with their vividly realized scenes of late Victorian England. Outside of those, only the science fiction continues to survive plus those propaganda novels that resemble science fiction.

What spark of vitality in Wells's science fiction has kept it alive while the rest of his fiction was dying, indeed while James and Conrad go unread except in classrooms, and while the science fiction of other authors of the nineteenth century, including Jules Verne, have faded from the public view?

Part of the answer is that Wells's science fiction, in spite of its Victorian furnishings, was timeless in other ways. The themes were large; the fears that he played upon were basic; and his approach was speculative rather that extrapolative. Extrapolation dates rapidly; speculation survives.

When, in *The Time Machine*, Wells imagines the troglodytic Morlocks as the degenerate descendants of the working class and the pretty but helpless Eloi as the devolved offspring of the leisure class, the political theory on which this outcome was based may seem antiquated but the irony of the situation and the horror of the imagery remain. *The War of the Worlds*, in various updatings and transplantings, has been kept continually in front of audiences because of the total savagery of the attack and the elemental terror of invasion by aliens. *The Invisible Man* and *The Island of Dr. Moreau* are not quite as timeless in their appeals, though they, too, continue to be revived. *When the Sleeper Wakes* and

The First Men in the Moon are one step farther down the ladder of universality.

Verne and other science-fiction writers of the period were clearly men of the nineteenth century, bound to it by idea, temperament, and style; Wells, who lived well into the twentieth century, seems curiously modern in his subjects, attitudes, and prose. When Wells is adapted to other media, his stories are translated into contemporary situations; Verne cannot be updated—he always is done as a period piece, as what might be called "historical science fiction."

Verne was concerned with the mechanics of getting there; he called his novels, appropriately, *voyages extraordinaires*. They were adventure stories built around an unusual journey, often by an unusual form of transportation: a balloon, a submarine, a cannon shell, a ship of the air, a comet. Wells was not concerned with how the Martians travel but what they are going to do; and Wells took the anti-gravity with which Cavor and Bedford got to the moon no more seriously than Lucian took his typhoon. Verne was concerned with the practicability of his Nautilus and his Columbiad; Wells described his time machine in considerable detail but didn't think for a moment that it would work.

In a celebrated exchange of views after Wells was called "the English Jules Verne," Verne commented:

> I do not see the possibility of comparison between his work and mine. We do not proceed in the same manner. It occurs to me that his stories do not repose on a very scientific basis. No, there is no rapport between his work and mine. I make use of physics. He invents. I go to the moon in a cannon-ball discharged from a cannon. Here there is no invention. He goes to Mars [sic] in an air-ship, which he constructs of a metal which does away with the law of gravitation. *Ça, c'est trés jolie*, but show me this metal. Let him produce it.

And Wells said:

> There's a quality in the worst of my so-called "pseudo- scientific" (imbecile adjective) stuff which differentiates it from Jules Verne, *e.g.*, just as Swift is differentiated from Fantasia—isn't there? There is something other than either story writing or artistic merit which has emerged through the series of my books. Something one might regard as a new system of ideas—"thought."

In 1902, when Arnold Bennett was writing a long article for *Cosmopolitan* about Wells as a serious writer, Wells expressed his hope that Bennett would stress his "new system of ideas."

Wells developed a theory to justify the way he wrote (he was fond of theories), and these theories helped others write in similar ways. He wrote:

> For the writer of fantastic stories to help the reader to play the game properly, he must help him in every possible unobtrusive way to *domesticate* the impossible hypothesis. He must trick him into an unwary concession to some plausible assumption and get on with his story while the illusion holds.

And he continued:

> The thing that makes such imaginations interesting is their translation into commonplace terms and a rigid exclusion of other marvels from the story. Then it becomes human. How would you feel and what might not happen to you, is the typical question, if for instance pigs could fly and one came rocketing over a hedge at you? How would you feel and what might not happen to you if suddenly you were changed into an ass and couldn't tell anyone about it? Or if you suddenly became invisible? But no one would think twice about the answer if hedges and houses began to fly, or if people changed into lions, tigers, cats, and dogs left and right, or if anyone could vanish anyhow. Nothing remains interesting if anything can happen.

In contemporary usage, Verne was writing an "if-this-goes-on" kind of story and Wells, a "what-if" kind. This fact alone is not enough to distinguish them and what they wrote; for occasionally they would switch, with Verne writing a what-if novel in *Hector Servadac, or Off on a Comet* and Wells writing if-this-goes-on kinds of novels in *When the Sleeper Wakes* and *The War in the Air.* Even then, however, the differences are great; with Verne the adventure is everything; with Wells the idea is king.

In his preface to *The Country of the Blind and Other Stories,* Wells wrote:

> I found that, taking almost anything as a starting point and letting my thoughts play about with it, there would presently come out of the darkness, in a manner quite inexplicable, some absurd or vivid little nucleus. Little men in canoes upon sunlit oceans would come floating out of nothingness, incubating the eggs of prehistoric monsters unawares; violent conflicts would break out amidst the flower-beds of suburban gardens; I would discover I was peering into remote and mysterious worlds ruled by an order logical indeed but other than our common sanity.

It may have been this floating of images and symbols out of his unconsciousness that gave them their power, their universality.

Part of Wells's modern appeal, however, lies in the way in which he saw the world changing and made that perception of change a part of his fiction and nonfiction. In his autobiography he described the changes that were occurring in his mother's world:

> Vast unsuspected forces beyond her ken were steadily destroying the social order, the horse and sailing ship transport, the handicrafts and the tenant-farming social order to which all her beliefs were attuned and on which all her confidence was based. To her these mighty changes in human life presented themselves as a series of perplexing frustration and undeserved misfortunes, for which nothing or nobody was clearly to blame—unless it was my father. . . .

Wells, on the other hand, saw change as providing opportunity to improve humanity's condition:

> Most individual creatures since life began have been "up against it" all the time, have been driven continually by fear and cravings, have had to respond to the unresting antagonisms of their surroundings, and they have found a sufficient and sustaining interest in the drama of immediate events provided for them by these demands. Essentially, their living was continuous adjustment to happenings. Good hap and ill hap filled it entirely. They hungered and ate and they desired and loved; they were amused and attracted, they pursued or escaped, they were overtaken and they died.
>
> But with the dawn of human foresight and with the appearance of a great surplus of energy in life such as the last cen-

tury or so has revealed, there has been a progressive emanci-
pation of the attention from everyday urgencies. What was
once the whole of life, has become to an increasing extent,
merely the background of life. People can ask now what would
have been an extraordinary question five hundred years ago.
They can say, "Yes, you earn a living, you support a family,
you love and hate, but—*what do you do?* . . .

In studies and studios and laboratories, administrative bu-
reaus and exploring expeditions, a new world is germinated
and develops. It is not a repudiation of the old but a vast
extension of it, in a racial synthesis into which individual
aims will ultimately be absorbed. We originative intellectual
workers are reconditioning human life.

Of his own efforts, Wells said:

I have found the attempt to disentangle the possible drift of
life in general and of human life in particular from the confused stream of events, and the means of controlling that drift,
if such are to be found, more important and interesting by
far than anything else. I have had, I believe, an aptitude for
it. . . .

Wells's attempts to look into the "confused stream of events" and find
"means of controlling the drift" found expression in 1901 with the publication of a series of articles in the *Fortnightly Review*, a series that
appeared toward the end of the year as a book entitled *Anticipations of
the Reaction of Mechanical and Scientific Progress upon Human Life
and Thought*. It was more commonly called simply *Anticipations*. It
was, as Wells wrote Arnold Bennett, a "rough sketch of the coming
time, a prospectus as it were of the joint undertakings of mankind in
facing these impending years."
  Anticipations was filled with predictions; some were remarkable
prescient, others were not. Wells saw how the automobile would change
society, for instance, from freeways to traffic jams and the development
of the suburbs, and he made a brilliant guess about the tank, but he
didn't foresee the development of the airplane (he dated the first successful flight of a heavier-than air machine as "very probably before
1950"). Mostly, however, the book did not deal so much with predictions as the business of predicting. As he pointed out in his 1902 talk to

the Royal Institution, "It is our ignorance of the future and our persuasion that this ignorance is incurable that alone has given the past its enormous predominance in our thoughts." He believed that it was possible, through the use of what he first called "inductive history" and later "Human Ecology" (defined as the working out of "biological, intellectual, and economic consequences"), to chart the possibilities of the future and to push people into making sensible use of those possibilities.

He was the first futurologist, the man who invented tomorrow, and perhaps the first "psychohistorian," in its Asimovian sense. In 1936, at the age of seventy-one, he proposed to the Royal Institution the creation of a "world knowledge bank, a world brain: no less." He asked scientists to put together a World Encyclopedia, a repository for the mind and knowledge of the race. He saw it as "a world monopoly" and through it the encyclopedists would acquire wealth sufficient to finance their activities and to manipulate "everyone who controls administration, makes wars, directs mass behaviour, feeds, moves and starves populations. . . ." It was remarkably like Hari Seldon's vision of the *Encyclopedia Galactica* and the Foundation in the *Foundation* stories, another of the many curious resemblances between Wells and Asimov.

But it is clear from Wells's nineteenth century science fiction that he was no simple believer in progress, even progress guided by such "innovative intellectual workers" as himself. Nor did he have an easy faith in the millennium he depicted in many of his propaganda novels, possibly arriving after some worldwide catastrophe like a world war, when a "new mass of capable men"—mostly scientists and engineers—would impose "social order" on "the vast confusions of the coming time." In the science fiction that he had just left behind, Wells saw longer-reaching problems having to do with the fate of the human species and of Earth itself.

He had foreseen those concerns, too, in an article—his nonfiction and his fiction were drawn from the same source—published in the *Pall Mall Gazette* in 1894 entitled "The Extinction of Man":

> What has usually happened in the past appears to be the emergence of some type of animal hitherto rare and unimportant, and the extinction, not simply of the previous ruling species, but of most of the forms that are at all closely related to it. Sometimes, indeed, as in the case of the extinct giants of South America, they vanished without any considerable ri-

vals, victims of pestilence, famine, or, it may be, of that cumulative inefficiency that comes of a too undisputed life.

No; man's complacent assumption of the future is too confident. We think, because things have been easy for mankind as a whole for a generation or so, we are going on to perfect comfort and security in the future. We think that we shall always go to work at ten and leave off at four and have dinner at seven forever and ever. But these four suggestions [the evolution of the ant and the cephalopod are two of them, foreshadowing two evolutionary competitors that Wells later would turn into fiction, "The Empire of the Ants" and "The Sea Raiders"] out of a host of others must surely do a little against this complacency. Even now, for all we can tell, the coming terror may be crouching for its spring and the fall of humanity be at hand. In the case of every predominant animal the world has seen, I repeat, the hour of its complete ascendancy has been the eve of its entire overthrow.

From these two poles—the hope for a better future and the fear that humanity may be extinguished—Wells's science fiction drew its inspiration and its energy. And from Wells's science fiction the genre itself would later draw not only inspiration but also ideas. His novels had the greatest impact on his readers, some of whom would turn into writers, but his short stories had the opportunity to explore more widely. He wrote only two novellas and five novels; he wrote some twenty science-fiction stories. This is not to insist that any succeeding treatments of Wellsian themes necessarily were derived directly from Wells, though some of them may have been, simply that in many cases Wells provided the first or the definitive version.

The linear descendants of the novels are clear enough: *The Time Machine* has spawned the most. It was the first story to incorporate a mechanical means for traveling through time and returning. Every other time-travel story since Washington Irving's "Rip Van Winkle" had used the mechanism that Wells re-used in *When the Sleeper Wakes*—a long period of sleep or suspended animation. Returning was the important aspect: to be able to return is to be able to bring the future back to the present, with its cautions and correctives. What *The Time Machine* did not do as far as the story goes was to venture into the past, with all its possibilities for paradox and ambiguity, although its potential to do so was seized upon by a hundred later writers; nor did Wells's novella consider the possibility of a mutable future. The future, if it could be traveled to, was as fixed as the past. At the same time, a vision of the future could serve as a cautionary tale in the real world of the reader.

The Island of Dr. Moreau was less seminal. Later stories often have dealt with vivisection, but usually it was practiced on human beings in efforts to test the irreducible human elements or to improve human abilities, or even to produce the superman. Thus Wardon Allan Curtis's "The Monster of Lake LaMetrie" published in 1899 may have owed something to *Dr. Moreau*, as well as A. E. van Vogt's *Slan* and even Frederik Pohl's *Man Plus*—although by the seventies independent inputs from cyborg developments and other real-life events may make simple literary derivations meaningless. The idea of evolution speeded up, slowed down, or reversed, on the other hand, has frequently been used; one example is Edmond Hamilton's "The Man Who Evolved" (1931), which even mentions that neighbors suspect a scientist of vivisection. Wells also may have been the first to suggest that the ability to tolerate pain for future good separates the human from the animal, an idea that John Campbell, long-time editor of *Astounding/Analog*, toyed with in editorial and story. Primitive rites of passage, he suggested, may have originated with the need to distinguish humans from reversions to the animal in the early days of humanity's evolution. One such story (though in *Fantasy and Science Fiction*) was Richard McKenna's "Mine Own Ways" (1960).

The Invisible Man has such fairy-tale resonances and wish-fulfillment appeal that the concept, rather than the fate of Griffin, has inspired writers to think of other possible uses—or drawbacks—of invisibility. There have been other film takeoffs and even an ill-conceived and ill-fated television series called "The Invisible Man," which owned little else to Wells's novel.

The War of the Worlds was followed by hundreds of alien-invasion stories in which humanity is challenged by superior science, more advanced technical development, greater intelligence, a more warlike society, or a more subtle danger. Sometimes humanity beats back the attack and sometimes it is conquered. Examples range from Edgar Rice Burroughs's *The Moon Maid* (1926) through Robert A. Heinlein's *The Puppet Masters* (1951) to Arthur C. Clarke's *Childhood's End* (1953) and John Varley's *The Ophiuchi Hotline* (1977). Christopher Anvil wrote a number of alien-invasion stories for *Astounding* in which the point usually centered on the difficulties of alien conquest.

When the Sleeper Wakes owes so much to the tradition described in the title that the mechanism becomes unimportant; it was a hoary convention even then. What Wells added was the concept that the Sleeper's fortune had grown over the centuries until he owned half the world; trustees act in his name to oppress the workers into the Labour Company. Harry Stephen Keeler used a similar notion in a 1927 story, "John Jones' Dollar," in which a single dollar grows by compound interest over the centuries to exceed the value of the solar system. Wells also envisioned, as he did in "A Story of the Days to Come" and *A Modern Utopia*, cities grown into great centers of population with the aid of machines while the land outside is virtually deserted. This concept of the future metropolis influenced generations of science-fiction writers and film-makers, including, no doubt, Fritz Lang, whose film *Metropolis* came out in 1927, and Isaac Asimov in *The Caves of Steel* (1954).

The First Men in the Moon also was less influential in its mechanism than in its message. Verne's objections to its plausibility had a firm foundation, and few subsequent writers used anti-gravity as a means of flying through space, one exception being James Blish in his *Cities in Flight* series. Other writers would seek more convincing methods of spaceflight: Verne had his cannon but Gernsback's writers had their rockets. Wells's anti-utopian civilization on the moon and the vision of workers so completely adapted for their tasks that they were little more than a giant hand to operate a machine contributed their share to the literature of humanity's subjugation to technology.

Not all of Wells's ideas were original with him. Some of them were in the air; others were inspired, in part or in whole, by other writings. *The Time Machine*, for instance, came out of a Debating Society talk given during Wells's college days by a fellow student named E. A. Hamilton-Gordon; it was about the theory that time was the fourth dimension, a notion that had been suggested in 1875 by Heinrich Czolbe, and C. H. Hinton included several essays about dimensions, including "What Is the Fourth Dimension?" in *Scientific Romances* published in 1884. Wells's biographers Norman and Jeanne MacKenzie noted:

> The quickness with which Wells seized on the notion of travelling through time illustrates the way he worked on his later scientific romances. He heard of some new concept or invention. He next set the novel theory in a conventional background. Then, having made the incredible acceptable by his attention to detail, his imagination was free to make what fantasies it pleased out of the resulting conflict.

Wells picked up ideas from his fellow fiction writers, as well. Oscar Wilde preceded Wells in the use of the fourth dimension as a means of escape in his 1887 story "The Canterville Ghost." And Bulwer-Lytton's *The Coming Race* (1871) and Samuel Butler's *Erewhon* (1872) contain a number of points of similarity with *The Time Machine*, including the fact that the traveler in all of them meets a girl (in *Erewhon* her name is even "Arowhena"). She becomes his companion and explains things to him, and takes him to a large public museum where a great deal of machinery is displayed.

The Island of Dr. Moreau is Wells's most Darwinian book and owes most of its inspiration to the theory of evolution. But there were other sources. Wells himself attributed the idea for Moreau to the downfall of a man of genius in the 1890s (Oscar Wilde). The mechanism and viewpoint of the novel owe much to Swift, particularly to *Gulliver's Travels*. Prendick, for instance, is castaway like Gulliver and rescued by Dr. Moreau; Prendick's first reaction to the Beast People is much like Gulliver's reaction to the Yahoos; and the final chapter, after Prendick's escape from the island and return to England, is virtually identical in impact to the conclusion of Gulliver's voyage to the land of the Houyhnhnms. Just as Gulliver sees Yahoos everywhere, Prendick recoils from the evidence of the Beast People in everyone. There also is something of Poe's *Arthur Gordon Pym* in Prendick's rescue, and Wells's "The Sayers of the Law" obviously is an imitation, if not a parody, of Kipling's "Law of the Jungle" in *The Second Jungle Book*.

The Invisible Man is one of Wells's most original concepts. It was preceded, nevertheless, by Fitz-James O'Brien's "What Was It? A Mystery" in 1859, Guy de Maupassant's "The Horla" in 1887, and Ambrose Bierce's "The Damned Thing" in 1893. The last two of these, to be sure, dealt with invisible creatures rather than men; the significant difference came from Wells's use of invisibility produced through scientific means while the others described strange (sometimes supernatural) natural phenomena. The basic idea Wells got, he said, from one of W. S. Gilbert's "Bab Ballads." Called "The Perils of Invisibility," it contains the lines:

> Old Peter vanished like a shot.
> But then—his suit of clothes did not.

The War of the Worlds was in the tradition of the future war novel pioneered by Lieutenant-Colonel Sir George Tomkyns Chesney's "Battle of Dorking" published in 1871 and followed by many others, twenty-two of them in 1871 alone, as I. F. Clarke has pointed out in *Voices Prophesying War*. Novels about life on Mars and the moon had been published before: Marie Corelli's *Romance of Two Worlds* was published in 1886, Tremlett Carter's *People of the Moon* in 1895, George du Maurier's *The Martian* in 1896, and F. R. Stockton's *The Great Stone of Sardis* in 1897, as well as Kurd Lasswitz's *Auf Zwei Planeten* in 1897. The speculations of Percival Lowell about the construction of canals on Mars by intelligent beings were first published in 1896, though Wells had published similar speculations a month or so earlier in an article entitled "Intelligence on Mars." The idea for the Martian invasion came from Wells's brother Frank. As Wells described it later:

> We were walking together through some particularly peaceful Surrey scenery. "Suppose some beings from another planet were to drop out of the sky suddenly," said he, "and begin laying about them here!" . . . That was the point of departure. . . .

Some of the physical descriptions of Mars may have been inspired by the work of a French writer of scientific and cosmic romances, Camille de Flammarion, particularly *La Fin du Monde* (1894) and *La Planète Mars* (1892). And the Martian heat-ray may owe something to Bulwer-Lytton's Vril, or perhaps to a description of John Hartman's electric gun published in London newspapers in the 1890s.

When the Sleeper Wakes was characterized by Wells as "a horoscope" and "a romance of the immediate future, somewhat on the lines of Mr. [Edward] Bellamy's *Looking Backwards* [sic]." *Looking Backward* was published in 1888, but the plot of someone falling to sleep and waking up in the future goes back at least to Washington Irving's "Rip Van Winkle" (1819). In fact, one character in Wells's novel comments that Graham's sleep is "Rip Van Winkle come real" and another that "It's Bellamy." Some of his ideas about the world to come Wells derived from theorists such as William James, but the highly mechanized future civilization he depicted leaned upon Flammarion's *La Fin du Monde*, which also may have influenced *Anticipations* and *In the Days of the Comet*, and in particular "The Star," in which the action of Flammarion's novel was condensed and refined into the artistry of the short story published four years later.

The First Men in the Moon is dependent on all the earlier moon voyages, particularly Edgar Allan Poe's "Hans Pfaal" (1835), in which a Dutch bankrupt ascends to the moon by balloon. Wells's descriptions of how the earth seems to diminish in diameter and the moon to increase during the flight is much like Poe's, as well as his description of the sunrise on the moon and the moon's atmospheric conditions. Wells followed Carter's *People of the Moon* in making his Selenites cave-dwellers and scientists. Wells also received help from a Normal school classmate, Richard Gregory, who sent him papers on moon craters and an article published in 1900 by *Nature* in which a Professor Poynting described experiments on the possibility of substances acting as a screen to gravity.

Similar materials from the real and fictional worlds found their way into his short stories. "The Diamond Maker" (1894), for instance, surely was inspired by the experience of James Hannay, who announced in an 1880 paper to the Royal Society of London that he had created artificial diamonds; Wells includes a description of a process for creating diamonds that is almost identical with Hannay's. Wells got a number of ideas from the inventor J. W. Dunne, including the basic notion of the tank that later was described in "The Land Ironclads." In a letter Dunne called them "big fat pedrail machines." Wells also used Dunne as a model for an aviator in several stories.

Wells acknowledged his indebtedness to a number of writers, including Hawthorne, Poe, Kipling, and others, particularly Sterne and Swift, although he rejected comparisons to Verne and never mentioned Flammarion. Ultimately all the material Wells touched, including his own life, became his subject, and he made it his own. His vision of humanity and its problems and its place in the universe sometimes transformed that material into art.

He ended his 1902 speech to the Royal Institution with a declaration of his faith in the power of the human mind to create a better future. There are two kinds of minds, he said. One, oriented to the past, regards the future "as sort of black nonexistence upon which the advancing present will presently write events." That is the legal mind, always referring to precedents. The second kind of mind, oriented to the future, is constructive, creative, organizing. "It sees the world as one great workshop, and the present as no more than material for the future, for the thing that is yet destined to be." Finally, he predicted what might be accomplished if the future-oriented mind were given freedom to express itself:

> All this world is heavy with the promise of greater things, and a day will come, one day in the unending succession of days, when beings who are now latent in our thoughts and hidden in our loins, shall stand upon this earth as one stands upon a footstool and shall laugh and reach out their hands amidst the stars.

Clearly Wells was finished with the pessimism of his early science fiction. But science fiction was not finished with him.

18

Robert A. Heinlein
The Grand Master

ROBERT A. HEINLEIN, who received the first Grand Master award from his fellow science-fiction writers, was recognized as a major author almost from the publication of his first story, "Life-line," in the August 1939 issue of *Astounding*. In the years that followed he influenced the evolution of science fiction more than any writer since H. G. Wells, not only with what he wrote but also with the new media he opened for science fiction: the slick magazines, the juvenile, film, and the best seller. Someone must go first to show the media and other authors what is possible, and Heinlein was first in all of them.

Most science-fiction readers and critics have personal favorites among Heinlein's books: *Double Star*, *The Moon Is a Harsh Mistress*, *Stranger in a Strange Land*, *Have Space Suit-Will Travel*. I would like to make a case that *The Puppet Masters*, which is not often given a prominent place in the canon of Heinlein's work, may be his most characteristic and perhaps his most artistic novel.

The Puppet Masters was serialized in *Galaxy* in September, October, and November 1951, and published in hardcovers by Doubleday the same year. Heinlein was forty-four years old and had been writing science fiction for twelve years.

There are two kinds of science-fiction writers: those who break into print at the top of their powers, like Edgar Rice Burroughs and A. E. van Vogt; and those whose later work shows significant improvement. In spite of Heinlein's early reputation—he and van Vogt, with occasional competition from others, were considered to be the two most popular writers of science fiction, and Heinlein was guest of honor at the third World Science Fiction Convention held in Denver in 1941 (and the third person to be named as a guest of honor at a world convention)—his writing grew steadily in skill and power, particularly in stories at the longer lengths.

The pulp magazines, even the science-fiction pulps, had the special advantage for the beginning writer that they were willing to pay while the writer learned. Heinlein's early stories were better than those of a beginner, perhaps because he was thirty-two when he started, but they were appealing more for their philosophy, toughness, and ability to evoke societies economically than their narrative skills.

This is not to say that Heinlein did not publish significant fiction in his early years. He soon was producing short stories of revolutionary insight and developing artfulness: "The Roads Must Roll," "They," "Solution Unsatisfactory," and "Universe," in particular. But the novel is more difficult to master.

Sixth Column, serialized in *Astounding* in January, February, and March of 1941, has many first novel faults plus, notably for Heinlein, a certain lack of seriousness. *Methusaleh's Children*, in *Astounding* in July, August, and September of the same year, was more serious but more fragmented; it was a better serial than a novel. And *Beyond This Horizon*, which appeared in the April and May 1942 issues of *Astounding* under the name of Anson MacDonald, was more fragmented yet; it was stuffed with ideas as if Heinlein were impatient to put everything to work at once, but the result was a kind of intellectual grab bag.

During World War II Heinlein, a graduate of Annapolis who had been retired from the Navy for medical reasons, worked as a civilian engineer in the Materials Laboratory at the Philadelphia Navy Yard. Nothing appeared between 1942 and 1947, and after 1942 he never wrote directly for *Astounding* again with the sole exception of the novella "Gulf," which he wrote to order for Campbell's special "anticipated" issue of November 1949. Two later novels, *Double Star* and *Citizen of the Galaxy*, were serialized in *Astounding* in 1956 and 1957.

After the end of the war Heinlein was ready to move in new directions simultaneously, into the slick magazines and into the juvenile magazines and the novel. Four stories appeared in *The Saturday Evening Post*, two in *Argosy*, one in *Town and Country*, a couple in *Boys' Life*, and one in *Blue Book*. Meanwhile he was feeling his way into the juvenile with *Rocketship Galileo* (1947) and *Space Cadet* (1948), two novels that many lesser writers would have been pleased to claim but were fashioned from standard juvenile elements. By 1949 he seemed to be filled with confidence and in control of story at the longer lengths. That was the year of "Gulf," the earliest example in which social background had been fully integrated with story and theme, and *Red Planet*, a true science-fiction juvenile with a mature SF plot, a fully realized background, and a carefully crafted narrative. In the ten years that followed he would experience a mid-career burst of creativity when, in demonstrating that he had fully mastered his style, his powers were at their peak.

Red Planet was followed by a series of successful and brilliantly original juveniles: *Farmer in the Sky* (1950), *Between Planets* (1951) *The Rolling Stones* (1952), *Starman Jones* (1953), *The Star Beast* (1954), *Tunnel in the Sky* (1955), *Time for the Stars* (1956), *Citizen of the Galaxy* (1957), and *Have Space Suit-Will Travel* (1958). One each year until Scribner's rejected *Starship Troopers,* Putnam picked it up, and Heinlein's juvenile-writing period was over except for *Podkayne of Mars* four years later. Seven of the juveniles were serialized, four of them—a tribute to their originality and maturity—in science-fiction magazines.

At the same time Heinlein was producing his juvenile novels he was writing adult science-fiction novels, though not as regularly nor as prolifically: *The Puppet Masters* appeared in 1951, *Double Star* in 1956, and *The Door into Summer* in 1957 (although it was serialized the year before). As intriguing as Heinlein's later novels are and as successful as they were financially and in breadth of readership—particularly *Stranger in a Strange Land* (1961), *I Will Fear No Evil* (1970), and *Time Enough for Love* (1973)—it seems to me that he never again combined theme and narrative so skillfully and so seamlessly as during the ten-year period between 1949 and 1958. The first adult novel in which this mastery was evident, and perhaps best achieved, was *The Puppet Masters*.

The story itself is straightforward and obvious. A race of parasitic slugs has invaded the earth and is subjugating humanity person by person and region by region. The aliens ooze to the top of the spinal column, insert their microscopic tendrils into the spinal column and the brain, and control the actions and thoughts of their human hosts. The plot develops naturally: How will the invasion be discovered? How can humanity be aroused to its danger and will it be in time to put up a fight? How can the puppet masters be defeated?

I can still remember my first reaction to reading the initial installment in the September issue of *Galaxy*: oh, no! not the parasitic aliens again! And then my surprise faded into admiration at the way Heinlein had rejuvenated the ancient idea. Heinlein had a talent for taking old ideas and making them new again: solipsism, time paradox, immortality, superman. It is likely that *The Puppet Masters* inspired me a couple of years later to write "A Monster Named Smith," in which a parasitic master is trapped in a human body.

The slugs of *The Puppet Masters* assume the proportions of Heinlein's worst nightmare; his skill makes it the reader's nightmare as well. The author's philosophy cannot necessarily be deduced from what his characters say and do. Ideas develop their own fictional imperatives, and few characters in literature differ as much in attitude as Sam of *The Puppet Masters* and Valentine Michael Smith of *Stranger in a Strange Land*, not to mention several dozen other characters in Heinlein novels and short stories.

But what Heinlein is concerned about in his fiction is not so obscure. One major theme is freedom. In story after story Heinlein explores the way in which people lose their freedom, have it taken from them, or surrender it casually. Political tyranny, military tyranny, religious tyranny, social tyranny—all of these he explores in detail through the length and breadth of his work. Worst of all, he says in *The Puppet Masters*, is to be totally deprived of will.

Other tyrannies may have redeeming aspects and therefore the Heinlein imperative to defeat them may be less convincing, but the ugliness of the slug and the total loss of humanity under their control leaves no room for debate. Heinlein intended to do something similar with "the bugs" in *Starship Troopers*; the war against them was supposed to be one that humanity could not have avoided so that Heinlein did not have to justify war itself. Disagreement about that novel indicates that the device did not work as well; *Starship Troopers* won a Hugo in 1960, but many readers and some writers criticized it for "glorifying" the military. Heinlein was concerned not with war but citizenship, and the war with the bugs was intended to be beyond debate so that this question would not be raised.

Repeatedly in *The Puppet Masters* Heinlein makes the reader share Sam's revulsion to the slugs and to the total degradation of being ridden by a master. The key scene of the novel, in which matters of the utmost importance to the plot and to the characters are revealed, is the scene in which Sam must conquer his revulsion and volunteer to renew the horror, and the aftermath of that decision. Anything is preferable to losing one's free will, and Sam hates the one who "had ridden my back for an endless time, spoken with my mouth—thought with my brain. My master. . . . If I killed this one I would be a free man, but I would never be free as long as *it* lived. . . . My master." Anything would be preferable to enduring its touch again—except to have it fasten itself onto someone you love.

Heinlein's characters believe in responsibility up to and including acceptance of total horror. In their fictional existences they act out their beliefs that life is an assumption of responsibilities that one shirks only by sacrificing one's humanity. One responsibility is to obey the orders of those people who have been placed in authority over you—if you recognize them to be wise; if they are ignorant or blind, you must try to convince them. Another responsibility is to grow wise as you grow old; in general, older people are wiser people if they have behaved responsibly, and younger people owe them respect. The point of growing old is to grow wise, and if a person shirks that responsibility he or she doesn't count for much in the scale of things. Similarly, it is the responsibility of the old to educate the young, to help them become wise. Thus another pattern has developed in Heinlein's fiction: the old educating the young— mutual responsibilities mutually honored.

Heinlein's work recognizes that freedom is worthless without responsibility. One form of responsibility is citizenship; the responsible citizen informs himself or herself about issues and votes intelligently. But what if voters do not value the ballot; what if they do not behave responsibly? In the United States, because we have seen how people can be deprived of the vote by poll taxes and corruption and tyranny, we tend to believe that no restrictions (except minimum age and criminal convictions) should be placed on suffrage; in *Starship Troopers* Heinlein speculates about the possibility of restricting the vote to those who have served. Wouldn't this make citizens value the vote and use it responsibly, he asks?

Heinlein's work also is concerned with competence. If a person knows what to do but is unable to do it because he doesn't know how to do it, wisdom is of little value. In general, competence is the natural consequence of wisdom; usually they are two aspects of the same character. Another process is at work in Heinlein's fictional universe: maturation and aging. The old may become wise but they also become gradually less capable of expressing their wisdom in action. At first they must use the young as extra sets of hands and then as the replacement of their own hands, and finally of themselves.

In Heinlein's fiction the reader comes across a great deal of process. The reader senses that Heinlein himself is fascinated by the way things are done and delights in describing it: the way spaceships fly, the way revolutions are made, the way society works. Process makes fascinating reading when it is properly handled, that is, when it develops out of the situation. It is at its best in Heinlein's work when it is implied rather than lectured about. In "Universe" the process by which reality becomes myth is implied by the way the reality of the self-contained spaceship is translated into religious imagery. An understanding of the ways things work is the result of wisdom and the basic requirement for competence.

The Puppet Masters is an adventure novel. It develops the way an adventure novel develops—the first appearance of the menace, the identification of the menace, the search for a solution to the menace while it grows more powerful, the discovery of a flaw in the apparent invulnerability of the menace, and its final defeat—but *The Puppet Masters* is not just an adventure novel. It also is an apprenticeship novel, what literary critics call a "bildungsroman," meaning "formation" or "development novel." Sam's competence is in question; he must prove his right to assume command. He is groomed for the leadership he eventually assumes, but he earns it by demonstrating his wisdom and the competence that is tested in every encounter—and found inadequate (no matter how superior to the ordinary citizen) until nearly the end.

Competence is continually on trial in Heinlein's novels. Some readers may object to the fact that incompetent people (which includes most of the population) don't count for much in the Heinlein novel. Bad things happen to them, and incompetent people who happen to find themselves in positions of authority—and hence in a position to thwart the wise and competent—are derided and exposed. Part of the problem of fighting the slugs is the need to get the incompetents out of the way so that the competent people can handle the situation.

This seems elitist and is sometimes condemned by people who are committed to democracy and a belief in the collective wisdom of the people under any circumstances—although most of them might agree that a suspension of democratic processes and guarantees is permissible in times of crisis, such as global war. What many fail to see is that Heinlein's worlds are worlds in crisis. Civilization or humanity are threatened, and competence is the single important quality. In time of all-out war innocent people get hurt. Their actions are important collectively, but someone must give the orders. Heinlein never starts a war, but his characters never stop fighting the war that others have started until final and total victory is achieved. Victory depends on people knowing what to do and being able to do it; sometimes this demands not only competence but toughness of character.

We do not know what qualities Heinlein would value in a world without crisis; perhaps the gentler virtues would be more honored. We know that in *Starship Troopers* an opportunity exists for alternative kinds of service, and *Stranger in a Strange Land* may describe a world in which no crisis exists. In that world there is, to use the title of another Heinlein work, time enough for love.

The Puppet Masters is narrated in a first-person, tough-guy style reminiscent of a generation of super-secret-agency spy novels such as those of Donald Hamilton. I'm no authority on spy novels, though I have read my share, but it seems to me, looking back, that Hamilton's "Matt Helm" series was the first of them. And the first Matt Helm novel appeared in 1960. Of course the hard-boiled detective had existed since the mid-twenties in *Black Mask* and the other pulp detective magazines, and Dashiell Hammett's first story was published in 1922. Ross MacDonald, the most prominent inheritor of the hard-boiled tradition, published his first Lew Archer mystery in 1949. So, without doing any literary sleuthing, one might guess that Sam, the hero of *The Puppet Masters*, is out of Hammett and Chandler, and that if Donald Hamilton didn't read *The Puppet Masters* before inventing Matt Helm it was an opportunity missed.

First-person narration has its weaknesses, but it is well suited to the detective story or the suspense novel where the narrator's ignorance of whodunit or the real state of affairs and the gradual discovery of meaning are essential to the structure of the work. So Philip Marlowe and Lew Archer (though not Sam Spade, for first-person is not compulsory) and many another detective tell their own stories. First-person narration also is particularly useful for the author of the apprenticeship novel; what the narrator learns and how he learns it are everything the novel is about. Dickens's *David Copperfield* falls naturally into the first person (though Joyce's *Portrait of the Artist as a Young Man* does not).

One problem with first-person narration is maintaining tone. Such narration is always colloquial to some degree, and Sam, like Philip Marlowe, is more colloquial than most. Colloquialism is the downfall of many a science-fiction story; the expression that rings false destroys the illusion of reality that the writer tries to create for his vision of the future, and those authors, like E. E. "Doc" Smith, who try to invent future colloquialisms run great risks. Isaac Asimov handles the problem of reflecting a believable future by having his characters speak contemporary language, perhaps under the rationalization that such speech has been translated from whatever future languages humanity may have created; he does give his characters different but plausible-sounding names and allows them an occasional new exclamation such as "Galaxy!" or "Sands of Mars!"

Heinlein is not immune to such problems. Occasionally his ear plays him false, and his later books, including *Stranger in a Strange Land* and I *Will Fear No Evil*, offer colloquialisms that sometimes seem out of touch with the times. But *The Puppet Masters* is placed in the not-too-distant future; outside of a few names for new products ("Gyro"; "tempus"), which like Heinlein's other sociological clues not only are appropriate to their context but sound right, the characters speak contemporary language. Sam, like Marlowe, speaks with a rude wit and ready metaphor that reveal a good but not scholarly mind in an active body; he is a man capable of good judgment if fallible, worthy of education, at home in any situation.

Another problem of science fiction arises out of the basic nature of the genre. It is idea fiction, and the ideas are often unfamiliar; the consequence often is the lecture. Stock characters developed to handle this need: the scientist's daughter, whose ignorance was a greater asset than her beauty; the hostile reporter; the loyal but not-too-bright sidekick. They were there so that the scientist could explain to them the way rocket ships worked or theories about the fall of night, the appearance of the stars, or Einstein's relativity.

In his most mature work Heinlein avoided these expository traps by the deceptively simple expedient of not explaining. He was helped by the development of a more sophisticated audience that already understood much that earlier authors had felt compelled to lecture about, and Heinlein learned to create future worlds by scattering cues to their origin and nature among the artifacts they create. Heinlein's economical and evocative techniques were adopted by a generation of science-fiction writers. John W. Campbell mentioned them in the introduction to Groff Conklin's great 1946 anthology, *The Best of Science Fiction*:

> In older science fiction—H. G. Wells and nearly all stories written before 1935—the author took time out to bring the reader up to date as to what had happened before his story opened. The best modern writers of science fiction have worked out some truly remarkable techniques for presenting a great deal of background and associated material without intruding into the flow of the story. This is no small feat when a complete new world must be established at the same time a story is being presented.

Heinlein, however, had another problem. Since his topic was wisdom (that is, learning the way things are, how people behave, and how to use this knowledge to obtain a desirable result) and the nature of responsibility (that is, growing wise and teaching others), his temptation was to present wisdom to the young (and to the reader) through lectures. This happens a bit in Heinlein's early fiction and later in *Stranger in a Strange Land* and in most of his fiction after 1958 to one degree or another. In *Time Enough for Love* Lazarus Long is allowed to impart his wisdom in the form of excerpts from his notebook. Heinlein's comments on life are always readable and frequently provocative, but lectures are nonfictionalized exposition.

In *The Puppet Masters* this kind of information emerges naturally from Sam in the course of his narration or comes to Sam, as it should in an apprenticeship novel, in the course of the action. Sam's education is not by instruction but by events. The adventure mode of *The Puppet Masters* works to enhance its artistry, and the total threat to humanity of the slugs requires no lengthy analysis of its dangers and provides no opportunity for equivocation.

Artistry is a word that is frequently misunderstood when used in connection with science fiction, and when used it frequently puts off science fiction readers and writers because it has so often been used to denigrate the qualities of science fiction that they like. By artistry the critic traditionally means a variety of aspects of a literary work that affect its total appeal. In an essay ("The Academic Viewpoint") in *Nebula Winners Twelve*, I categorized them as: consistency of story, story premises and their application, credibility of characters, consistency of theme, imagery, style, total artfulness, challenge to the imagination, and overall impression.

Science fiction's traditional concern for ideas and the magazines' traditional concern for action have minimized the authors' concerns for this kind of artistry; part of the challenge of the critic or the teacher who wants to deal with science fiction has been to defend its artistry, either in the form of its ideas or its handling of action, or in more traditional terms. I consider *The Puppet Masters* to be an artistic book according to most of the criteria by which it can be analyzed.

The style, the story premises, and the theme have been discussed already. The characters are not complex, but they are adequate for their purposes in an adventure story. That brings us to the imagery, the challenge to the imagination, the total artfulness, and the overall impression. Certainly the slugs challenge us; as imaginary creations and as an image they repel and fascinate us. They may be more nightmarish to Heinlein than to the reader (who may not share Heinlein's total commitment to freedom), but the author succeeds in communicating his horror. The image of the humpbacked humans who are being controlled by their masters and the disregard of the humans' welfare by their masters

function better for me than does the comparable image of dehumaniza-
tion in Jack Finney's *The Body Snatchers*. Finney's pod creatures may
look like humans but are aliens; Heinlein's puppets are still human, still
capable of knowing what it is to be human at the same time that they
cannot function humanly.

In *The Puppet Masters*, as perhaps in no other Heinlein novel, everything works together. In an exercise of artistic skill paralleled only in
the best of his shorter pieces, Heinlein prepares the reader for everything that happens. As a consequence, events are as surprising as an O.
Henry short story but they arrive with the inevitability of a Theodore
Dreiser social tragedy. One example may be sufficient. On the second
page of the novel Sam describes his boss in these terms:

> He was quite capable of saying, "Boys, we need to fertil-
> ize this oak tree. Jump in that hole at its base and I'll cover
> you up."
> We'd have done it. Any of us would.
> And the Old Man would bury us alive, too, if he thought
> that there was as much as a fifty-three-per-cent probability
> that it was the tree of Liberty he was nourishing.

In the hands of some writers, this would be simply a way of characteriz-
ing the director of the U.S. secret intelligence section that even the C.I.A.
doesn't know about. In the hands of a skillful writer, everything works
not only to characterize and advance the plot but to prepare the reader
for what is to happen. The image of "the Tree of Liberty" is no accident; liberty—not just democracy—is what *The Puppet Masters* is all
about. The Old Man asks that kind of obedience from his agents and
they provide it. Sam, before the novel is over, is going to be asked to
fertilize the tree of Liberty not simply with his body but with his soul,
and, although he hesitates, he does it. All this Heinlein has told the
reader. It is a promise he keeps, as he keeps all the promises he makes
within the novel.

At the same time, Sam's reasons for sticking with an unpleasant,
dangerous, unrewarding job are foreshadowed, as well as other kinds of
relationships with other characters: "the Old Man," for instance, whose
name is not selected casually. At least once he is accused of manipulating people as if they were puppets; at another time military officers are
accused of playing god like the puppet masters.

In this novel at least Heinlein proves himself in total command of
his art. He is the master.

19

Isaac Asimov
The Foundations of Science Fiction

Writing about the life of Isaac Asimov is like pouring water into the ocean. Asimov has written more about himself than any living author, and generally with frankness and insight. His autobiographical output began in 1962 with the first of his anthologies, *The Hugo Winners*, in which he inserted references to his own life in the introductions. Like many of the events in his life, this happened by accident. In his autobiography, Asimov mentions that he had never edited an anthology, though it would be fun to try, but he was not sure of his judgment in choosing the stories. The stories in *The Hugo Winners* already were chosen (they were the less-than-novel-length stories awarded Hugos by the World Science Fiction Conventions, beginning in 1955), and even the order was evident. All Asimov had to do was to write introductions. Since there was no question about the reason for the stories' inclusion, he decided to deal with the authors, and in a humorous way. The general introduction would be funny too and would deal with the fact that the editor had never won a Hugo. *The Hugo Winners*, indeed, became a highly personal book, as much about Asimov as about the Hugos or their winners. After that, Asimov went on to edit dozens of anthologies and added comfortably to his nearly five hundred volumes.

The Hugo Winners was a breakthrough for Asimov in another area as well. Up to that point, Asimov says, his attempts at humor had been well received in person but poorly in print. Many readers of *The Hugo Winners* wrote to tell him that the introductions were the best part of the book. After that, collections of his own stories began appearing with introductions, at first *(The Rest of the Robots*, 1964) with notes about the stories salted with a few personal comments, and later with full-blown autobiographical detail. This technique reached its grandest expression in *Opus 100* (1969), the story of how Asimov came to write one hundred books, with excerpts by category; *The Early Asimov* (1972), a kind of autobiography with illustrations from his early writing; and *Before the Golden Age* (1974), which carried Asimov back to his earliest memories of reading SF and brought his life story up to *The Early Asimov*, illustrated with his favorite science-fiction stories among those he read between 1931 and 1933.

All of these works were limbering-up exercises for the massive autobiography in two volumes, the first of which came out in 1979 as his
200th book (along with *Opus 200*, which he put together in fairness to
Houghton Mifflin, which had published *Opus 200*). The autobiography
offers 1,560 pages of Asimov's life story, complete with photographs, a
list of his two hundred books, and indexes (which, he informed his
readers, he did not trust anyone else to do). In 1994, two years after his
death, *I. Asimov: A Memoir* was published, adding some 562 pages to
the story of his life.

Asimov devoted hundreds of thousands of words—perhaps as much
as a million—to his self-description of a man who, he admitted, had
"never done anything." The recollections progressed from "and then I
read" to "and then I wrote" because Asimov's life has been woven from
the warp and woof of reading and writing. The triumph of his writing
skill was that he made it all so readable.

This kind of obsession with self might have been insufferable in a
person who was not at the same time openly amazed at the good fortune, success, plaudits, renown, and wealth that came his way. Asimov
was greatly honored and richly rewarded for remarkable achievements.
Even so, to interpret everything in terms of one's own reaction to it,
including World War II, may seem excessively egotistical. But Asimov's
attitude of "cheerful self-appreciation," which sometimes broke over
into "charming Asimovian immodesties" (a phrase coined by a Doubleday
editor in response to a *Time* magazine article quoting some of Asimov's
self-praise), was balanced by disarming Asimovian self-denigration.

In his autobiographical writings and comments, Asimov continually
invited the reader to share his triumphs, to laugh at his blunders and
lack of sophistication, and to wonder, with him, at the rise to prominence of a bright Jewish boy brought to this country from Russia at the
age of three and raised in a succession of Brooklyn candy stores. Asimov
was aided too by the fact that his readers were predisposed to enjoy his
success with him. Some were admirers of his science popularizations
and other nonfiction books and were curious about his earlier life; others were science-fiction readers and fans, and the science-fiction community still retains much of the solidarity and lack of envy of its early
ghetto days.

The problem remains: What more can a critic say about Asimov's
life and work that Asimov himself didn't say already in nearly a million
well-chosen words? Asimov's autobiographical writings are both an as-

set and an intimidation, revealing valuable information about the circumstances of creation and publication but also rendering redundant the critic's job of digging out little-known facts about life and work. Asimov's life is an open book—in fact, four hundred and seventy open books.

Well, the critic can tell the Asimov story more selectively and send the still curious on to Asimov's own fuller accounts, bring the details of the life into focus in illuminating the work, and explain the work in terms of a thesis that may have been too close to Asimov for him to perceive. The critic also has an opportunity to comment on the state of criticism as well as the work and the author at hand. One reason for first undertaking this study, more than a dozen years ago, was the conviction that much criticism of science fiction has been misguided and particularly that critics of Asimov's work have headed up false trails, trying to bring to the analysis of Asimov's fiction traditional methods and traditional criteria that are unproductive when applied to Asimov and to much other science fiction. What I found myself doing as I began writing, then, was blending biographical, sociological, publishing, and critical considerations into what I later perceived (perhaps without sufficient perspective) to be something a bit unusual in criticism, perhaps unnatural in normal circumstances, that I eventually thought of calling "criticism in context." In the book I wrote about him, I included a number of plot summaries. These were desirable for several reasons: first, because the reader may be familiar with many Asimov works but certainly not all; second, because the reader may remember the general outlines of stories and novels but not the revealing details; and third (and most important), because what happens is the most important aspect of Asimov's fiction (and most other science fiction) and what happens is revealed in plot.

Other matters that I found important as I got into my consideration of Asimov's work were the conditions under which the fiction was written and the way in which it was published. Asimov himself kept referring to these matters in his autobiographical writings; he thought they were important to what he wrote and didn't write, and so do I. In one footnote in his autobiography, he wrote:

> In this book I am going to pay considerable attention to the details of the money I received for stories and other things. Perhaps I should be noble enough to rise above such sordid things as money, but the fact is I couldn't and didn't. The money I earned or didn't earn has influenced my pathway

through life, and I must go into the financial details if the
pathway is to make sense.

The goal of the science-fiction writer was to get published, and the
writing done was shaped by what was read in the magazines, what was
said by an editor, what was paid for a story, and sometimes how readers
responded. More traditional critics may feel that such concerns disqual-
ify the writing from serious literary study. And yet scholars have been
trying for centuries to ferret out the same kind of information about
Shakespeare's plays.

Asimov's early ambition, for instance, was to sell stories to *Astounding Science Fiction*. Two of his stories were published in *Amazing
Stories* before one appeared in *Astounding*; to get published was a triumph, but only the *Astounding* story meant true success. The relationship between Asimov and John W. Campbell, editor of *Astounding* beginning in 1937, was influential in Asimov's development. Asimov gave
Campbell most of the credit for his early science fiction and even his
later writing career.

Asimov's life is best related through his writing. As Asimov himself
recognized, his life was his writing, and his other relationships were
either detractions from or contributions to it.

Asimov provided several illustrative anecdotes. When he received
copies of his forty-first book from Houghton Mifflin, he mentioned to
his wife the possibility of reaching a hundred books before he died. She
shook her head and said, "What good will it be if you then regret having
spent your life writing books while all the essence of life passes you
by?" And Asimov replied, "But for me the essence of life is writing. In
fact, if I do manage to publish a hundred books, and if I then die, my
last words are likely to be, 'Only a hundred!'"

On another occasion his beloved daughter Robyn asked him to suppose he had to choose between her and writing. Asimov recalled he
said, "Why, I would choose you, dear." And added, "But I hesitated—
and she noticed that, too."

Asimov was born January 2, 1920 (as nearly as his parents could
calculate; it may have been as early as October 4, 1919), in Petrovichi,
U.S.S.R. Petrovichi is a small town about fifty-five miles south of
Smolensk and about two hundred fifty miles southwest of Moscow. When
Asimov was three, his parents emigrated with him to the United States,
at the invitation and sponsorship of his mother's older half-brother. They
settled in Brooklyn where Asimov's father, handicapped by his lack of

English and of job experience, bought a candy store in 1926. The candy store, and its successors, became a major part of Asimov's existence. "It was open seven days a week and eighteen hours a day," he reported in his autobiography, "so my father and mother had to take turns running it, and I had to pitch in, too."

The other important fact of Asimov's youth was his precocity. He had an unusual ability to learn and, as he later discovered, an unusually retentive memory. They were to be major assets in his life and career. He taught himself to read at the age of five, entered the first grade before he was six (his mother lied about his age), and became the brightest student in his class early and continuously, even though he skipped half a year of kindergarten, half a year of first grade, half a year of third grade, and changed schools a couple of times.

Asimov's schoolboy practice was to read all his school-books the first couple of days after he got them and then not refer to them again. He acquired a reputation as a child prodigy and a sense of his own superiority that he didn't mind letting other people see. That did not add to his popularity—he was considered a smart-alecky kid—but he did not have much association with others anyway. His work in the candy store kept him busy after school, and the seven-day week meant that he and his parents never visited anyone or had anyone visit them.

Asimov recalled that he was orphaned by the candy store (since he was deprived of his parents' companionship) as well as protected by it (since he knew where his parents were at all times). The candy store constricted and shaped his life until he left home. It also meant that he grew up largely in the company of adults when he was in the store, or in the company of books when he was not. Both no doubt contributed to his precocity.

Asimov completed junior high school in two years instead of three and entered Boys High School of Brooklyn, which at the time was a selective high school that had an excellent reputation for mathematics. He was twelve and a half upon entering, two and a half years younger than the normal age of fifteen. He continued to be sheltered: he had almost no contact with girls, as he might have had at a coeducational school. But in the world encapsulated in his autobiography almost everything happened for the best—how could it not have happened for the best when he rose so far from such humble beginnings?—and he reasoned that, though being segregated from girls may have kept him naive far into his adolescence, it also may have protected him from more severe symptoms of rejection, for he was so much younger than his female classmates. Moreover, he had a bad case of acne from twelve to twenty.

High school, however, was the beginning of a series of disillusionments. Asimov discovered limits to his intellectual ability. He was not as good a mathematian as some of the other boys, who may not have been as intelligent but had a special feeling for math. He never made the math team. He discovered as well that other students could study harder and accomplish more; Asimov stuck by his "understanding-at-once-and-remembering-forever" pattern. He had to abandon his illusion of universal brilliance when he discovered, for instance, that he disliked and could never understand economics. And even his attempts at creative writing were ridiculed in a high-school writing class. This bothered him more than anything else, because his ambition to write fiction had been growing since the age of eleven, when he had begun writing a series book for boys called *The Greenville Chums at College*, copying it out in longhand in nickel copybooks. When Asimov was fifteen his father had found $10 to buy his son a much-longed-for typewriter, an office-size model.

More disappointments awaited him. His father wanted his elder son (there were two other children, a girl, Marcia, and a boy, Stanley) to become a physician, and the fifteen-year-old Asimov had come to share this ambition. But getting into medical school was not easy; medical schools had quotas on the number of Jewish applicants they would accept. For a variety of reasons, Asimov was never to be admitted to the study of medicine. By the time he was ready to apply, however, his goals had changed. After high school, he applied to Columbia College, but was rejected, possibly, he speculates, because he did not make a good showing in interviews. He was asked to change his application to a Brooklyn branch of Columbia University called Seth Low Junior College, where enrollment was heavily Jewish.

Asimov also applied to City College of New York, which had no tuition and accepted him because his grades were excellent. He actually spent three days there before receiving a letter from Seth Low asking why he had not showed up. When his father explained to Seth Low authorities that the family could not afford the tuition, Seth Low came up with a hundred-dollar scholarship and a National Youth Administration job for $15 a month. Asimov switched colleges. His second year, after a summer spent in manual labor to earn enough money, was at the

Morningside Heights campus because Seth Low had closed at the end of its tenth year. He was enrolled in Columbia University, not its more prestigious undergraduate college. Asimov was a second-class citizen throughout his undergraduate education, and he never forgot it. When he was graduated, he received a bachelor of science degree in chemistry instead of the bachelor of arts degree, for which University undergraduates were not eligible, he wrote.

In his second year of college, Asimov's distaste for zoology (he killed a cat and dissected it but never forgave himself) and embryology (he was not good at picking out details through a microscope and even worse at drawing them) led him to drop the biological sciences and switch to chemistry as a major. He liked chemistry and did well at it. After graduation from Columbia he applied (somewhat halfheartedly because of his distaste for biological courses) to a number of medical schools and was rejected by all of them. He went on with the study of chemistry in Columbia's graduate school, but only after some difficulty because he had not taken physical chemistry. He had to spend a troublesome year on probation. As usual, his problem had not been his grades or test scores but his "wise-guy personality."

Asimov obtained his M.A. in 1941 and was working toward his doctorate when the United States entered World War II. A few months later he suspended his studies in order to work as a chemist at the U.S. Navy Yard in Philadelphia, where for the first time he was free of his duties at the candy store and where the steady income gave him the opportunity to marry the woman with whom he had fallen in love, Gertrude Blugerman.

Asimov's autobiography suggests that he was good at the theory of chemistry but not at the practice. He refers to his poor laboratory technique and his difficulties getting the correct results. His talents were probably not those of a research chemist, nor those of a practicing scientist of any kind. But at the end of the war he returned to his doctoral program at Columbia, earned his degree in 1948, did a year of postdoctoral research at Columbia, and finally was offered a position as instructor in biochemistry at the Boston University School of Medicine.

Asimov's discovery of science fiction and his attempts to write it were more important to his final career than his studies. He had come upon *Amazing Stories* in 1928, its second year of publication, when he was eight years old. His father's candy store carried magazines, but the young Asimov was not allowed to read them because his father considered them a waste of time and a corrupting influence. They would turn him into "a bum," his father said. The boy had been reading library books of all kinds, but he longed for the brightly colored pulp magazines with their cover paintings of futuristic machines and planets and alien menaces. Finally, when Hugo Gernsback lost control of *Amazing* and brought out a competitor, *Science Wonder Stories*, the then nine-year-old boy brought the magazine to his father, pointed out the word "Science" in the title, and won his battle. Possibly his father just did not have the spirit to fight because his mother was about to give birth to Asimov's younger brother, Stanley.

The science-fiction magazines filled Asimov's imagination with ideas and dreams. They did not consume all his reading time because there weren't enough of them (only two a month at first, and only three a month in 1930). He kept up his omnivorous reading of other books, mostly library borrowings, but science fiction became what he lived for. Oddly enough, Asimov's early writing efforts did not focus on science fiction. "I had the most exalted notion of the intense skills and vast scientific knowledge required of authors in the field, and I dared not aspire to such things," he remembered.

On his new typewriter, however, he ventured into fantasy and then into science fiction. Like almost every aspiring author, Asimov started many stories and finished none, and what he wrote was derived mostly from what he liked to read. His derivative writing was to persist through several years of his career as a published writer until he finally rid himself of what he called his "pulpishness." He got his inspiration, his plots, even his vocabulary from other science-fiction writers. From them came the blasters and needle guns and force beams that litter his stories and early novels, and even, by an analogous process of invention, such concepts as neuronic whips and psycho-probes, hyperspace and Jumps. When he turned to more unique concepts such as psychohistory and the Foundations, the logical development of robots, a radioactive Earth and the lost origin of man, and particularly human reactions to overcrowded cities, his fiction began to glow with its own fire.

Not long after he got his typewriter, Asimov wrote a letter to *Astounding Stories* that was published in 1935. Two years later, when Campbell had become editor of the magazine and had changed its name to *Astounding Science Fiction*, Asimov began writing letters again, "commenting on the stories, raking them, and, in general, taking on the airs of a critic." Such letters became a monthly event; usually Campbell published them in a letters-to-the-editor section called then, as now, "Brass Tacks."

One Tuesday in May when the new *Astounding* was scheduled to arrive in his father's package of new magazines, it did not show up. The eighteen-year-old Asimov was terrified that it had ceased publication. He called the publisher, Street & Smith, and was assured that the magazine still was being published. But when the new issue had not arrived by the following Tuesday, he ventured off on the subway to the Street & Smith offices in Manhattan, where an executive told him that the publication date had been changed from the second Wednesday to the third Friday of the month. Two days later the magazine arrived.

His panic at the thought that *Astounding* might vanish sent Asimov to the typewriter to finish a story he had been working at for some months titled "Cosmic Corkscrew." He completed the story on June 19, 1938, and took it personally to the editor. Campbell was familiar with Asimov's name from his frequent letters and talked for more than an hour with the aspiring author, read the story overnight, and mailed it back two days later with a polite letter of rejection. That sent Asimov back to his typewriter to work on a story titled "Stowaway." He finished it in eighteen days and took this in person to Campbell. That story came back with a rejection in four days. A pattern had been established. A rejection would come from Campbell but phrased in ways that would encourage Asimov to turn immediately to a new story. "It didn't matter that he rejected you," Asimov recalled. "There was an enthusiasm about him and an all-encompassing friendliness that was contagious. I always left him eager to write further." "Stowaway," however, did not end up lost for all time with "Cosmic Corkscrew." It eventually found its way into print, in the April 1940 *Astonishing Stories* edited by Frederik Pohl (as youthful an editor as Asimov was a writer), as "The Callistan Menace," though Asimov's third story, "Marooned Off Vesta," had appeared first, in the March 1939 *Amazing Stories*.

Meanwhile, Asimov had discovered other science-fiction readers, and not just readers but fans, fanatics like himself. This led progressively to fanzines, club meetings, and the organizing of the Futurians, a fan group that included many of the later writers and shapers of science fiction, including Pohl, Donald A. Wollheim, Cyril Kornbluth, Robert W. Lowndes, Richard Wilson, and later Damon Knight and James Blish. Asimov attended monthly meetings, became involved in the debates and schisms to which fandom was so susceptible, began meeting other authors, and talked about his writing ambition and finally getting published. All culminated in the first World Science Fiction Convention held in Manhattan on July 2, 1939. Every Futurian but Asimov was excluded by the organizer, Sam Moskowitz, as disruptive influences. Asimov went as an author and felt guilty about it ever after. But as he became more and more an author, he became less and less a fan.

By the time of the World Convention Asimov was a bona fide author in his own eyes because *Astounding* had published his tenth story, "Trends," in its issue of July 1939. Almost two years later it published the second of his robot stories (the first, "Robbie," was published in the September 1940 *Super Science Stories* as "Strange Playfellow"), and within the next fourteen months, two more robot stories, plus "Nightfall," and "Foundation" and its sequel. Though Asimov didn't know it at the time, "Nightfall" alone made him, in his own words, "a major figure in the field." The stories did not earn that much money, but what they brought in was put to good use, paying for his tuition or accumulating in a bank account. He had three stories published in 1939, seven in 1940, eight in 1941, ten in 1941, only one in 1943, three in 1944, four in 1945, one in 1946, one in 1947, two in 1948, three in 1949, and six in 1950.

It was not a remarkable record of productivity or success; it brought Asimov a total of $7,821.75, which amounted to little more than $710 a year. It was not enough to encourage him to consider a career as a full-time writer, but it did provide a growing feeling of economic security. Finally, Doubleday published his first novel, *Pebble in the Sky*, in 1950. A specialty house called Gnome Press began publishing his robot stories and then his Foundation stories as books. His income from writing slowly began to equal and then to exceed his income from teaching at Boston University School of Medicine, and, after a disagreement with his superior, he turned to the career that had seemed impossible for all those years.

The impression even the casual reader may obtain from Asimov's autobiography is that he was shaped by his childhood. He referred continually to the way in which the candy store controlled his early life and the way the habits of those years had carried over into his later life. His industry—he still wrote seven days a week and ten hours a day until the poor health of the last two or three years of his life, turning out six to ten thousand words on an average day—he traced to the long hours at the candy store, for instance, and to his father's accusations that he was lazy when found in a corner reading.

In a similar way, Asimov traced his ability to eat anything to his mother's hearty, indigestible cuisine, and his habit of eating swiftly to the fact that he and his mother and sister had to eat in a hurry so that his father could be relieved of his duties in the candy store and eat his supper in a more leisurely fashion. He read while he ate because he loved to read, his father wasn't present, his mother was busy cooking and serving, and in any case reading was a sign of studiousness.

His uneasiness with strangers Asimov traced to the fact that during his childhood his family visited no one and no one visited them. The fact that he read newspapers and magazines so carefully that no one could tell they had been read started, he believed, when he had to return magazines to his father's rack looking unopened. As a boy he had to awaken at 6 a.m. to deliver newspapers before school. If he wasn't down on time, his father would yell at his window from the street below, and later lecture him about the "deadly spiritual dangers of being a *fulyack* [sluggard]." To his last years, Asimov awakened without an alarm clock at 6 a.m.

He described his infatuation with baseball when he was in junior high school: he became a Giants fan, which was odd because Brooklyn had the Dodgers. "By the time I found out there was a Brooklyn team, it was too late; I was imprinted." He was "imprinted" in other ways as well. He blamed his fear of flying on his mother's oversolicitude about his health. "My parents . . . trembled over my well-being so extremely, especially after my babyhood experience with pneumonia, that I could not help but absorb the fact and gain an exaggerated caution for myself. (That may be why I won't fly, for instance, and why I do very little else that would involve my knowingly putting myself into peril.)"

His mother's insistence that he keep her informed of his where-abouts meant that when he was out he had to report in at frequent intervals by telephone. "I've kept that habit all my life," he wrote. "It is a bad habit. It ties me to the phone, and if forgetfulness or circum-stances get in the way, everyone is sure something terrible has hap-pened." He traces his avoidance of books on how to write and of col-lege-level courses on writing to "the ever-present memory of that hor-rible course in creative writing in the sixth term of high school."

It may not be surprising that someone who can find so many habits of the man in the experience of the boy would imagine a science of predicting human behavior, called "psychohistory," in his Foundation stories. On the other hand Asimov could relate anecdotes that seemed to demonstrate just the opposite principle of behavior. He recalled his father struggling to balance the books of the candy store every evening, being a dollar over or a dollar under and staying until he had straightened it out. Later in his life, when money was easier, Asimov remembered handing his father five dollars to make up the difference, and his father commenting, "If you gave me a million dollars, that dollar would still have to be found. The books must balance." Asimov never could understand why the books had to balance. Rather than carrying that trait into his own life, he said, "In later life, when I had occasion to balance accounts, I never bothered over trifling discrepancies. I just made arbitrary corrections and let it go. My father did enough searching for both of us in his lifetime."

At the same time, Asimov was capable of seeing his explanations for behavior as "probably simple rationalizations designed to resign me to things as they are." After all, what is an autobiography? It is not so much the finding of the truths in one's existence as a rationalization of how one got from one place to another when there were so many different places at which one could have arrived. Asimov had much to explain, and his autobiography was a search for explanations.

Asimov also was a supreme rationalist, a searcher for explanations in his fiction as well as in his life. The reason for his faith in rationalism and his distrust of emotions may be no easier to come by, however, than any other speculation about his life. Asimov did not rely totally on environment to rationalize his life; some traits were implicit, or genetic, and Asimov simply did not mention them. His intelligence, for instance, and his ability to learn and remember must have been inherited. His habit of counting objects (light bulbs, repeated decorations, holes in soundproofed ceilings) whenever he was bored in public places he traces to his counting automobiles as they passed on Van Siclen Avenue when he was three. He found no reason for his idiosyncratic fondness for enclosed places. He liked the candy store on Decatur Street because it had a kitchen in the back that had no windows. "Why it should be, I don't know, and psychiatrists may make what they like of it (for I will not ask them, and I will not listen if they try to tell me), but I have always liked enclosed places." He remembered that he thought display rooms in department stores looked better than real rooms and finally realized that it was because they had no windows. He envied the people who ran newsstands in subway stations, "for I imagined that they could board it up whenever they wanted to, put the light on, lie on a cot at the bottom, and read magazines. I used to fantasize doing so, with the warm rumble of the subway trains intermittently passing." Asimov's claustrophilia and agoraphobia had their impact on the Robot Novels *The Caves of Steel* and *The Naked Sun*.

A psychiatrist (one of that group to whom Asimov will not listen) might suggest that Asimov's distrust of emotions and faith in rationalism are his responses to "being orphaned" by the candy store at the age of six. Being deprived of his parents' companionship ("never again, after I was six, could I be with him [his father] on a Sunday morning, while he told me stories") came at a difficult time: he was in the middle of second grade. Moreover, his father had admired his son's abilities from an early age. When Asimov taught himself to read at the age of five, his father asked him how he had done it, and Asimov replied that he just figured it out. "That gave my father the idea that there was something strange and remarkable about me; something he clung to for the rest of his life." But the high regard in which Asimov's father held his son's abilities meant that when the schoolboy brought home less than perfect marks from school, he could expect his father's disapproval for not living up to his potential. In his autobiography Asimov recalled many instances of his father's disapproval, few of his approval.

His mother also spent much of her time in the candy store with customers, or with her two younger children. She had a terrible temper, Asimov recalled, and unlike his father "raised her hand to me any time she felt she needed a little exercise. . . ." He also recalled, seemingly without rancor, being beaten with a rope his mother kept in her closet. When he mentioned it to his mother in later life, she did not remember it. His parents, though a devoted couple, were not demonstrative. There were few if any expressions of affection between them, and Asimov presents the births of three children as the only proof that there was any at all. Certainly Asimov had reason to distrust emotion and to seek rational explanations for why he was deprived of parental closeness, perhaps even love.

Asimov, nevertheless, always knew that he was his parents' favorite, and his brother knew it as well, apparently without resentment. Asimov spoke bitterly about the series of candy stores but remembered his father and mother with great fondness. The family was always in close touch until the death first of his father (in 1969, at the age of 72) and then of his mother (in 1973, at the age of nearly 78), even though, because of his fear of flying, Asimov did not go to see his parents after they moved to Florida a year before his father's death.

In his typical rational way, he looked back upon his childhood as a generally happy period: "I know perfectly well it was a deprived one in many ways, but the thing was, you see, I never knew it at the time. No one is deprived unless and until he thinks he is."

A more general mystery than the origin of Asimov's traits and neuroses is why certain young people turn to reading, and sometimes writing, science fiction. Asimov is a case study. When he began reading science fiction, the number of readers was small—Damon Knight has called science fiction the mass medium for the few—but intensely involved. Most had turned to science fiction out of some kind of youthful frustration with their lives. A profile of new readers would reveal them to be mostly boys; mostly brighter than their schoolmates; mostly social misfits because of personality, appearance, lack of social graces, or inability to find intellectual companionship; unsophisticated about girls (the study of women readers and writers still is in its infancy) and ill at ease in their company. Science fiction was a kind of literature of the outcast that praised the intellectual aspects of life that its readers enjoyed and in which they excelled, and a literature that offered more hope for the future than the present. When people like these discover others like themselves, fan clubs spring up, sometimes fanzines are published, conventions are organized, and writing science fiction becomes a virtually universal ambition. When people like these begin to write, they write science fiction.

Asimov was like that. The Futurians were like that. Damon Knight says that "all we science-fiction writers began as toads." When Robert Silverberg read the first volume of Asimov's autobiography, he wrote for the galley proofs of the second volume because he couldn't wait: there was so much in Asimov's life that paralleled his own that it gave him a sense of déjà vu.

There are certain curious resemblances between the characters and careers of Asimov and H. G. Wells, who is often called the father of modern science fiction. Both spent their early lives in unsuccessful shops, were precocious students, quick to learn with good memories, and began by writing science fiction but turned to popularizations (Wells's biggest financial success was his *Outline of History*). Both were selective in what they liked, Wells with biology and evolution, Asimov with chemistry, and both were fond of history. Both became known as pundits, experts in almost everything, and both were attentive to the ladies. Still, the analogy can be carried too far. Wells, for instance, became a serious novelist of contemporary life. Asimov varied his science fiction and nonfiction with detective stories and novels.

Asimov, in spite of his success at other kinds of writing and public speaking, never thought of himself as anything but a science-fiction writer who sometimes wrote other, often easier, things. He introduced himself as a science-fiction writer. Some writers of science fiction have gone on to other kinds of writing and some, like Kurt Vonnegut, Jr., have denied that they ever wrote science fiction. Not Asimov, who always remained true to his boyhood love. In his autobiography he described a fancy *World Book* sales meeting at which the board members were introduced with orchestral motifs—to his chagrin. Asimov was introduced as a science writer by "How deep is the ocean? / How high is the sky?" "No matter how various the subject matter I write on," he added, "I was a science-fiction writer first and it is as a science-fiction writer that I want to be identified."

In an interview in 1979, I said to him that his autobiography revealed a great deal of loyalty to what he was, to the boy he was, and to what science fiction had meant to him when he discovered it. Asimov replied that he had deliberately not abandoned his origins. He had made up his mind when he was quite young, and said it in print, that no matter what happened to him or where he went, he would never deny his origins as a science-fiction writer and never break his connection to science fiction, and he never did.

He considered loyalty a prime virtue. In 1976 when he started *Isaac Asimov's Science Fiction Magazine*, he told publisher Joel Davis that he wouldn't give up his *Magazine of Fantasy and Science Fiction* science articles.

> I probably bore everybody with my endless repetition of how much I owe to John Campbell, because I figure I would rather bore them than be disloyal in my own mind. It is the easiest thing in the world to forget the ladder you climb or to be embarrassed at the thought that there was a time when somebody had to help you. The tendency is to minimize this, minimize that, and I'm normal enough and human enough to do the same thing if it were left to itself, but this is a matter of having once made a vow and sticking to it.

He pointed out that it was inconvenient to always have to tell people that Campbell made up the Three Laws of Robotics, and the more important the Three Laws became the more he wanted to be the originator and take the credit, but he couldn't. "Why this is so I never really thought about. I guess I like to think about it only as a matter of virtue. I don't consider myself a particularly virtuous person, but I like to think I have some virtues, of which loyalty is one."

Possibly, however, his insistence on being considered a science-fiction writer was like his relationship to his racial origins. He said he was not a good Jew. Asimov attended no Jewish religious functions, followed no Jewish rituals, obeyed no Jewish dietary laws, and yet he never, under any circumstances, left any doubt that he was Jewish.

> I really dislike Judaism. . . . It's a form of particularly pernicious nationalism. I don't want humanity divided into these little groups that are firmly convinced, each one, that it is better than the others. Judaism is the prototype of the "I'm better than you" group—we are the ones who invented this business of the only God. It's not just that we have our God and you have your God, but we have the only God. I feel a deep and abiding historic guilt about that. And every once in a while, when I'm not careful, I think that the reason Jews have been persecuted as much as they have has been to punish them for having invented this pernicious doctrine.

Asimov suggested that because he felt that in some ways he had been a traitor to Judaism ("which I try to make up for by making sure that everyone knows I'm a Jew, so while I'm deprived of the benefits of being part of a group, I make sure that I don't lose any of the disadvantages, because no one should think that I'm denying my Judaism in order to gain certain advantages"), he made up his mind that he was not going to be disloyal in any other way. "I'm not saying I believe this," he concluded, "but this is the sort of thing that people do work up for reasons, and, after all, I'm imaginative enough to think up such reasons, too. . . . I don't guarantee it's correct."

The characteristic that began to appear in Asimov's science fiction, which gave his writing its unique quality and made it so typically Campbellian as well as Asimovian, was its rationality. Asimov agreed with

Randall Garrett's assessment that the relationship between Asimov and Campbell was symbiotic. In the interview Asimov commented that he must have been the perfect foil for Campbell.

> On the one hand, I was close to him. I lived right in town and I could see him every week. And, for another, I could endure him. I imagine that a great many other writers found him too rich for their blood—at least to sit there and listen to him hour after hour. But I was fortunate in the sense that he was in some ways a lot like my father. I had grown up listening to my father pontificate in much the same way that John did, and so I was quite at home. I suppose if you took all the time that I sat there listening to John and put it all together, it was easily a week's worth—of just listening to him talk. Day and night, 168 hours. And I remember everything he said and how he thought and I did my best—because I desperately wanted to sell stories to him—to incorporate his method of thinking into my stories, which, of course, also had my method of thinking, with the result that somehow I caught the Campbell flavor.

The Campbell flavor was the solution of problems. Much of Asimov's early writing did not quite capture that quality of problem-solving that became characteristic of his later work; those stories were less successful, neither identifiably Asimovian nor distinguished science fiction. His first published story had it, "Marooned Off Vesta," and later it would find its best expression in the robot stories and the Foundation stories, among his early science-fiction successes, and, of course, in the science-fiction mystery novels *The Caves of Steel* and *The Naked Sun* that came so naturally just before he switched to writing non-fiction.

I made these suggestions to Asimov, and he agreed that they seemed right. "Certainly the stories that really satisfied me and made me feel good about my writing were my robot stories, and the robot stories, of course, virtually every one of them, had a situation in which a robot—which couldn't go wrong—did go wrong. And we had to find out what had gone wrong, how to correct it, within the absolute limits of the three laws. This was just the sort of thing I loved to do."

At its most typical, in "Nightfall" for example, Asimov's science fiction demonstrates the triumph of reason, or the struggle of reason to triumph, over various kinds of circumstances, including irrational or emotional responses to situations. If reason is going to prove superior as an approach to life, the mystery is the natural form in which that superiority will be demonstrated.

Asimov has said that his villains generally are as rational as his heroes. "In other words, it's not even a triumph of rationality over irrationality or over emotion, at least not in my favorite stories. It's generally a conflict between rationalities and the superior winning. If it were a western, where everything depends upon the draw of the gun, it would be very unsatisfactory if the hero shot down a person who didn't know how to shoot."

Growing up as he did, excelling at intellectual pursuits but uneasy in personal relationships in which he found himself ignorant of the proper thing to do or uncertain how the other person would respond, Asimov found himself coping in a variety of ways. One way, which he adopted when he was young, was to distance himself from the rest of the world with wit. To the end he delighted in puns and wordplay, which found their most typical expression in personal banter with his friends but also enlivened his limericks and verse parodies and displayed themselves in the titles of and occasional lines in articles and stories. Another way to cope was to demonstrate his greater knowledge or superior mind. His adoption of these two characteristics gave him a reputation as a smart-aleck and a know-it-all with a mission to enlighten everyone around him.

Asimov gave as an example of his behavior the assignment of Leigh Hunt's "Abou Ben Adhem" in his high-school English class. Anticipating the teacher's question about the last line ("And lo! Ben Adhem's name led all the rest"), his hand shot up, and he answered the inevitable question, "Why did Ben Adhem's name lead all the rest?" with "Alphabetical order, sir?" He was sent to the principal, but he felt the quip was worth it.

Asimov finally gave up his mission to educate the masses. He traced his decision to a time when he was in the army in Hawaii, waiting for the H-bomb tests at Bikini. A couple of soldiers in the barracks were listening to a third explain, inaccurately, how the atom bomb worked.

> Wearily, I put down my book and began to get to my feet so I could go over and assume the smart man's burden and educate them.

Halfway to my feet. I thought: Who appointed you their educator? Is it going to hurt them to be wrong about the atom bomb?

And I returned, contentedly, to my book.

This does not mean I turned with knife-edge suddenness and became another man. It's just that I was a generally disliked know-it-all earlier in my life, and I am a generally liked person (I believe) who is genial and a nonpusher later in my life. . . .

Why? I'm not sure I know. Perhaps it was my surrender of the child-prodigy status. Perhaps it was my feeling that I had grown up, I had proved myself, and I no longer had to give everyone a headache convincing them that I was, too, smart.

One other way in which Asimov learned to cope socially was his adoption of a flirtatious attitude toward women—all women—what he called his "all-embracing suavity," by which he meant that he was willing to embrace any female within range and usually did. From a gauche, inexperienced, tentative young man he turned into a good-natured, public Casanova with a "penchant for making gallant suggestions to the ladies." Yet Asimov speculated about his behavior as an adult that "you don't really change much as you get older." The uncertain young man might still have been there inside the "all-embracing" older one.

Asimov denied being anything other than direct and clear in his writing, and that may apply to his personal life as well. Certainly he was open about his life, even on those matters that most people are most closed about: money and sex—and, more important to Asimov, his writing. I asked him in our interview if his disclaimer of knowledge about the craft of writing wasn't a pose. Clearly, he had thought about it, I pointed out. He had criticized other people's stories in his teenage letters-to-the-editor days; he had noticed Clifford Simak's way of leaving space to indicate a break between scenes and, after having had it explained, had adopted it himself; he had even attended the Bread Loaf Writers' Conference several times as a member of the faculty. Asimov responded that he did not deliberately set up a pose. He really thought he did not know much about writing, but, as he pointed out in an afterword to the collection of essays about his work edited by Martin Greenberg and Joseph Olander titled *Asimov*, "without very much in the way of conscious thinking I manage to learn from what I read and what I hear."

As the young Asimov became the older Asimov (still in his late youth, as he would say), what he had been became what he was, either conditioned by his early experience or in reaction to it. Asimov recognized both processes. In one sense he was a rational man in an irrational world, puzzled at humanity's responses to change, unable to understand humanity's inability to see the clear necessity, if it is to survive, to control population and pollution and eliminate war, still assuming "the smart man's burden" to educate the bewilderingly uneducable, even taken aback at times when the people he dealt with behaved irrationally.

Joseph Patrouch, in his *The Science Fiction of Isaac Asimov* (1974), commented that Asimov had not written in his fiction on the subjects about which he was most concerned, the subjects he wrote on in his nonfiction and spoke about in his public talks: pollution, overpopulation, and so forth. I asked Asimov about this, saying that in his talks and articles and books he seemed to exhibit a kind of alarm about our world situation that was not in his fiction—a kind of public despair that contrasted with his fictional optimism. In his science writing he tried to persuade by showing the terrible consequences of what would happen if people do not act, and in his science fiction he tried to persuade by showing how the problems could be solved. Asimov agreed.

> In my public statements I have to deal with the world as it is—which is the world in which irrationality is predominant; whereas in my fiction I create a world and in my world, my created worlds, things are rational. Even the villains, the supposed villains, are villainous for rational reasons. . . .
>
> You can see for yourself in my autobiography that I had a great deal of difficulty adjusting to the world when I was young. To a large extent the world was an enemy world. . . . Science fiction in its very nature is intended to appeal (a) to people who value reason and (b) to people who form a small minority in a world that doesn't value reason. . . . I am trying to lead a life of reason in an emotional world.

Asimov, no doubt, still was trying to please his stern father with industry and productivity. Asimov would have been the first to admit it. He also would have said that it didn't matter how the past had shaped him. He was satisfied to be what he was: a claustrophile, an acrophobe, a compulsive writer. When he was a teenager, people complained about his eccentricities: his walking home from the library with three books, reading one and holding one under each arm; his love of cemeteries; his constant whistling. Their complaints didn't bother him (though he did, when asked, stop whistling in the cemetery). "I had gathered the notion somewhere that my eccentricities belonged to me and to nobody else and that I had every right to keep them." He added, "And I lived long enough to see these eccentricities and others that I have not mentioned come to be described as 'colorful' facets of my personality."

He ended up rationalizing everything that had happened to him. He was a rational man who knew that the past cannot be changed, it can only be understood. Moreover, the things that he became were rewarded by the world. He had his many triumphs. Scientists applauded his science books: Professor George G. Simpson of Harvard called him "one of our natural wonders and national resources." He was guest of honor and toastmaster at World Science Fiction Conventions. He won Hugos and Nebulas, was named a Grand Master by his fellow science-fiction writers, and, perhaps best of all, John Campbell told him, "You are one of the greatest science-fiction writers in the world."

As a rational man, Asimov knew that the present must be accepted, and as a rational man, he knew that what he was was an excellent thing to be. So the world said, and so he agreed. That life of reason found its expression in his fiction as well as his nonfiction.

20

Henry Kuttner, C. L. Moore, et al.

The year was 1942. The attack on Pearl Harbor was a few weeks in the past. The United States had declared war on Japan and Germany, and was in the midst of frantic military preparations. Men were volunteering for service; others were being drafted.

Even science fiction was affected. L. Ron Hubbard's *Final Blackout* had been serialized in *Astounding* in 1940. Robert Heinlein's prophetic atomic weapon story "Solution Unsatisfactory" (published under the pseudonym of Anson MacDonald) appeared in 1941. These were only the leading edge of a wave of war-related stories: the science-fiction magazines, too, were being retooled for war.

By 1942 John Campbell had been editor of *Astounding Science Fiction* for five years. Three major new writers had come into prominence in 1937 and 1938: Eric Frank Russell, L. Sprague de Camp, and Lester del Rey. Four more had been introduced in *Astounding* in 1939: Isaac Asimov, Robert Heinlein, Theodore Sturgeon, and A. E. van Vogt. Together with other writers (and a decade later, with other editors and magazines), they would begin the development of what has become known as modern science fiction and the creation of what some have called science fiction's "golden age."

By 1942 Heinlein was well launched into his "future history" stories (he had completed all of them that would appear in *Astounding*) and had nearly perfected his major technical innovation—the naturalistic revelation of carefully constructed future societies. Asimov had brought his scientific mind to bear upon the explication and codification of science-fiction concepts, had launched one major series (his robot stories), and had written the first two stories in his "Foundation" series (although they would not appear for some months). Sturgeon had completed a series of highly personal stories, mostly fantasy, and one significant science-fiction story, "Microcosmic God." Van Vogt had created a major impact both with his superman and superpowers themes and with his breakneck, scenic style.

But by the beginning of 1942, or shortly thereafter, Heinlein had joined the Naval Air Experimental Station of the U. S. Navy Yard in

Philadelphia as a civilian engineer, where L. Sprague de Camp, followed by Asimov, came to join him. Sturgeon had gone to the British West Indies in 1941, managed some mess halls and barracks for the army, operated a gas station, and was to take a job as a bulldozer operator on an island where he remained until 1944. Van Vogt had become a clerk in the Canadian Department of National Defence but continued to write; after *Slan* appeared in 1940, however, he published little of significance (with the single exception of "The Seesaw") until "Recruiting Station" in March 1942.

As a direct result of the war, then, only three Heinlein stories (all under his Anson MacDonald pseudonym) appeared in *Astounding* in 1942 and none thereafter; only two Asimov stories were published in *Astounding* in 1942, one in 1943, three in 1944, and a scattering thereafter; only one Sturgeon story appeared in *Astounding* in 1942, and twelve in the years thereafter, beginning with "Killdozer!" in November 1944. Van Vogt continued his production with seven stories in 1942 and a substantial number in the years up to 1950.

But if some inputs into *Astounding* were dwindling, one was to start up in 1942. It would be a significant event in the evolution of science fiction: the publication of three stories over the name of an author never before published anywhere—Lewis Padgett. The stories were "Deadlock" in August 1942, "The Twonky" in September, and "Piggy Bank" in December. In addition, C. L. Moore, a familiar name in fantasy though not unknown in science fiction, had a story, "There Shall Be Darkness," in the February issue.

The following year *Astounding* published eight stories by Padgett, one short story and two short-shorts by Henry Kuttner, a two-part serial by C. L. Moore, and a story by Lawrence O'Donnell; in 1944, one by Padgett, one by Moore, and one by O'Donnell; in 1945, seven by Padgett and one by O'Donnell; in 1946, six by Padgett and two by O'Donnell; in 1947, four by Padgett and one by O'Donnell; in 1948, one by Padgett; in 1949, two by Padgett; in 1950, three by O'Donnell; and in 1953, one by Padgett. These stories, as well as dozens of others published in other magazines, some under other names, were written, of course, by two authors, Henry Kuttner and Catherine Moore, who were at the time these stories appeared—and until Kuttner's death in 1950—Mr. and Mrs. Henry Kuttner.

As Lewis Padgett and Lawrence O'Donnell—and under their own names—they helped carry *Astounding* through the war years. More important, they contributed substantially to the evolution of science fiction during the formative early stages of the modern period.

The accidents and influences that bring two people together are always mysterious in retrospect. Thomas Wolfe noted in the opening sentence of *Look Homeward, Angel*:

> A destiny that leads the English to the Dutch is strange enough;
> but one that leads from Epsom to Pennsylvania, and thence
> into the hills that shut in Altamount over the proud coral cry
> of the cock, and the soft stone smile of an angel, is touched
> by that dark miracle of chance which makes new magic in a
> dusty world.

The inexplicable workings of chance or the inevitable operations of destiny brought together an Indianapolis bank secretary and a sometime Los Angeles literary agent turned fantasy writer to make not just a marriage but at least two different major literary gestalts. Or, more precisely, fantasy introduced Henry Kuttner to Catherine Moore.

Catherine Moore was born in Indianapolis in 1911. Her childhood and adolescence were marred by periodic illness; her necessary withdrawals from a more active life—like H. G. Wells's famous broken leg—may have opened to her an inner world of books and stories, particularly Greek mythology, the Oz books, and Edgar Rice Burroughs. In 1931 she discovered *Amazing Stories*. "From that moment on," she has recalled, "I was a convert. A whole new field of literature opened out before my admiring gaze, and the urge to imitate it was irresistible."

She attended Indiana University for a year and a half, but the Depression forced her to take a job as a secretary in a bank. She wrote in her spare time, and in 1933 produced and had published her first story in the November 1933 issue of *Weird Tales*. It became a fantasy classic, "Shambleau." Over the next few years she continued to write romantic fantasies for *Weird Tales,* featuring such epic characters as Northwest Smith and Jirel of Joiry, but she also was having some success with science fiction, selling four stories to *Astounding* between 1934 and 1939.

Henry Kuttner was born in 1914 in Los Angeles, where his father ran a bookstore. His father died when Kuttner was five, and he spent his early years in San Francisco. He moved back to Los Angeles about the time he entered high school. Like Catherine Moore, he went from the Oz books to Edgar Rice Burroughs and then to *Amazing Stories* in 1926.

Upon graduation from high school, he began working for a Los Angeles literary agency run by a cousin. His enthusiasm for *Weird Tales* fantasy brought him into contact with the Lovecraft circle of correspondents, and his first publications were in *Weird Tales:* first a poem, "Ballad of the Gods," in February 1936, and then "The Graveyard Rats" in March. He became a regular contributor to *Weird Tales* and to such hybrid magazines as *Strange Stories* and *Thrilling Mysteries.* Kuttner began to write science-fiction stories in 1937, with publications in *Thrilling Wonder Stories*, *Marvel Science Stories*, and one in *Astounding*, "The Disinherited" (August 1938).

Five years into his career Kuttner seemed primarily a fantasy writer—certainly his fantasy writing represented not only the bulk of his production but the chief source of his reputation—and in 1939 when *Astounding* brought out its sister fantasy magazine, *Unknown*, Kuttner began to contribute stories immediately: one in 1939, two in 1940, 1941, 1942, and 1943. Moore contributed one story in 1940.

In 1938, through the Lovecraft circle, Kuttner became acquainted with Indianapolis writer C. L. Moore and began to visit Indianapolis on his trips between New York and Los Angeles. In 1939 he quit his job with the literary agency and moved in with his mother in New York City to write full time.

On June 7, 1940, in New York, Henry Kuttner and Catherine Moore were married. They lived there a year before moving to Laguna Beach, California. In 1942 Kuttner entered the Medical Corps and served until 1945 at Fort Monmouth, New Jersey. His wife lived nearby in Red Bank. After the war they bought a house at Hastings-on-Hudson, New York; in 1948, they could afford to move back to Laguna Beach. There Kuttner attended the University of Southern California, with the aid of the G. I. Bill. He earned a bachelor's degree in three and a half years, and had nearly completed a master's degree in English (he was going to write a thesis on the works of H. Rider Haggard) when he had a heart attack and died on February 4, 1958. Moore also attended Southern Cal; she earned a bachelor's degree in 1956 and a master's in 1963, also in English.

After her husband's death, Moore completed the screenplay for "Rappacini's Daughter" that they had been writing for Warner Brothers, and she later wrote scripts for such television shows as "Maverick" and "77 Sunset Strip." She also carried on the teaching of Kuttner's writing course at U.S.C. and continued it two mornings a week for four years. She married Thomas Reggie in 1963 and died in Los Angeles in 1987.

The marriage of Henry Kuttner and Catherine Moore was more than a wedding of man and woman; it was also a fusion of writers into a series of *personas* that may represent a unique experience in collaboration. In an introduction to a recent paperback edition of *Fury*, Moore wrote, "We collaborated on almost everything we wrote, but in varying degrees." And in a private letter, she wrote, "Everything we wrote between 1940 and 1958, when Hank died, was a collaboration. Well, almost everything."

"It worked like this," Moore wrote in that introduction to *Fury*:

> After we'd established through long discussion the basic ideas, the background and the characters, whichever of us felt like it sat down and started. When that one ran down, the other, being fresh to the story, could usually see what ought to come next, and took over. The action developed as we went along. We kept changing off like this until we finished. A story goes very fast that way.
>
> Each of us edited the other's copy a little when we took over, often going back a line or two and rephrasing to make the styles blend. We never disagreed seriously over the work. The worst clashes of opinion I can remember ended with one of us saying, 'Well, I don't agree, but since you feel more strongly than I do about it, go ahead.' (When the rent is due tomorrow, one tends toward quick, peaceful settlements.)

Either separately or together, Kuttner and Moore used seventeen different pen names: the principal ones were Paul Edmonds, Keith Hammond, Hudson Hastings, Kelvin Kent, C. H. Liddell, Lawrence O'Donnell, Lewis Padgett, and Woodrow Wilson Smith. Donald B. Day, in his *Index to the Science Fiction Magazines 1926-1950*, lists another seven, most of which may have been "house" names.

The Lewis Padgett pseudonym was adopted, probably, at the suggestion of Robert Heinlein, as a rate-raising device, not, as Sam Moskowitz has stated, "because of his tarnished reputation." It was the Kuttners' first deliberately chosen communal name, and it was placed on stories that hoped to command the Kuttners' top going rate. "If the editor wouldn't pay," Moore wrote in a private letter, "he had to use one of many other pseudonyms, and there were so many because we were producing so much copy in the 1940's that often we had two or three stories in the same issue of a magazine, and it looked rather stupid to use the Kuttner name three times in the table of contents. So either we or the editor would pick alternative names more or less out of thin air."

One of the names, Hudson Hastings, was picked because the Kuttners at that time were living in Hastings-on-Hudson. C. H. Liddell began as the author of "The Sky Is Falling" and "was simply the formal name of Chicken Little."

But the only important pseudonyms, Moore recalls, were Lewis Padgett and Lawrence O'Donnell. Neither name appeared outside the pages of *Astounding*, except for later reprints. O'Donnell "emerged gradually as the name we used for many of our more favorite stories. And gradually it became the one we used for those which were mostly mine. I didn't use C. L. Moore except in very rare cases, because I just didn't feel these were C. L. M. stories we were writing, but I could feel comfortable as Lawrence O'D."

As an illustration of how pseudonyms came into being, take 1943, the Kuttners' most prolific year in *Astounding*, when they had thirteen stories, including a two-part serial, plus two contributions by Kuttner to a department of short-short stories called "Probability Zero." In January Lewis Padgett was represented by "Time Locker," the first of the Gallegher stories, and Henry Kuttner had to use his own name on "Nothing but Gingerbread Left," the first story in *Astounding* under his name since 1938. In February Lewis Padgett had a story called "Mimsy Were the Borogoves" and Henry Kuttner had to be pressed into service again for the "Probability Zero" offering called "Blue Ice." The same situation prevailed in March, with a Lewis Padgett story entitled "Shock" and a Henry Kuttner short-short in "Probability Zero" called "Corpus Delicti." But a third Kuttner story that month demanded a new name: Lawrence O'Donnell was invented as author of "Clash by Night," which contained the first mention of the Venus undersea "keeps" and would provide setting and background for the later novel Fury. The Kuttners had stories, but no conflicts, in the April, May, June, October, November, and December issues. However, another problem arose in the August issue: Padgett had a story called "Endowment Policy" and the Kuttners had a two-part serial beginning—it appeared under the name of C. L. Moore and was called "Judgment Night." Much later, so intimately had Moore become identified with her favorite pseudonym that she could not recall whether "Judgment Night" had not, in fact, appeared under the name O'Donnell.

During the period between 1942 and 1947, Kuttner and Moore contributed forty-one stories to *Astounding*—forty-eight by 1955—including three two-part serials and one three-part serial. The significance of their contribution, however, lies not in the quantity nor in the continuation of the thrust of Campbell's new ideas about science fiction through difficult years, although these factors are meaningful. They were one (or two or four) of the finest writers to marry magazine science fiction to literary form, to do it sufficiently often to be noticeable and effective, and to do it—though perhaps without deliberate intent—with increasing skill.

They did it so effectively that two of their stories—one by Lewis Padgett and one by Lawrence O'Donnell—were selected by their fellow science-fiction writers for inclusion in *The Science Fiction Hall of Fame*. And their contributions to the wartime magazine period sustained the level of that "golden age" that had begun around 1938 or 1939.

The Kuttners built their reputations slowly: novels, though not the ideal form for science fiction, are the quickest and most spectacular routes to recognition. The Kuttners were primarily authors of short stories and novelettes. They produced only one significant novel, *Fury* (1947). But their shorter works created an immediate impact upon readers and writers alike, and made a substantial contribution to the development of science fiction.

Contributions to the development of science fiction can be categorized in several ways: in terms of content and technique; in terms of source; and in terms of the change, evolutionary or revolutionary.

Editors have exerted a disproportionate influence on the field because the science fiction magazines were virtually the only medium for science-fiction in the United States between 1926 and 1946, and predominantly the medium between 1946 and 1960. A history of American science fiction cannot be written without substantial discussion of the contributions of Hugo Gernsback, John W. Campbell, Anthony Boucher, and Horace Gold, to mention only the major figures. The editors served not only as gatekeepers, deciding what would get through to the public, but in the case of Campbell, Boucher, and Gold they intervened in the creative process and actively helped shape science fiction to their desires through suggestions to authors, requests for particular kinds of stories or rewrites, and sometimes rewriting by others, including the editor himself.

But they could not do the writing, and sometimes they were surprised by unexpected contributions through which the writers themselves shaped the direction in which science fiction would go. Even though these new developments usually fit into the policy already set by the editor, or were recognized by him as a logical extension of that policy, sometimes they helped reshape that policy through innovations in content or technique.

In just this way Heinlein would bring to science fiction a method of constructing future societies and revealing them, from within, by the use of naturalistic detail; Asimov would bring his analytical mind to bear upon the myths and conventions of traditional science fiction, and would begin a process of codification and logical consideration exemplified in his robot series; van Vogt would bring to science fiction the narrative techniques of John Gallishaw and Thomas Uzzell, and his own "intensively recomplicated story," as James Blish called it. And Theodore Sturgeon would pursue his own individual style and ideas wherever they led.

These same four authors would also pioneer in subject matter: Heinlein through his "future history" of the next two hundred years and his engineer-heroes; Asimov through his robot stories and his Foundation and its psychohistory; van Vogt with his supermen and superpowers, as well as his treatment of science as magic; and Sturgeon, ultimately, with his treatment of the varieties of love and sexual experience.

The ways in which a genre develops can be further divided into either abrupt breaks with the past (Campbell's emphasis on an accurate representation of the scientific and engineering culture was something of a revolution, as was Gold's emphasis on the reactions of the average citizen, and the New Wave was an even greater departure in style, viewpoint, and subject matter) or a slow evolution. As Darko Suvin has pointed out in *Science Fiction Studies*, "A literary genre is a collective system of expectations in the readers' minds, stemming from their past experience with a certain type of writing, so that even its violations—the innovations by which every genre evolves—can be understood only against the backdrop of such a system."

Evolutionary development comes about through increments of new areas of experience or imaginative concept. Edward Elmer (Doc) Smith, for instance, brought into science fiction the concept of universe-wide civilizations. Stanley Weinbaum brought realism to the romantic concept of aliens. Dr. David H. Keller added a concern for psychology, which the Kuttners would later reinforce. After 1946 when Groff Conklin lamented "the paucity of stories dealing with the social sciences and with the sciences of the mind," both subsequently were brought more fully into science fiction by a variety of writers, particularly after 1949 in *Galaxy*. Frederik Pohl and Cyril Kornbluth brought into science fiction (or brought back) the anti-utopia. Currently science fiction is expanding into biology and genetics.

What the Kuttners brought to science fiction, which broadened it and helped it evolve, was a concern for literary skill and culture. The Kuttners expanded the techniques of science fiction to include techniques prevalent in the mainstream; they expanded its scope to include the vast cultural tradition available outside science fiction, just as, in their ways, Heinlein would draw upon and bring into his fiction the engineering and military education he received at Annapolis, Asimov would open to science fiction the concepts and methods of the working scientist, and Hal Clement and Larry Niven would expand science fiction into the physical sciences in such works as *A Mission of Gravity* and *Ringworld*. The significance of the Kuttners' work rests in the fact that much of the development in science fiction over the past twenty years has come along the lines they pioneered.

This is not to say that everything the Kuttners wrote (not even the stories they wrote for *Astounding*) was without precedent; certainly man's cultural heritage and a concern for style were a part of science fiction in its beginnings, in the work, for instance, of Mary Shelley and Edgar Allan Poe, both of whom, directly or indirectly, benefited from a classical English education. And there was H. G. Wells. But those classical and literary traditions were lost in the science-fiction ghetto created by Hugo Gernsback in 1926. They were replaced by newer pulp traditions of action and adventure, and eventually of scientific accuracy and informed speculation about one science after another, beginning with geography and mesmerism and progressing through chemistry, electricity, physics, and mathematics to computers, psychology, sociology, and biology.

Many areas of human experience, as contrasted with human knowledge, were considered unimportant or inappropriate to science fiction, either consciously—as in the case of sexual relationships and such other basic functions as eating and excreting—or unconsciously in areas in which writers were unaware or uneasy, such as cultural traditions and stylistic methods.

In the latter areas the Kuttners moved with growing skill and familiarity. Insofar as one can disentangle the gestalts they created, Moore seems to have contributed most of the unusual romantic involvements and perhaps all the classical references to myth, legend, and literature that served to expand and enrich the Kuttners' best work. Kuttner provided insights into the minds of children—he seemed to have a particular fondness for what has become known as the generation gap—and his literary references, perhaps appropriately, were almost entirely restricted to *Alice in Wonderland* and *Through the Looking Glass*.

I intend to examine a number of the Kuttners' stories, almost all of which were printed in *Astounding*. I believe that the magazine and the stories printed in it had the greatest influence on the development of the field between 1938 and 1950. Stories printed in other magazines usually were *Astounding* rejects, and even when original and effective (some were outside Campbell's definition and others slipped through one of the chinks in his editorial judgment) and possibly individually significant, they never had the cumulative impact of *Astounding* stories. I will proceed chronologically, examining each story for subject, theme, and technique.

Kuttner had one story in *Astounding* in 1938 (August), "The Disinherited"; Moore had four prior to their marriage: "The Bright Illusion," (October 1934), "Greater Glories" (September 1935), "Tryst in Time" (December 1936), and "Greater than Gods" (July 1939).

As fantasy writers, the Kuttners were attracted first to the new *Unknown*, introduced by Campbell as a companion fantasy magazine to *Astounding* with the issue of March 1939. Kuttner's "The Misguided Halo" appeared in the August issue. In April 1940, two months before their marriage, came Kuttner's "All Is Illusion"; in October, Moore's "Fruit of Knowledge"; and in December, Kuttner's "Threshold." In 1941 *Unknown* (it would change its name to *Unknown Worlds* with its October issue) published Kuttner's "The Devil We Know" (August) and "A Gnome There Was" (October); in 1942, "Design for Dreaming" (February) and "Compliments of the Author" (October); and in 1943, when *Unknown Worlds* discontinued publication, probably because of the paper shortage, "Wet Magic" (February) and "No Greater Love" (April).

But after their marriage the Kuttners turned most of their efforts toward science fiction, particularly during the 1942–1945 period when Kuttner was serving in the Medical Corps in New Jersey. "There Shall Be Darkness" (February 1942) by Moore was the first, followed by "Deadlock" (August 1942), "The Twonky" (September 1942), and "Piggy Bank" (December 1942), all by Lewis Padgett.

"The Twonky" was a memorable story frequently anthologized and adapted for other media. What makes it distinctive is its domestic setting and matter-of-fact tone; into this situation is introduced a console radio-record player. Kerry Westerfield, a likeable professor at the university, does not know that it is actually a Twonky, manufactured by a workman from the future who was caught in a temporal snag and, while under partial amnesia, created a Twonky with the materials at hand in a radio factory. The Twonky analyzes Westerfield, performs services for him—such as lighting his cigarette and washing the dishes—and then begins to censor his reading and his personal habits. Westerfield's reactions run through amazement, interest, and finally consternation. In the end, the Twonky blocks his friend's memory, destroys his wife when she starts toward it with a hatchet, and then disintegrates Westerfield when he attacks it, saying, "Subject basically unsuitable. Elimination has been necessary." And then, "Preparation for next subject completed." The story ends with a newly married couple looking over the house and admiring the console.

The story is pleasantly and efficiently told, with some effective references to music and literature (including *Alice in Wonderland*). "The Twonky" suggests one other observation: without its introductory exposition about the Twonky's origin, "The Twonky" would have had a Kafkaesque mainstream quality; explanations seem to be one aspect which distinguishes science fiction from mainstream stories. The mainstream cherishes its ambiguity.

"Piggy Bank" includes significant mythological references, as well as an unusual plot for science fiction. Ballard, a robber baron who has climbed to power with a stolen, secret process for manufacturing diamonds, finds his empire threatened by a series of seemingly unstoppable diamond thefts probably conducted by a criminal gang encouraged by a rival baron. He instructs his technological genius, Gunther, who makes the diamonds for him and protects the secret for his own survival, to make him a diamond-studded, invulnerable gold robot conditioned for self-preservation through flight, thus providing Ballard with a piggy bank containing all the wealth he will need in any emergency. When Gunther delivers the robot, Ballard calls it "Argus" because "his eyes had diamond lenses, specially chosen for their refractive powers":

> He was blazingly beautiful, a figure out of myth. In a bright
> light he resembled Apollo more than Argus. He was a god
> come to Earth, the shower of gold that Danae saw.

Secure at last, Ballard has Gunther killed in such a way that he tricks from Gunther the telephone number of the man who is to make public the patent number of the diamond-making process. But Ballard's business rival begins to assault his commercial castle, and Ballard must obtain some of the diamonds from Argus. The phrase, "implanted in Argus," fails to stop the robot from fleeing, and a posthumous note from Gunther informs Ballard that the key phrase will not work unless Gunther has made a daily adjustment. Argus cannot be captured by any of Ballard's ingenious traps; at last he finds himself ruined in the presence of riches. In final desperation, surrounded by his rival's guards, he shouts at Argus the phrase relayed through his rival from Gunther—the phrase that will immobilize Argus but make all its diamonds worthless—the patent number of the artificial diamond process.

A critic might quibble with the plot. Like the Doomsday machine in "Dr. Strangelove," the fact that Gunther needed to reindoctrinate Argus every day should not have been kept secret if Gunther wished to continue living; but the writing and the concept are excellent, and the imagery is refreshing. In "Piggy Bank," also, we see at work a narrative method that Kuttner perfected, if he did not invent—a method that James Blish described in *The Issue at Hand*:

> Padgett stories for years have begun in just this way: The narrative hook, almost always dealing with incipient violence, madness, or both; enough development of the hook to lead the story into a paradox; then a complete suspension of the story while the authors lecture the reader on the background for a short time, seldom more than 1,000 words. The lecture technique is generally taboo for fiction, especially in the hands of new writers, and only two science fiction writers have managed to get away with it and make the reader like it, Heinlein being the other.

I'm not sure I would go along with all the specifics of Blish's outline, but I agree with its thrust; the Kuttners were masters of plot, and their manipulation of exposition was masterly. In the expository section of "Piggy Bank," incidentally, the Kuttners (the story was largely Kuttner's) set down a background for a world similar to that which Pohl and Kornbluth would describe in greater detail ten years later in the more famous *The Space Merchants*:

> The stranglehold of the robber barons was still strong. Each one wanted a monopoly, but, because they were all at war, a species of toppling chaos was the result. They tried desperately to keep their own ships afloat while sinking the enemy fleet. Science and government were handicapped by the Powers, which were really industrial empires, completely self-contained if not self-supporting units. Their semanticists and propagandists worked on the people, ladling out soothing sirup. All would be well later—when Ballard, or Efoulkes, or All-Steel, or Unlimited Power took over. . . .

In the Kuttners' big 1943 year, three of the thirteen stories—"Time Locker" (January), "The Proud Robot" (October), and "Gallagher Plus" (November)—belonged to Kuttner's series about the drunken inventor Gallegher (Galloway in the magazine version of "Time Locker"), which later were collected into a book entitled *Robots Have No Tails*. A significant two-part serial by Moore, "Judgment Night," was published in August and September. Kuttner's "Clash by Night" introduced, for the first time, the concept of a Venus on which the land and its various life forms were so deadly that man had built his cities under impervium domes in the oceans. It contained, also, one of the early suggestions that an atomic accident might consume the Earth. Earth had been turned into another sun:

> A star—all that remained of Earth, since atomic power had been unleashed there two centuries ago. The scourge had spread like flame, melting continents and leveling mountains.

The concept would be used again by Kuttner, not only in *Fury,* the novel built upon the same background, but in the two-part 1947 serial, "Tomorrow and Tomorrow." In response to the catastrophe on Earth, scientists on Venus had outlawed atomic research and adopted a peculiarly modern "Minervan Oath":

> to work for the ultimate good of mankind . . . taking all precautions against harming humanity and science . . . requiring permission from those in authority before undertaking any experiment involving peril to the race . . . remembering always the extent of trust placed in us and remembering forever the death of the mother planet through misuse of knowledge. . . .

However accidental the choice of the O'Donnell pseudonym, in the first of these stories some of the characteristics, which would be developed and enlarged in later work to be published under that name, are already apparent. They include the use of chapter epigraphs, literary quotations, and mythological references (in this case to the Greek gods Mars, Minerva, and Aphrodite); relatively complex characterization (in "Clash by Night," Captain Scott is torn between two different kinds of life and between his loyalty to his Free Companions and the military life and his knowledge that it is meaningless and doomed); and conflict and complication, which are not altogether linear. The usual Kuttner story, even the customary Padgett narrative, is slick and controlled; "Clash by Night" approaches the texture of real life. Moore, in a private letter, attributes this first O'Donnell story to Kuttner, but internal evidence suggests that she may have had a significant hand in it.

In 1943 *Astounding* also published one of the Kuttner classics, the story that placed seventh for inclusion in *The Science Fiction Hall of Fame,* "Mimsy Were the Borogoves." The story introduced one of Kuttner's favorite notions: namely, that children are aliens. This quiet, controlled tale begins with a scientist in the future stuffing into a time-travel device some of the toys that had helped his son "pass over from Earth"; Scott, the son of Dennis and Jane Paradine, discovers the faulty device, extracts the toys, and, along with his younger sister Emma, begins to play with them. The toys teach Scott and Emma how to perceive and manipulate different kinds of space and relationships because, unlike adults, they're "not handicapped by too many preconceived ideas." Eventually, while their parents puzzle out what the children are doing, learning, and becoming, the children discover the way to pass over into a larger world through a strange physical parallel to the equation described in the *Through the Looking Glass* quatrain beginning: 'Twas brillig. . . ."

Science fiction and fantasy have discovered many ways to achieve conviction; science fiction, in particular, has struggled for verisimilitude. One fantasy technique is the final triumphant display of the key artifact, as in many a tale of horror: "He unwrapped the scrap of dirty yellow silk and I saw, nearly blinding me with its radiance, the diamond eye of the Hindu idol!" or "There in his hand was the tiny figure of a man only three inches high, *and he was alive!*" Science fiction refined and sophisticated the technique. Kuttner used it almost unchanged in "The Third Eye"—also called "Don't Look Now"—the frequently anthologized and dramatized 1948 *Startling Stories* tour-de-force that ends with the Martian opening his third eye and looking after the man leaving the bar. In "Mimsy" Kuttner does it more subtly. A series of references to *Through the Looking Glass* leads to the revelation that Alice Liddell also had found a box of toys from the future (and the reader realizes that the opening section describes *two* time-travel experiments) and that she had told Charles Dodgson the songs and verses that he sprinkled through the book he would later write.

Kuttner brought in other references: Hughes's *High Wind in Jamaica,* the nature of education, the spawning patterns of eels and salmon. And the quiet tone builds to a final climax in which the sensible father sees his son and daughter disappear like smoke. We feel his horror and his wife's horror yet to come, as well as the potential horror of the children when they arrive in a larger world where there are no adults and where they will be alone, possibly helpless, and afraid.

The next year, 1944, *Astounding* published only three stories by the Kuttners, but each was important. "When the Bough Breaks" by Lewis Padgett plays upon the notion introduced in "Mimsy" that children are aliens. Almost as soon as Kuttner has introduced Joe and Myra Calderon (Joe is a favorite Kuttner character, a reasonable, rational university professor) as the new parents of the infant Alexander, he insinuates that "babies are a great trial. Still they're worth it." But then goblin-like men from the future arrive at their door and acclaim Alexander as a mutant, the father of their race, and a long-lived "x-free superman" of the future. They have traveled through time to his childhood so that they can remove the frustrations Alexander suffered as a child and begin his education early enough so that he can attain still greater feats of intellect and insight. Joe and Myra are unable to discipline Alexander, at first because of the powerful gadgets of the dwarfs from the future and then because of the growing powers of the infant superman. His parents can only watch nervously as Alexander grows more powerful but not more mature. He teases and torments his parents through his abilities of teleportation, telekinesis, and energy control, with "a child's normal cruelty and selfishness." One dwarf informs them:

> "tolerance for the young is an evolutionary trait aimed at providing for the superman's appearance. . . . Infants are awfully irritating. They're helpless for a very long time, a great trial to the patience of parents—the lower the order of animal, the faster the infant develops."

Joe and Myra realize they can look ahead to nineteen more years of torment as Alexander progresses socially from well-trained monkey to bushman to super-powerful cannibal and eventually to practical joker. Driven beyond endurance, they allow Alexander to play with a blue ovoid his dwarf mentor has forbidden him, and Alexander destroys himself.

Besides the insights into infant irritation and parental patience, the story is enriched with references to biology ("parthenogenesis, binary fission") and mythology ("Deucalion and what's her name—that's us. Parents of a new race"; "I feel more like Prometheus. . . . He was helpful, too. And he ended up with a vulture eating his liver.") And the story includes comments about riddles, the nature of humor, and comic strips. Moore estimates that "When the Bough Breaks" was seventy per cent Kuttner.

"The Children's Hour" in the March issue was pure Moore, although published under the name of O'Donnell and apparently the first in which the O'Donnell pseudonym was used by choice rather than necessity. The story is a rich exploration of three months lost from the memory of a soldier named Lessing. Through hypnosis by a camp officer, Lessing begins to remember a strange and wonderful girl he had met and loved two years ago, a "glamorous" girl named Clarissa, whose presence made "a world a little brighter than human." Eventually, as he works his way back to their meetings and at last to their final parting, he realizes that Clarissa was a superbeing growing toward maturity on an infinity of worlds. "After that, the destiny of *homo superior* has no common touching point with the understanding of *homo sapiens*. We knew them as children. And they passed. They put away childish things."

The narrative itself would be unexceptional without the description of scene and situation, which creates images in much the way Moore built them in the fantasy adventures of Northwest Smith:

> In atmospheres of oxygen and halogen, in lands ringed with the shaking blaze of crusted stars beyond the power of our telescopes—beneath water, and in places of cold and darkness and void, the matrix repeated itself, and by the psychic and utterly unimaginable power and science of *homo superior*, the biological cycle of a race more than human ran and completed itself and began again. . . .

Significantly, the story reflects more than the events it relates: an insight into the child's world ("Everything shone, everything glistened, every sound was sweeter and clearer; there was a sort of glory over all he saw and felt and heard. Childhood had been like that, when the newness of the world invested every commonplace with particular glamour.") and into the shared experience of mythology and literature, with quotations from Longfellow and Shakespeare and a comparison (again) to Danae when Lessing sees Clarissa standing in an impossible golden shower and compares her with Danae whom Zeus visited in a shower of gold.

The third story of 1944 would have made any writer's year; it became an instant classic. It was clearly Moore, and, in fact, was published under her own name: "No Woman Born." The story line is simple and effective: a lovely woman, a singer and actress, has been so horribly burned in a theater fire that her brain has had to be transferred into a metal body. Harris, her manager, is going to see her for the first time since the accident, a year before; he is reluctant because she had been so beautiful and now is cold and unfeeling metal. Maltzer, the scientist who had overseen the secret collaboration of artists, sculptors, designers, and scientists that had constructed her new body, is worried about how Deirdre will appear to the public and how she, in turn, will react to that reaction. This concern builds throughout the novelette—through Deirdre's ability to project an image of herself as a beautiful woman, her desire to perform in public again, her triumphant return to the stage with a single dance and a single song, Maltzer's apprehension that Deirdre is worried, and his final attempt at suicide as punishment for creating her beautiful, fragile, and vulnerable, without weapons to fight her enemies. In a final scene, Deirdre flashes across the room with superhuman speed to save Maltzer from throwing himself out the window. She tells him and Harris that she is worried, true, not because she is defenseless but because she is superior to humanity, with weapons, strength, new skills, and even new senses; her concern is that she will grow away from humanity, that she will change.

The story is distinguished by a skillful use of what Henry James created and called the technique of the central intelligence: Harris plays the same role for "No Woman Born" that Strether plays for *The Ambassadors*. Even more than the technical excellence of the story, its observations, texture, and extensions round it into three dimensions. Deirdre is a real woman (I find myself identifying her with the author), and Maltzer is an understandably concerned creator with a Frankenstein complex. The descriptions of Deirdre, so essential to conviction, provide what James called "the specifications": golden metal, bare skull with the delicate suggestion of cheekbones; a crescent-shaped mask across the frontal area where her eyes would have been, filled in with something translucent and aquamarine; a body clad in a fine metal mesh shaped like a longer Grecian chlamys; and arms and legs formed from diminishing metal bracelets—"she looked, indeed, very much like a creature in armor, with her delicately plated limbs and her featureless head like a helmet with a visor of glass, and her robe of chain-mail. But no knight in his armor ever moved as Deirdre moved, or wore his armor upon a body of such inhumanly fine proportions." Other comparisons help extend the story into different areas of experience: James Stephens's poem with its lines, "There has been again no woman born / Who was so beautiful; not one so beautiful / Of all the women born—" In addition, certain perceptions emerge about the nature of humanity, not only the power of the human soul to impress human form on metal but the nature of creation: "The thing we create," Maltzer says, "makes living unbearable." And the final opening up of the story at the end, with the speculation as to what Deirdre will become before her brain wears out in another forty years or so. She thinks of herself as unique, like the Phoenix; there never will be another like her, and she wonders, in a moving final paragraph, how she will change:

> Her voice was soft and familiar in Harris' ears, the voice Deirdre had spoken and sung with, sweetly enough to enchant a world. But as preoccupation came over her a certain flatness crept into the sound. When she was not listening to her own voice, it did not keep quite to the pitch of trueness. It sounded as if she spoke in a room of brass, and echoes from the walls resounded in the tones that spoke there.
> "I wonder," she repeated, the distant taint of metal already in her voice.

The next year, 1945, was another big year in *Astounding*: eight stories, all of them competent but none outstanding. Four of them—"The Piper's Son," "Three Blind Mice," "The Lion and the Unicorn," and "Beggars in Velvet"—belonged to Kuttner's "Baldies" series about mutant telepaths trying to remain a part of human society through restraint and good manners while they cope with paranoia among themselves: effective stories, competently done, sensibly conceived, but seldom touched with greatness or special insights.

"What You Need" (October) and "Line to Tomorrow" (November) demonstrate Kuttner's ingenuity with stories about time, one of his favorite subjects. In these two stories he is concerned with the problems of foreknowledge. In "Line to Tomorrow" a character named Fletcher finds himself listening to a telephone conversation between a student, who is doing research in what seems to be approximately Fletcher's period, and his professor in the future. Fletcher overhears and writes down what seems to be a cure-all and an equation that demolishes an entire laboratory when a scientist tries to apply it; he finally overhears enough to deduce that the student is a decade or so in his own future and that when Fletcher reaches that time period he will go mad. "What You Need" begins with a man entering a shop that advertises, "We have what you need"; continues with a commercial transaction with the proprietor who sells his customers objects, such as a pair of scissors, which they will need desperately at some time in the future; and ends with the proprietor selling his customer slick shoes that doom him to death, because otherwise he would kill the proprietor and stop him from reshaping the world into a better place. "The future is a pyramid shaping slowly, brick by brick, and brick by brick Talley had to change it. . . ."

Eight more stories appeared in *Astounding* in 1946, one of them a two-part serial, in spite of the fact that the Kuttners were venturing into other fields. They were turning out magazine-length novels (about 40,000 words) for both *Startling Stories* and *Thrilling Wonder Stories*; these were primarily adventure stories, with a strong element of fantasy and some scientific explanation. Their first of this type had been "Earth's Last Citadel," a 40,000-word serial for *Argosy* in 1943. In 1945 they published a 20,000-word short novel, "Sword of Tomorrow," in the fall issue of *Thrilling Wonder Stories*; in 1946, a 40,000-word novel, "The Dark World," in the summer issue of *Startling Stories* and an 18,000-word short novel, "I Am Eden," in the December issue of *Thrilling Wonder Stories*. In addition, Duell, Sloan & Pearce published the first two Kuttner mystery novels in 1946: *The Brass Ring* and *The Day He Died*.

But the influential stories were those published in *Astounding*. Of the eight, two deserve special notice. "The Fairy Chessmen," a two-part serial in the January and February issues, should be discussed in conjunction with another two-part serial in the January and February issues a year later, "Tomorrow and Tomorrow." Both begin with similar scenes in which a man with overpowering responsibilities fears that he is beginning to lose his sanity. In "The Fairy Chessmen," the protagonist is Robert Cameron, civilian director of psychometrics in Low Chicago. (Life on the surface is no longer possible in a United States that has been at war for decades with "the Falangists.") Cameron fears he is losing his mind when reality begins to change around him; the story opens with a great line: "The doorknob opened a blue eye and looked at him." In "Tomorrow and Tomorrow," Joseph Breden has nightmares about blowing up the atomic pile of which he is a guardian; he lives in a world the antithesis of "The Fairy Chessmen": a Global Peace Commission, set up after an abortive World War II, has kept peace for one hundred years, but the price of peace has been a stern maintenance of the status quo, including a ban on new research.

The stories have more similarities than differences: both involve mutations caused by proximity to radiation; both include interaction with strange, extra-temporal forces (in "Chessmen" a genetically bred and conditioned warrior from the future named Ridgeley, whose nation has been defeated in his own time, has escaped by means of one-way time travel to Cameron's world and is manipulating the war on both sides, while in "Tomorrow" a mutant called "the Freak" perceives alternate worlds created by decisions made during World War II); and both progress by means of plots and counter-plots. Both have some nice touches, including in "Chessmen" effective description of Low Chicago; and both have well-calculated surprises at the end. In "Chessmen" Cameron solves his problem, but now fears that what he must do will bring about Ridgeley's world. Before his aide can propose an alternative to a world continually at war by directing man's need for an enemy toward the stars, the hostile universe, Cameron goes mad; the final sentence repeats the first. In "Tomorrow" Kuttner suggests that the world should have its atomic war and then get on to a beneficent, peaceful world where progress is possible (compare H. G. Wells's utopian novels). But the two short novels, though readable enough, do not represent major additions to the science-fiction canon, possibly because they never suggest universals.

"Vintage Season," published in the September 1946 issue of *Astounding* under the name of Lawrence O'Donnell, may be the ultimate expression of Catherine Moore's art. An immediate sensation when it appeared, the novelette still retains its evocative appeal, as evidenced by its inclusion in *The Science Fiction Hall of Fame* volume II, where it was ranked sixth among the novelettes. The narrative is relatively simple: a young man named Oliver Wilson rents his house to three foreigners, Omerie, Klia, and Kleph Sancisco; they are perfectly dressed but as if for a part, they are arrogantly assured, and they look "expensive." The complication comes through Oliver's fiancée, who wants him to get out of his lease and accept a better offer from another "foreigner." The substance of the story involves the Sanciscos, who move into the house with him and conduct themselves strangely, and Oliver's growing involvement with them and gradual understanding of what they are: time-travelers, dilettantes of the future making a sort of pilgrimage of the seasons—autumn in Canterbury in the fourteenth century, Christmastime in Rome at the Coronation of Charlemagne in 800, and May in Oliver's house and time. The time-travelers have rules, and Kleph breaks one when she tells him:

> Now this month of May is almost over—the loveliest May in recorded times. A perfect May in a wonderful period. You have no way of knowing what a good, gay period you live in, Oliver. The very feeling in the air of the cities—that wonderful national confidence and happiness—everything going as smoothly as a dream. There were other Mays with fine weather, but each of them had a war or a famine, or something else wrong.

At the end all the Sancisco's friends from the future gather in the three front bedrooms of the house to watch a small meteor strike the city. The city burns; Oliver falls ill; the character who has been largely an observer becomes the central figure as he awakens to find the future's great composer of music and visual images, Cenbe, finishing his composition from the inspiration of the city's destruction, with Oliver's death-marked face one of the major motifs. Fatally ill, Oliver writes down a message about the time-travelers who might be captured and forced to warn about impending disasters, but six days later the house is dynamited as part of a futile attempt to halt the relentless spread of the Blue Death.

The impact of the story comes from two elements: the gay mood of the pilgrims in time contrasted with the cataclysmic events involving the protagonist and his city; and the distancing effect from contemporary man—which lies at the heart of all good science fiction—achieved through Oliver's inability to understand the Sanciscos: what they do and why, their pleasures, their lives, their values, and their attitudes toward his present. As he observes Cenbe:

> suddenly Oliver realized from across what distances Cenbe was watching him. A vast distance, as time is measured. Cenbe was a composer and a genius, and necessarily strongly

empathetic, but his psychic locus was very far away in time.
The dying city outside, the whole world of *now* was not quite
real to Cenbe, falling short of reality because of that basic
variance in time. It was merely one of the building blocks that
had gone to support the edifice on which Cenbe's culture
stood in a misty, unknown, terrible future.

Oliver had succumbed to the lure of the delightful and the unknown,
including Kleph, who had seemed more human than the others but was
only weaker and more foolish; he now realizes that "all of them had
been touched with a pettiness, the faculty that had enabled Hollia to
concentrate on her malicious, small schemes to acquire a ringside seat
while the meteor thundered in toward Earth's atmosphere. They were
all dilettantes, Kleph and Omerie and the others. They toured time, but
only as onlookers. Were they bored—sated—with their normal existence?" Stories are great as they exhibit uniqueness of idea; specificity
of character, setting, and action; suitability of diction and style; and
universality of theme. All of these qualities can be found in "Vintage
Season."

Similar statements, though more qualified, might be made about the
Kuttners' 1947 *Astounding* serial, *Fury*, another story by O'Donnell.
The novel was eighty-per-cent Kuttner. The setting, a watery Venus still
in its ravening Jurassic period, has been rendered improbable, perhaps
impossible, by recent scientific observations and unmanned rocket explorations. But the storyline, the driving of a decaying humanity out of
its undersea paradise onto the hostile surface, retains its universality.
The Kuttners attack the problem that defeats most utopias, how to make
people do what is good for them.

The story begins seven hundred years after the undersea Keeps were
created, six hundred years after Earth was turned by atomic holocaust
into a star, and three hundred years after "Clash by Night." The Keeps
are ruled by immortals—tall, slim, aristocratic mutants who outlive normal humanity by centuries and can make their plans for the long term.
For lack of a challenge, because life is too easy, the Keeps have become
"the tomb, or womb, or both for the men of Venus."

To a couple of immortals, at the cost of the mother's life, is born a
child. Turning insanely on the infant, the father has the child operated
upon and converted, by endocrinological tampering, into someone who
will grow up fleshy, thick, and bald—obviously not an immortal. The
child grows up to be Sam Reed; as a street urchin he comes under the

tutelage of a master criminal named the Slider and learns to live ruthlessly and savagely, using others before they can use him. He lives with fury, in constant rebellion against the shortness of his life measured against his needs and ambitions, not knowing that he is immortal. The plot brings him into contact with his own Harker family of immortals (he has an affair with a woman who may be his great-great-grandmother); with Ben Crowell, a one-thousand-year-old immortal who can predict the future and has become the Logician at the Temple of Truth; and with Robin Hale, an immortal who is the last surviving Free Companion and wishes to persuade the people of the Keeps to go landside. Sam uses Hale to work a stock swindle based on conquering landside, but in the moment of his triumph his mistress, bribed by the Harkers, gives him dreamdust. Normally dreamdust is fatal, but Sam is nursed through forty years of unconsciousness. He awakens to the realization that he, too, is immortal. The remainder of the novel consists of Sam's efforts to force the people of the Keeps to the land surfaces, deadly with Venusian life forms though they are; his plans culminate in a simulated rebellion that turns the impervium domes of the Keeps radioactive.

Woven through the plot are the kinds of insights seldom found in science-fiction novels: immortals view life differently (they can take up occupations that require fifty or one hundred years of preparation; they have time to let their enemies die); a workless society provides limited alternatives (a person can be a technician, an artist, or a hedonist); an unrelenting search for pleasure must go continually further for satisfaction (deadly "happy clocks" and "dreamdust"); foreknowledge has built-in difficulties (which is why the utterances of oracles are always cryptic).

The novel is rounded with literary touches which satisfy the reader looking for some extension of the work beyond the here-and-now (or there-and-then): epigraphs, a prologue and an epilogue, quotations, mythological references. In the prologue the word "fury" is applied to the deadly, teeming land surface of Venus; later the word describes Sam Reed. After Sam awakens, a character comments, "Someone had fed him dream-dust forty years ago. *The voice is Jacob's voice, but the hand is the hand of Esau.*"

Finally, wounded, defeated through treachery, Sam is spirited away by Ben Crowell, who tells him:

> "Up till now we've needed you, Sam. Once in a long while a
> fella like you comes along, somebody strong enough to move

a world. . . . There's nothing you wouldn't do, son, nothing at all—if it would get you what you want. . . . If you hadn't been born, if Blaze hadn't done what he did, mankind would be in the Keeps yet. And in a few hundred years, or a thousand, say, the race would have died out. . . . But now we've come landside. We'll finish colonizing Venus. And then we'll go out and colonize the whole universe, I expect. . . . All you could think of was repeating the thing that made you a success—more fighting, more force. . . . You had the same drive that made the first life-form leave water for land, but we can't use your kind any more for a while, Sam. The race has got immortality, Sam, and you gave it to 'em. . . ."

Ben Crowell puts Sam to sleep where he will stay until he and his "fury" may be needed again:

"I hope you die in your sleep. I hope I'll never have to wake you up. Because if I do, it'll mean things have gone bad again. . . . Maybe we'll need a man like you again, Sam. I'll wake you if we do. . . ."

The novel concludes with an epilogue that, in spite of its gimmickry, opens up the novel for further speculation and suggests eternal principles at work rather than the special circumstances that so often weaken the endings of science-fiction novels: "Sam woke—"

By mid-1947 the Kuttners' contributions to *Astounding*—and to the genre—were almost over. In addition to the two serials, three more stories would be published that year, one in 1948, two in 1949, three in 1950, and one in 1953. Other stories appeared in the *Magazine of Fantasy and Science Fiction* in 1951, 1955, and 1956, and in *Galaxy* in 1952.

Two worth special mention are "Private Eye" in the January 1949, *Astounding* and "Two-Handed Engine" in the August 1955 *Magazine of Fantasy and Science Fiction*. Both are mature considerations of crime prevention worked out through the experiences of a single criminal. In "Private Eye" science has discovered how to pick up visual and aural impressions from matter so that investigators can, in effect, look into the past and trace a person's actions before he committed a crime, thus documenting motive and premeditation. The story is about Sam Clay, who sets up a crime so carefully that he cannot be convicted. But he discovers as he is committing the murder that he likes the job he has taken as a coverup, he doesn't want to be a murderer, and the chain of events he has initiated cannot be stopped. Freed, he is blackmailed by the onetime fiancée for whom he had planned the crime: he kills her, with clear intent and motive, and triumphantly satisfies the big, floating, staring eye he used to see during his unhappy childhood, with its legend: THOU GOD SEEST ME. "Two-Handed Engine" envisions a human utopia of self-repairing and self-constructed machines after a devastating war, which is also a time of ultimate individualism with no deterrent to crime. In an effort to restore the human conscience, the machines have been instructed to create "Furies"—giant, indestructible robots—as externalized consciences to follow persons convicted of murder until, at a moment known only to the Furies, they carry out their execution. The narrative concerns a man hired to kill another after he has been convinced that false data can be fed into the computer to redirect a Fury. But a Fury comes after him anyway. Finally he confronts the computer scientist who had tricked him, and the computer scientist kills him while the Fury is watching. Desperately, knowing he will be pursued by a Fury, the scientist codes false information into the computer—and it works. Yet he finds himself pursued by something even worse, an internalized conscience. The Furies may not be incorruptible, but they have succeeded in the task they were assigned.

Both stories were very nearly fifty-fifty collaborations; both are rich plum-puddings of stories. In "Private Eye" the fullness comes in large part from psychology; in "Two-Handed Engine," from legend and literature. Even the titles are revealing: "Private Eye" is a psychological pun; "Two-Handed Engine" is a quotation from Milton:

> But that two-handed engine at the door
> Stands ready to smite once, and smite no more. . . .

The Kuttners' decline in production for *Astounding* is easily explained. In 1948 they had returned to California and had started their college studies. The two mystery novels they had published in 1946 would lead to five more: *Man Drowning* for Harper in 1951 and four mysteries for Pocket Books between 1956 and 1958. In addition, they produced nine novels or short novels for *Startling Stories* and *Thrilling Wonder Stories* between 1947 and 1952. These stories alone represented a production of nearly 300,000 words. Probably they were easy words, compared at least with the difficult, tightly woven words of the Kuttners' *Astounding* stories. Interesting reading in their way, they usually feature a heroic man precipitated into strange circumstances and required, in the end, to do battle against strange, unearthly powers. "The Mask of Circe," for instance, begins in traditional Edgar Rice Burroughs and A. Merritt fantasy style. A man named Talbott is sitting in the north woods listening to a story told by Jay Seward, a restless, haunted man with a bronze face—"it might have been a mask hammered out of metal, with the tall Canadian pines a background and the moonlight silvering it with strange highlights." They sit in a "moon-drenched clearing" and Seward says, "Tonight something's going to happen. Don't ask me what." Seward had been doing psychological research on ancestral memories and had unleashed within himself the memories of Jason; a voice kept calling for Jason to return to the sea. One night he did return, leaping to the deck of a ghostly Argos, and found himself at last the pivotal figure in a battle between Hecate, the last of the alien beings who became gods on Earth, and Apollo, the beautiful, powerful machine created by the gods that draws upon the sun for atomic power. In the end Jason-Seward prevails, with the help of the Golden Fleece, which Hephaestus had created before his death to destroy Apollo by bottling up within him the sun's energy.

Such stories achieve their tone, in part, through the use of elevated diction. As A. Merritt's *The Moon Pool* speaks of "shafts of radiance," "cylindrical torrents," "amber," "amethyst," "molten silver," "phosphorescence," "coruscations," and "incandescence," so, too, in "The Mask of Circe" a "Nubian face" is ebony, not black; hemispheres are milky; water is opalescent; walls are mirror-silver; glow is crepuscular; and the glare of gold is intolerable. The air of the alien and the ineffable is achieved by mating contradictory adjectives: in *The Moon Pool* the narrator's wife disappears into the pool in the arms of the dweller, and "her eyes stared up to me filled with supernal ecstasy and horror"; in "The Mask of Circe" the Kuttners write of Apollo's "beautiful, hideous face." Yet they departed from the Burroughs-Merritt fantasy tradition by frequently providing a rational explanation for their mysteries—the walls of Jericho, for instance, leveled by supersonic vibrations.

The Kuttners' significant work, however, was their science fiction, particularly that written for *Astounding*, although several noteworthy stories escaped Campbell, such as "Absalom," another child-father conflict of superpowers *(Startling Stories*, Fall 1946); "Call Him Demon," in which a child destroys a meat-hungry alien with strange mental powers by feeding him the child's grandmother *(Thrilling Wonder Stories,* Fall 1946); and "Don't Look Now" *(Startling Stories,* March 1948).

The Kuttners' range of subjects, in their production for *Astounding,* at least, was somewhat limited. Like a dog with a favorite bone, they would pick up an idea, chew on it for a while, bury it, and then dig it up again and again to begin the process all over. Psychology, for instance, seemed to be much on their minds, for their stories are filled with men going mad, fearful that they are going mad, or suffering from paranoid symptoms or serious neuroses, as in "The Piper's Son," "Tomorrow and Tomorrow," "The Fairy Chessmen," "Line to Tomorrow," "Private Eye," "No Woman Born," *Fury,* "Endowment Policy," "The Children's Hour," "The Cure," and others. Other favorite subjects included androids, robots, and what we now call cyborgs, as in "Android," "No Woman Born," "The Twonky," "Home There's No Returning," "Piggy Bank," and "The Proud Robot"; foreknowledge and time travel, as in "Vintage Season," "Line to Tomorrow," "The Cure," "What You Need," "The Fairy Chessmen," "Mimsy Were the Borogoves," "Time Locker," and "When the Bough Breaks"; supermen and superpowers, as in "The Children's Hour," "Margin for Error," "The Piper's Son," "Absalom," "The Fairy Chessmen," "When the Bough Breaks," "Mimsy Were the Borogoves," and others; crime and punishment, as in "Private Eye," "Two-Handed Engine," "Time Locker," "Piggy Bank," and others. Several favorite possible events sometimes provided central themes but more often background: atomic catastrophe in "Tomorrow and Tomorrow," *Fury,* "The Piper's Son," "Two-Handed Engine," "Margin for Error"; meteor and plague in "Vintage Season"; and children as aliens, often inhuman, sometimes monsters, in "Call Him Demon," "When the Bough Breaks," "Mimsy Were the Borogoves," "Absalom," and "The Piper's Son."

The Kuttners did not deal with such themes as "the wonderful journey," or man and the future (in any extrapolative sense, with the possible exception of *Fury,* "Judgment Night," and—in lesser ways, because they are not extrapolative but thematic "The Fairy Chessmen" and "Tomorrow and Tomorrow"); cataclysm (they dealt entirely with pre-cataclysm or post-cataclysm, and never in a cataclysmic vein); and only in a limited way with man and his environment, man and alien, and man and religion.

The Kuttners concerned themselves principally with man and society: How is man going to function in the new worlds that will be created by changes in technology, science, and social restructuring? To this theme they brought perceptions and techniques refined by their fantasy writing. Every writer seeks to convince his or her readers that what they are reading is, in some sense, real. The fantasy writer tries to achieve this conviction through psychological or mythic truth; the naturalistic writer, through verisimilitude. Even the romantic or the satiric writer believes that he is reflecting reality. Tobias Smollet asserted, "Every intelligent reader will, at first sight, perceive I have not deviated from nature in the facts, which are all true in the main, although the circumstances are altered and disguised to avoid personal satire." Jean-Jacques Rousseau wrote, "In an imaginary picture, every human figure must have traits common to men, or the picture is worthless." Fanny Burney explained in her preface to *Evelina*, "The heroine of these memoirs, young, artless, and inexperienced is 'no faultless monster, that the world ne'er saw,' but the offspring of Nature, and of Nature in her simplest attire."

The fantasy writers of the early twentieth century, it is true, had no such belief. They overwhelmed the reader with the sweep of their imaginations, the pace of their adventures, and the color of their descriptions; in fact, the more fantastic the writers wrote them, as in one all-time A. Merritt favorite, *The Ship of Ishtar*, the better their readers liked them. Science fiction struggled in the other direction, toward realism and credibility, and achieved its ends through different means—perhaps, thereby, contributing to the fabled loss of Sam Moskowitz's "sense of wonder," for something that is explained is no longer a miracle: the rainbow, God's covenant with man that there will never be another flood, becomes only another natural phenomenon when science explains that it is caused by the refraction of sunlight by raindrops.

In its search for credibility, science fiction tried pseudoscientific explanations or explanations by analogy (as in "Doc" Smith's epics), scientific logic (as in Isaac Asimov's robot stories), extrapolation from present possibilities or trends (as in a host of rocketry and atomic bomb stories), naturalistic detail (as in Robert Heinlein's early novels and juveniles), ordinary heroes or antiheroes (as in Pohl and Kornbluth's *The Space Merchants* and other *Galaxy* stories), to cite some of the most important methods.

Science fiction is most obviously distinguished from the best of mainstream literature by its thinness, its orientation toward plot to the exclusion of other qualities of literature. What the Kuttners brought to science fiction from fantasy were the qualities of literature: the quest for conviction through characterization and individualization, through set-ting, through symbol and myth. Fantasy always has been close to main-stream literature, if not indistinguishable from it; in our times, at least, both are concerned with private visions rather than the public—or shared-visions—of science fiction. The mixture of the two brought back from beyond the grave of years what might be called literary science fiction, or science fiction that attempted to meet the standards of mainstream literature. It was not an easy task, for elements on both sides are antago-nistic. At best, an uneasy balance could be struck: too much science-fiction convention, too much explanation, and the characters seem ma-nipulated by the story. The non-initiated reader is lost. Too much con-cern for style, for myth, for the individual, and the heart of science fiction—the idea—is buried beyond recall. In the 1940s the Kuttners provided the best mixture.

They were not without predecessors: Stanley Weinbaum, John Campbell writing as Don A. Stuart, and, of course, the man who de-serves more than anyone the name of father of science fiction, H. G. Wells. The Kuttners had contemporaries: Theodore Sturgeon; some-times Clifford Simak and Lester del Rey; Jack Williamson and Ed Hamilton in their later styles; James Blish; Damon Knight; Phil Klass writing as William Tenn, to name the most obvious. Most of all, they had successors.

It is tempting to say that the Kuttners drove science-fiction writers out of their impervium magazine domes onto the literary landside where they had to face ravening readers and critics. But the Kuttners were professionally quiet and gentle; they never drove anyone. What they did was show the way, making their toves slithy and arranging them so that they would gyre and gimbel, and, if other momes could follow, they would, like the Kuttners, rath outgrabe.

Appendix A

Notes from a Workshop

In 1998 a writer from Minneapolis attended the Writers Workshop in Science Fiction. A year later she surprised me with the notes she had taken during the Workshop discussions. My surprise was not only at her enterprise and her expertise but at her ability to organize and make sense out of what were, at best, comments and asides. I also was surprised at how well the notes reflected my approach to writing and my attitudes toward the writing craft, and I thought the readers of this book might read them with the feeling that they, too, had been present. So, thanks to Mary Sue, the following reflections of a Writers Workshop:

NOTES FROM THE 1998 SF WRITERS WORKSHOP
Instructor: James Gunn. Notes: M. S. Lobenstein

Some overall considerations

- Science Fiction (SF) is the fiction of ideas. If the story is more about character, then it should probably be a mainstream story. Also, a derivation of this first definition: SF shows the adaptability of humanity. Specifically, what separates humanity from the rest of the creatures that share our planet is the fact that we can decide to do it differently—through intelligence and rationality. And, what distinguishes SF from mainstream is its "worldview."
- A writer should only write a story as SF if it can't be written as mainstream (i.e., the story can't be told except as SF). That way the SF story will be more powerful. The reverse is also true: if it can be written as mainstream, it is usually more powerful written as mainstream rather than as SF.
- Someone once said that fiction is "interesting people in difficult situations." You need to have both things.
- Someone said once that a story ought to be picked up like a puppy: in the middle, then go back to the front and finally to the end.
- Stories are not written, they are rewritten.
- Reality is not an excuse for bad writing!

- Anything is acceptable if you can make it work. However, you have to learn the standard rules before you can decide to break them. And, it helps to thoroughly understand them so that you fully understand the consequences of breaking them.

Some specifics to remember about writing in general and writing SF in particular

- There is very little that's new in SF. There is a way in which SF is just one big volume—the more you read, the more you would know about it and what has gone before. As a result, the SF writer has to think of what to do with a familiar idea: he or she either needs to do something different with the same idea, or else do something better with the idea than anyone has done before.

- It's important to think in terms of the "reader's" story, not "your" story. The writing of fiction is the "management of the reader's expectations." You can have surprises, but you don't want to "disappoint" the reader. Neither do you want the reader to lose confidence in you as an author.

  - The ending of the story should be implicit in the first sentence (e.g. Hemingway and the opening line of *The Old Man and the Sea*).
  - Authors want to ease into a story; readers want to jump into it.
  - The reader wants the twin pleasures of "surprise" and "rightness."
  - Need to somehow suggest to the reader all along what's going to happen without giving it away. If done well, the reader doesn't get it until the end—then she/he can see the "clues" the writer has placed throughout.
  - Early on in the story, the writer needs to establish what is going to happen as the thing that the reader wants and needs to have happen.
  - What leads a reader through the story is unanswered questions. The writer needs to raise these questions for the reader and guide him/her through them. Writers are in the pleasure business. We all have an inner need to become involved in a story and characters—to care about them so much that we want to

find out what's going to happen to them. A good writer knows this and sets the story up accordingly.

- The reader expects to see several stages of the learning process for the main character. The character learns through repeated failure until at last he/she succeeds, or at the very least knows how to succeed.

- The reader needs to have validation, and validation within the story, for all the things the characters say and do, otherwise he/she will loose confidence in the story and in the author. Avoid statements that come out of thin air (at least as far as the reader can tell), in order to just get on with the story. Instead, provide an authentication so that the reader believes it. When you have a character do or say something, ask yourself if this is something you would do or say. If not, go back and provide the required motivation or background information.

- Avoid undercutting your own writing. Don't write in a way that gives the reader the sense that you (the author) are not taking yourself or your story seriously.

- In SF, since anything is possible, the reader is looking for the author to narrow down the possibilities to only those that are consistent with the particular world the author has created.

- In every story, the reader needs to know what's at stake and it has to be relevant to the reader (i.e., stories are more powerful if they are close to our lives). Therefore, every story you write must pass the "so what" test. It fails if it is a "slice of life" rather than a story, which has a purpose.

- Remember: we read fiction to involve ourselves in the fictional lives of people we care about, and to have our concerns intensified until the end where our concerns are released in a way that is both satisfying and plausible.

- The basic strategy of SF is to make the reader reevaluate his/her world. At the heart of it is gaining the reader's agreement to buy into one of his/her preconceptions about the world and then pulling that preconception apart, forcing the reader to rethink his/her world and to reconsider his/her prejudices. (The uninspected belief is not worth holding; if you haven't examined what you believe and held it to an outside source, you shouldn't accept it.) As a result, one way to write a SF story is to take something that people really feel strongly about and then turn it on it's head. Set up the situation so that it is exactly the opposite of the assumption.

- Fantasy says that we can escape this world and get to something that is better. SF says that our world is not perfect, but we can make it better. Therefore in general SF is a public vision, whereas fantasy is a private vision.

- In SF, the science fiction or fantasy elements must be interwoven with other aspects of the story into a seamless whole. Can't just place a random technology/magic here or there. Must be integrated into the underlying world, and must be believable.

- What happens in a SF story has to be important for everyone (i.e., relevant for humanity at least by implication). If it is only related to the particular characters in this particular situation, then it's not good SF, and you might as well write mainstream fiction. Making it relevant for humanity raises the stakes and makes it relevant/interesting to the reader (e.g. Asimov's *Caves of Steel*).

- Creating new technologies or magic in SF/Fantasy

  - In any story where you have a new development (or magic) of some sort, you almost always have to deal with the unintended consequences of that development, and it is these consequences that make the story interesting. It's not the initial prediction that is important in SF; it's what wasn't anticipated that is.
  - If you invent something (whether it's magic or technology), you also have to consider what is the drawback. What's the cost or penalty? If you want to do something, you have to be willing to pay the price. In fantasy, for example, it is important that the magic not be too easy. There needs to be a payment of some sort. Either it takes a lot of work to do magic, or it has a consequence that you have to live with. For every action, there must be a reaction. Nothing comes free and in some cases, the payment may be worse than the value of the magic.
  - In fantasy, it's important for things to be psychologically true, not necessarily technically true.

- A problem with SF is that *anything* can be literal. As a result, metaphors are always a risk in SF. When you do use a metaphor, you have to be very careful to show that it is clearly a metaphor and not a literal possibility. Some examples of ambiguous metaphors: "her world exploded," "he turned on his left side."

- SF is the kind of writing that specializes in great beginnings, but there aren't as many great endings. That's because it's often hard to live up to the beginning. Usually the writer starts at a high point and then tries to make the ending even higher. In fact, the better the beginning, the higher the reader's expectations. So if you don't have a good ending, you better not set it up so that the reader expects one. Don't promise what you can't deliver.

- The one mistake you can't afford to make in writing SF/fantasy is to be "ordinary." SF is smart, so the story and everything about the story should be smart.

- Avoid the arbitrary in stories.

  - You want things to happen in a story because it's the only thing that can happen right then. You should be able to look back and notice that things couldn't have happened any other way than the way they did, and that nothing was accidental.
  - Frivolous motivations lead to uninteresting narratives. Your characters must have believable motivations.
  - In SF if you have a native population doing something, you have to have them doing it for a reason, even if we don't understand the reason for it right away, or ever.

- Anything that you *can* leave out, leave out. If left in, it *will* weaken the story. Either eliminate it, or else change it into something that is relevant to the story. It's particularly important to be a harsh critic of your "darlings" (e.g. favorite scene, plot twist, character) and consider eliminating them. (A darling is anything that is meaningful to you as a writer, and that you want to write about, but that never really becomes meaningful to the reader. These just get in the way and we need to cut them.)

- Always ask yourself: what is the most dramatic way to tell this particular story, or what is the way I can best reveal this story through what the characters' do? You must think dramatically when you are telling the story. Two types of scenes that are useful to use:
  - Panoramic—covers a lot of distance and scenes in a short time
  - Dramatic—close up of the action

- If the more interesting story is the one that you aren't telling (i.e., it's implicit within your story, but not specifically being told) your story is in real trouble. It's hard for the reader to get interested in a story when there's obviously a more interesting one underneath.

- Rule of Three regarding conflict:

  - Set the conflict early
  - Mention the conflict later to keep it going
  - Resolve the conflict at the end

- Necessarily, the art of writing a short story versus a novel is different and what is good about each of them is different.

  - When we read a short story, we expect to read it at one sitting, so *everything* the author tells us should be important, and that's the way the reader expects it to be. Anything extraneous is annoying. Needs to have a beginning, a middle, and an end.
  - In a novel, what is important is the situation and the characters. However, a novel ought to be as thoughtful and well-organized as a short story. Each chapter (like each short story) should have a beginning, a middle, and an end to be really effective.

- The typical form of the modern short story at one time was a naturalistic story (i.e., things happen in our world in a way that we can understand based on nature; Darwinian) transformed into something supernatural by a single, massive metaphor. This form is embodied in the work of James Joyce (e.g., "The Dead.") The idea is to imbue the story with something more than just the words themselves.

- Most fiction has the same dynamic: people *earn* their fates. As a result, in fiction we find meaning, truth, and justice, and we know why people do what they do. However, horror stories have an entirely different dynamic because the characters live in a universe that hates people. Therefore, in most horror stories things don't work out because the world itself is against us.

• SF mystery is different from a regular mystery in that the outcome or solution of the mystery is crucial to the societal issue that's at work in the SF story.

• Function must be as important as structure to our writing. As you go along, ask yourself: What is the story I want to tell and how does what I've written further that story? At the same time you are telling the story you must also answer these questions for the reader:

1) What is happening?
2) Why is it happening?
3) Where is it happening?
4) Why should we (the readers) care about it?

• A piece of fiction has to operate at all levels. The reason a story does not work well is often because it is only working at one level (e.g., plot). But language, action, setting, subtext (i.e., the level of meaning below the surface actions and dialogue), cultural assumptions, metaphors, etc. all must be working together to reinforce the idea of the story. If the author does not actively notice and work at all these levels, at best it is a lost opportunity to reinforce the idea of the story, and at worse it risks allowing these factors to unknowingly work against the story (especially with subtext and metaphor).

• A lot of stories are simply old plot elements rearranged into new writing. That's not what you want to do. The process of becoming a good writer is in three stages and you want to get to stage 3.

1) Fall in love with writing.
2) Recapitulate what you've read.
3) Discover what you have to tell people that nobody else knows; what you can write that nobody else can write. This is the only thing that people (readers) want: what is unique about you, what is your vision, what speaks to your experience or your knowl-

edge in a way that nobody else can. It comes from your need to reflect your understanding of what life is really about.

- Ending Chapters

  - A good time to end a chapter is when the situation is changing or being reevaluated.
  - A good chapter ending needs a note of suspense or an aspect of the story that is left hanging.

- Plots

  - According to Heinlein, there are three kinds of people stories in SF (and this is sometimes a useful way to organize thinking about your story:
    - Boy meets girl (basically a love story)
    - Little tailor (person rises from the lowest to the highest through ingenuity)
    - The man who learned better (see concept of epiphany below).
  - Alternatively, Marilyn Zimmer Bradley says that there is basically only one kind of SF story: "Joe gets his ass caught in a bear trap and tries like hell to get it out."
  - Concept of an "Epiphany" as first noted by James Joyce is useful in SF. An epiphany is that moment in the plot when the main character has a revelation—when he/she sees things the way they really are. The story in this case is all about the education of that character to come to this grand moment of epiphany. If you are writing this kind of story, it is useful to make sure that the epiphany is clear to the reader.

- Exposition is what the reader needs to know in order to understand the story, but that the reader doesn't really want to know. Therefore, the writer needs to figure out a way to give it to the reader in a way that the reader wants. Otherwise, it risks just being one big information dump. There are several ways to do this:

  - The writer can dole it out, bit by bit as the story progresses;
  - The writer can create an appetite in the reader which the information then satisfies.

- Alternatively, if you do it boldly enough, and are a good enough writer, you can sometimes state the facts directly without having to explain the details of why something is so.

Note: Hemingway once said something like: "It's not what you put into the story that matters so much as what you know and leave out."

- Description

  - Perhaps more than anything else, description establishes the reality of a place. If you don't describe a place (e.g., odor, sound, look, feel), the reader doesn't really believe it. The reader may accept it, but it is not real to him/her.
  - The problem with a lot of nonprofessional writers is that they don't look at what they are seeing in their head and incorporate it into their writing. Good writing reflects good observation, not just of reality but of senses as well. The more intimately you can describe the scene, the more real it will be to the reader.
  - There is an idea that nothing (i.e., no place) really exists in fiction unless it appeals to at least three of the five senses (sight, sound, smell, touch, taste).
  - It is always better if description is effectively dramatized by being part of somebody's psychological awareness. The writer should strive to render it emotionally in the story so that the place is "there" as the characters in the story experience it.
  - Location will always have a value for the sake of general description and a sense of place, but it is better if every location is part of the emotional structure of the story—if it is dramatically necessary for the story. If something is happening in a story and it is happening in a place that is not necessary or essential to the story, try to change it. Put the action in a different place that is important to the story.
  - In order to evoke a sense of reality, you really need that which says this is "X" and nothing else but "X." You must use what is characteristic and specific to whatever you are describing. Otherwise it's just a device or abstraction and it will seem to the reader as if he/she is not really there, or is not really seeing it. It will not be real. You can't just use generic terms. Try to pin it down as much as possible and use something that will evoke the image for the reader. Along that line, there are only four

basic tastes (sweet, sour, salty, and bitter) and the sense of taste is dependent on only seven basic odors (e.g. pungent, floral, musky, etc.)

- Characters

  - You must use every sentence and every character optimally to express the story and move it along. Think about the idea you are trying to convey and ask yourself: How does this particular sentence or this particular character carry out the idea?
  - Characters should always act for their reasons, not for the writer's reasons. Actions have to come out of the characters themselves, not because it is convenient.
  - If you have a character who lacks integrity in the beginning of your story, but who will come around to do the right thing by the end of the story (at the epiphany), it is useful for the reader to see that there is at least the potential there for the person to act correctly—that he/she would be OK if he/she would just do "X" or "Y." The reader needs to see that the character can redeem herself/himself from the beginning even if it doesn't happen until the end.
  - In a story, the reader always wants to see the protagonist take action—to do that which finally resolves the problem/challenge. The protagonist can't just be a meek and mute observer in the story. Things can't just happen to her/him or for her/him. She/he must *make* them happen.

- Dialogue

  - Dialogue, even well written dialogue, is often a trap. Even though it reads quickly, it takes a lot longer to move the story along with dialogue than with narrative. As a result, always question what you have put into dialogue and see if you can do without it, or whether the scene could be moved along better in any other way.
  - Dialogue drains the drama and emotion out of a story. Whenever people start talking, the dramatic intensity droops. It's when people are silent and suffering that the drama rises. It's then their inability to talk that raises the level of drama.
  - Good dialogue is that which is credible on the page, not that

which mimics real life. The printed word is much more intrusive than the spoken word. Written words have more impact; they are more solid and significant. (One person said something like: printed words have seven times the impact of the spoken word.) As a result, the writer should use one-seventh of the words that might actually be spoken if the scene were real life. The writer should strive to "suggest" the conversation, not re-create it. Writing is not real life and written dialogue should not be a direct imitation of a real life conversation.

- When you do use dialogue, have the characters doing something while they are talking (something that moves the story along). Don't just have them in a static situation when they are talking.
- Remember that nobody needs to say anything that the reader already knows by some other means. If it's not necessary, leave it out.
- Generally, you should use "said" as the dialogue verb unless there is some specific reason why you have selected some other verb (e.g., the character really does "scream" or "snarl" his/her response.) Either use "said" or better still skip it altogether if it is clear from the context who is speaking, or if you can indicate who is speaking by the action. Why?
  - The adage that one should not use words repeatedly in close proximity doesn't apply to words that are so common they tend to fade out, words like "the," "a," or "said."
  - Using a word other than "said" tends to draw attention to it and bogs the narrative down. You don't want the reader's attention drawn to it unless it is intentional (i.e., to add to the reader's understanding of character, to give depth to the plot, etc.)
  - The search for color in this way is usually a cover-up for the fact that there is not enough else going on to keep the reader's interest.
- *Ideally*, anytime you have a dialogue between two people, their voices should be distinctive enough so that the reader can tell who is speaking without the author always saying "he said," "she said."

- Point of View

  - It's a dramatic principle that in a story, the reader is asked to be concerned about one person. If more than that, the reader can get confused. As a result, the writer should generally follow that viewpoint character throughout the story. (You can use first or third person.) If the writer switches around to more than one character's point of view, it is often because the writer either is not confident of the dramatic quality of the chosen character, or can't figure out how to do it any other way. (If the latter, it's just the easy way out.)
  - If you are planning to switch viewpoints at the end of a story, you must establish that second viewpoint somewhere earlier in the story. You can't just introduce it at the end.
  - First person viewpoint is effective when it's personal—when what happens to the person and what is going on inside the person's head is important.
  - Third person viewpoint is effective if you want readers to have confidence in what you tell them (i.e., that it's objective).

- Points of proper English

  - Terms in direct address should be set off in commas.
  - Never use a descriptive word or verb adjunct as a dialogue verb (e.g., don't write, "he smirked," instead write, "he said with a smirk.")
  - Avoid misplaced modifiers. It's a common problem with writers and it bogs down the writing and risks confusing the reader.
  - Avoid overuse of adjectives. Generally, the use of adjectives is a substitute for the exact noun you are looking for. As an exercise, it is useful to re-write something you've written, but cut out *all* the adjectives.
  - Periodic sentence is one in which the meaning is not clear until the end. One way to do this is to put the noun at the end of the sentence if possible. This often makes for a stronger sentence.
    - Passive constructions are death to storytellers. Try to get people in the action whenever possible.
    - Go through your work and get rid of words like: just, merely, really, actually, etc.

- It takes work to write and writers get paid (psychologically or materially) because they do the work of writing. In addition, authors should never be lazy or take the convenient way out. If it's hard, it's a better story. Therefore, don't look for the easy way out. If it's the first thing that occurs to you, it's probably the first thing that occurs to the reader as well. You should discard the first solution you think of and keep thinking until you've come up with at least several other less likely solutions. Don't be afraid of working harder to get the job done; your story will be that much better as a result of the hard work.
- Don't settle for the first idea you have about how to do something in your story. It is usually the easy (lazy) way out. Typically, in order to have *one good* idea, you have to go through a lot of mediocre ideas until you get the right one.
- There is nothing magic about writing. It's hard work, but you can do it bit by bit. You may not be a great writer, but you can be a competent one. The business of writing really just consists of writing one good sentence after another. If you write good sentences, you can carry the story along.

General strategy for getting published: don't give the editor a chance to say "no."

- Re-read your story as an editor might; think about what she/he is thinking when he/she reads your story. Editors seldom read in the office; usually they read at home or on commute. The only thing an editor wants to do is read until he/she can say "no," and they want to say no fast.

- Some things that **guarantee** the slush pile:

  - Poor (i.e., unprofessional) formatting—make sure you know how to submit a professional manuscript.
  - Uninteresting title.
  - First sentence that does not grab you.
  - Subsequent sentences that are uninteresting. Every sentence in manuscript is a challenge to the editor to say no.

- A good title:

  - Need to use a strong noun, perhaps with an adjective;
  - Prepositions and verbs do not make good titles;
  - Must be appropriate to the story and say something about the story;
  - It should be essentially dramatic—making the reader want to read it;
  - Ideally it should catch the attention of the reader.

- A good opening:

  - An opening not only has to grab the reader, it must also prepare the reader for the story that is to come.
  - It's best not to start with dialogue because you don't know who is talking or what the situation is.

- An editor likes to see evidence of an author's authority over the story, so you *must* demonstrate that authority in the text, including:

  - Authenticity—the story, details, technology, etc. has the ring of truth/probability.
  - The writing is under control.
  - The story raises no questions that can't be answered or verified within the story.

- Know who your readership will be. When you are selling a novel in particular, it helps to have a clearly identified audience because the people who will buy and sell it will have to think about how to market it. That's also why it helps to write in a particular SF category and to tell your publisher what the category or audience is for your particular novel.

- Once you've written your story as good as you can do it, you have to learn to do it better.

  - Platonic version of any story: This is the idea that there is an ideal way to write each story; and that it's the author's obligation to figure out what that ideal is for each particular story and to try to achieve it, or to get as close to achieving it as possible.

- You have to lift your story out of the level of just competent—you must distinguish it from the rest. It must be competent plus, but it doesn't matter what the plus is. You can do it through voice, diction, description, place, or idea (idea is especially pertinent in SF). Your story must be special in at least one way and competent in all ways.

Appendix B

Syllabus for a Workshop

A writers workshop operates in many different ways, depending upon the talents and preferences of the workshop leader (or teacher) and the experience of the writers involved. I started my beginning class in fiction writing with the fundamentals of idea, character, setting, and dialogue, and, most of all, the development of these in the form of scenes—the crafts that are special to the creation of fiction. After that the class moved on to the writing and critiquing of stories. More advanced classes started with the writing and critiquing of complete stories. I have always felt that story writers ought to have stories to tell, and if they don't have stories they should go away and live a little and observe a lot until they do have stories that must be told.

When I was asked to develop an on-line course in science-fiction writing, I constructed a syllabus based on a four-week series of reading and writing assignments, with critiques, and then four weeks more for the completion of a science-fiction story and its critique by the other workshop participants. What follows is that syllabus, with assignments and readings from *The Science of Science-Fiction Writing*. Individual writers can follow it to construct a story, or workshop leaders (or teachers) can use it with a group. The most important part of the workshop, however, is the establishing of standards and the elevating of aspirations. Critiquing by other writers is essential until standards get internalized—and sometimes critiquing helps even then.

Writers Workshop in Science Fiction

Week One

Ideas! Science fiction is a literature of ideas (as well as the literature of change and the literature of the human species, and a lot of other literatures), and an SF story ought to have an original idea, a concept that hasn't been used up, a novel insight into the workings of the universe or the human condition under change. Unlike many readers, who like the comfort of the familiar, SF readers demand something different. Although complete originality is unattainable, a new twist on an old idea, a new way of expressing an old concept, or a new way of telling an old story often will work.

Everyone will be expected to evaluate (when the stories themselves are posted during the second four weeks, we'll call these critiques) the story ideas, as they will the later assignments. The instructor will evaluate last so that other evaluations will not be influenced and can be compared to the instructor's so that this, too, can be a learning experience. Story ideas should be evaluated for originality and workability. That is, do they embody characteristics that can be developed into a satisfying narrative, and, if the story is written, will it be different enough from other SF stories that an editor might consider it for publication? Can you suggest improvements?

Ernest Hemingway once said that writing a novel was getting into the ring with Mr. Tolstoy. For SF writers, writing an SF story is getting into the ring with Mr. Heinlein—and Mr. Asimov and Mr. Clarke and all the other great SF authors. That's the competition.

Readings: *Where Do You Get Those Crazy Ideas?; The Origins of Science Fiction; The Anatomy of a Short Story.*

Assignment: *Outline an idea for a short story in a paragraph, describing the concept and suggesting the dramatic development.*

Tip: H. L. Gold once said that if you can't put the idea for a story in a sentence you won't be able to turn it into a good story.

Week Two

Characters. Fiction is "interesting people in difficulties." Who are the people in the difficulty (the situation) you conceived in the first assignment? One way to decide who you need as characters in your story is to ask yourself who would hurt the most in this situation. A character must be moved to action by the situation, and unless someone is hurt (in pain, pushed to the wall), he or she isn't going to act, or isn't going to act definitively. Make characters "interesting" by inspecting their lives in detail—avoid "typical housewives" or "ordinary college freshmen." Everyone is special if you look at them intently, particularly if they are suffering (let your characters suffer—most authors are too soft-hearted and want to save their characters pain).

In your evaluation of these scenes, ask first if the scene works dramatically and is a complete dramatic unit. Then, is/are the character(s) interesting, understandable, and well presented? How can the scene and the characterization be improved?

Reading: *Heroes, Heroines, Villains: The Characters in Science Fiction*; *The Issue Is Character*; *Scene—The Smallest Dramatic Unit*

Assignment: *Write a scene of 750-1,000 words, which will serve as a dramatic unit of your story, in which you present character(s).*

Tip: A scene must do many things at the same time: advance the story (move the character toward epiphany), characterize, dramatize, and involve the reader.

Week Three

Setting. A story can be narrated—that is, it can be communicated to the reader through someone's *impressions* of events and comments upon it and the circumstances that led up to them. That usually occurs through the use of a first-person narrator or an omniscient narrator, or sometimes through a limited third-person narrator. The other method of presentation is by dramatization—that is, the story is allowed to unfold in front of the reader's eyes, like a play. The difference between a story and a play, however, is that in a story the setting can't be viewed; it must be described. The arts of description are many and the kind of description used will differ according to the kind of story. One method, that improves other aspects of the story, is to render a sense of place through the perceptions of one of the characters—that is, transformed by the character's response, conditioned as it is by the situation and his or her emotional state.

In evaluating scenes for this assignment, consider how the scene itself works as a dramatic unit, then whether the place where events happen has been made real. How could both be improved?

Reading: *A Local Habitation and a Name*; *Toward a Definition of Science Fiction*

Assignment: *Write a scene for your story emphasizing a sense of place, and appealing to at least three senses.*

Tip: Flaubert was the master of description; as Carolyn Gordon pointed out, he discovered the principle that nothing exists in fiction until it happens *somewhere*, and he achieved reality by appealing, in each setting, to at least three senses.

Week Four

Dialogue. One of the principles of story writing that runs contrary to intuition and to reading experience is that dialogue is a trap for the unwary. Dialogue is so easy to write (and so easy to read) that the author thinks the story is moving forward when, as a matter of fact, the story is stalled in inconsequentia (particularly if dialogue is used as a way of providing background, often called exposition). People should talk, in fiction, only when they have something that must be said, and what they say should be necessary to the story and should advance the plot. Stories move best when characters are acting, not talking, and authors are advised to see how much dialogue they can do without (as is the case with everything else in a story; if it isn't essential, leave it out). Nevertheless, a story often is judged by the strength of its dialogue, and writers must learn how to handle it skillfully.

As before, evaluate the scene as a scene and then whether the dialogue is effective, believable, necessary, and in character. Can you suggest improvements?

Reading: *Speaking Well in Print*; *Why People Read Fiction*

Assignment: *Write a scene for your story in which characters have to confront each other with dialogue; make sure that what they have to say is essential and dramatic.*

Tip: The written word has several times the impact (some authorities say "seven times") of the spoken word, so the wise author includes only one-seventh of what he or she hears—dialect, verbal mannerisms, vulgarities, etc.

Weeks Five through Eight

Story. Write your story. You have a head start with the idea you have developed and the three scenes—amounting, perhaps, to more than half your story—you have already written. You will want to revise your scenes, however, and add those necessary to complete the narrative, supplying characterization and setting to those scenes in which these aspects of the scene were not stressed, and inspecting, adding, deleting, or revising dialogue. Good stories are not written; they are rewritten. Pay particular attention to the opening sentence and the opening paragraph; get the story started characteristically (in the midst of the protagonist's response to the situation is a good place) and get it ended definitively (with the protagonist's resolution of the situation or his or her inability to cope, even though he or she now knows what is required). As soon as the story is finished, deliver it to the Workshop. The Workshop wants your best work, not what you know is flawed; at the same time, you must be willing to submit a manuscript when revision no longer helps. The second four weeks is an opportunity to critique each other's complete short stories and have your own critiqued. This is the moment for which everyone has been working, the moment of truth. As in my face-to-face workshops, I will offer my comments last.

Reading: *How to Be a Good Critiquer and Still Remain Friends; Suspense in Fiction; Getting the Words Right; Why a Formula Is Not a Formula*

Assignment: *Complete and post your story; read the stories of everyone else and comment on them.*

Tip: Good stories are the result of good ideas effectively dramatized. They also are the result of good judgment about what to include and what to omit. Hemingway once said that a story is like an iceberg—90% of it is below the water; it isn't what you put in a story that matters; it is what you know and leave out.

Index

About the Author

James Gunn, emeritus professor of English at the University of Kansas, has published thirty-six books and nearly one hundred short stories. His novels include *The Immortals*, *The Joy Makers*, *The Listeners*, *Kampus*, and *The Dreamers*. He has published seven collections of short stories, including *Future Imperfect* and *Breaking Point*. As a professor, he taught fiction writing and science fiction, including a long-running intensive Writers Workshop in Science Fiction. His books about science fiction include *Alternate Worlds: The Illustrated History of Science Fiction*, *Isaac Asimov: The Foundations of Science Fiction*, *Inside Science Fiction*, and the six-volume anthology series *The Road to Science Fiction*. Now he has pulled together his experience in writing science fiction and helping others write fiction as *The Science of Science-Fiction Writing*.